PETER DAVISON

IS THERE LIFE OUTSIDE THE BOX?

AN ACTOR DESPAIRS

JOHN BLAKE

Published by
John Blake Publishing,
3 Bramber Court, 2 Bramber Road,
London W14 9PB, England

www.johnblakebooks.com

www.facebook.com/johnblakebooks
twitter.com/jblakebooks

First published in hardback in 2016
This paperback edition published in 2017

ISBN: 978-1-78606-290-1

British Library Cataloguing-in-Publication Data:
A catalogue record for this book is available from the British Library.

Design by www.envydesign.co.uk

Printed in Great Britain by CPI Group (UK) Ltd

1 3 5 7 9 10 8 6 4 2

Text copyright © Peter Davison 2016

Papers used by John Blake Publishing are natural, recyclable products made
from wood grown in sustainable forests. The manufacturing processes conform
to the environmental regulations of the country of origin.

Every attempt has been made to contact the relevant copyright-holders,
but some were unobtainable. We would be grateful if the appropriate people
could contact us.

John Blake Publishing is an imprint of Bonnier Publishing.

www.bonnierpublishing.co.uk

This book is dedicated to my sister,
Shirley J. Bignell 1948–2016

CONTENTS

FOREWORD
BY DAVID TENNANT

As a child who grew up obsessed with television, I recall Peter Davison was absolutely all over my childhood. Of course there were only three channels in those days. That ballooned to four in the heady days of 1982 when the launch of Channel 4 made us feel drunk with choice, but there weren't a lot of different things to watch, and as a child who spent hours in front of the box, with an undiscerning capacity for consuming anything that came on, Peter Davison seemed to feature in a disproportionately large number of programmes.

I am sure he was in three different sitcoms at the same time, there was definitely an advert or three – most significantly the slightly space-age one about...was it saucepans? And then of course there was *All Creatures Great and Small* – the *Downton Abbey* of its day, which was a massive hit across the nation, *and* in our house. Somehow this story of a gentler time, of an England carved in jaw-dropping countryside and peopled with honest, simple folk struck a chord in post-industrial Paisley, as it did across the nation. My mum loved it, and of course she particularly loved the youthful, slightly cheeky blonde-ish one: the winsome Tristan Farnon, everyone's favourite.

To be perfectly honest, *All Creatures Great and Small* annoyed me. It was on at the same time as *The Muppet Show* and there was no such thing as a video recorder or a second television to allow diversity of viewing in the house. As a fairly annoying eight-year-old my viewing habits were usually indulged, but an exception was made for *All Creatures*. I was outnumbered and Sunday nights were all about the vets, the rolling hills and lovely, fresh-faced Tristan.

But then of course in 1981 it all changed and Peter was announced as the next face of *Doctor Who*. Although he had been part of the televisual furniture for as long as I could remember, he was suddenly plopped into the centre of my ten-year-old world. Tom Baker had been the Doctor since I was tiny, he was the only one I really knew. I understood that it was a revolving door and that other actors could take the part but I had never lived through that. I had pictures of Tom on my bedroom wall, my granny had knitted me a long multi-coloured scarf. Could a new Doctor ever mean as much, ever make the TARDIS fly with quite the same excitement?

I can still taste the sense of anticipation and excitement and nervous-ness I felt sitting down to watch the first episode of *Castrovalva*. It was just after Christmas, only a couple of days into 1982. It was initially so disconcerting to see a different face stream through that famous title sequence. How could this be the Doctor? Could we ever get use to this fresh-faced pretender? He had floppy hair and no scarf. He was all breathless energy and confounded enthusiasm. This wasn't right. Could I ever accept this?

It took me about two episodes. My granny knitted me a cricket jumper.

Then a lot of years passed. Lots of other things happened to me and to TV's Peter Davison and it isn't for me to go into them all here because a lot of it is about to be covered in the book you are now holding. Suffice to say that Peter Davison continues to be a big presence in my life, not only because he is still all over the telly, and on stage and on the radio, but more significantly he is also the grandfather of my children.

I don't know what the odds of this happening are. It's a weird quirk of fate, or possibly a stutter in the space-time continuum that has led me here. Yet for all its unlikeliness it all makes a sort of sense. You might occasionally meet the people who influenced you as a child and that can be gratifying or disappointing depending on the individual or the circumstances. It is pretty rare to find yourself related to one of them.

My ten-year-old self would be, I think, delighted, if not a little mystified.

My forty-five-year-old self is, I am sure, delighted – and still a little mystified.

I can't wait to read this book – not least to find out if he says anything about me – but also because after thirty-five years I remain a fan.

Peter is a great actor, a beloved granddad and a lovely man.

I feel very lucky that he has been such a constant presence in my life, in such a variety of unlikely ways.

Thank you Peter. Well done for finishing the book – and can you babysit Friday night?

DT

PREFACE

Where do I start? More particularly, given that I'm still breathing, and available for work, where do I finish? And anyway, how much of what I remember will be of interest to anyone, other than my children (at some point in the future obviously), or those searching for actionable libels, and the most devoted followers of certain iconic TV series?

It's hard work too. I'm not a writer, which makes the decision to eschew the services of a proper one all the more questionable. Instead, my friend Andy Merriman, who years ago had written a radio series I was in, and who now cannot avoid blame for this book as it was his idea in the first place, has dispatched himself to all parts of the kingdom to interview friends and family, hoping their fragmented memories will fill in the gaps in mine. This has presented its own problems as it turns out no two people have the same memory of the same event. Apparently, this is the case even if the event happened yesterday let alone fifty years ago. So when I have come across contradictions which haven't been ironed out by a light bulb switching on in my head and me leaping from my chair and exclaiming, 'Yes, that's right, of course it is!', I have trusted my own recollections over those of others. Partly because I have the usual conviction that I am always right, and partly because where the odd disputed memory has surfaced, closer examination has often revealed I was right (although I admit the closer examination was done by me).

None of which matters because it's my book. Go and write your own.

All the words in it are my own, although I'm sure, before you read this, Andy will have taken a view on the exact order they end up in. I'm also grateful to my wife Elizabeth, who whenever I've asked her to read a page or two, hopeful of a bucketful of praise, has spent her time adding or subtracting commas, apostrophe's (are you *sure* that's right, Elizabeth?) and full stops.

Not being a writer, I then made the huge mistake of reading other autobiographies. I stuck to those actually written by the subject, which, while illuminating, became a depressing exercise when comparing them with my own efforts. There was the politician whose vivid account of childhood deprivation in London made my own South London, lower-middle-class, walk-in-the-park life seem trivial. Then there was the writer and comedian whose brilliantly funny and honest book was only marred by him spelling my name wrongly on page 22.

Finally, there was Mark Twain. Two volumes of it. Big fat books which, at his insistence, remained unpublished until a hundred years after his death, to be absolutely sure everybody mentioned in it would be properly dead.

This was either an overly cautious man or one who showed enormous confidence in the advancement of medical science in the twentieth century. He started writing his life story at the age of forty-two (two years after the ideal age, he was told), stopped, started again, stopped for a bit longer, and thirty-three years later had finally figured out how to do it.

This is one of the greatest writers of all time – what chance do I have? I am already twenty-two years behind schedule, and my original plan of starting at the beginning, and proceeding in an orderly manner has been blown out of the water by Twain's moment of epiphany. In June 1906 he announced the 'right way to do an autobiography' was to start at no particular time of your life, and wander about all over it, talking only about what interests you, and stopping the moment you're bored, or when something else interesting comes to mind. When I read this, I sprang up from my chair exclaiming, 'Yes, that's right, of course it is!'

Whether he leapt from his chair or not, Arthur Miller used the same approach in his memoir, *Timebends*, and, as you will discover if you delve further into this book, Arthur and I were like two peas in a pod.

When I told Andy about writing the book myself, he said I should do as much as I wanted. I had ambitious plans. My initial thought was that only *Doctor Who* fans would read it so why not call the book *Volume Three – The Doctor Who Years,* thus eliminating the need to write about anything else before or after, and while it was meant to be a joke, it gave me the option to work on volumes one and two later, if volume three proved to be a publishing sensation.

After our first meeting, I started to write with great excitement; that is to say, I sat down with great excitement, and looked out of the window with much less of it. At the end of each day I would reflect, and delete all but a few lines. At the rate I was going this would be a book the length of an average school essay. The problem with a book about *Doctor Who*, even one written by a former Doctor, even one whose son-in-law is also a former Doctor, even one whose daughter is a Time Lord, and who herself is the daughter of her own husband, is that there are just too many of them (books – not Doctors).

I could tell the story of how and when each episode was made – but a good many have done that before me. There are always tit-bits about the costume and make-up and thoughts about the scripts, but I've given so many interviews about that stuff, and there's always someone who's written it down, and slapped in yet another book.

So I stopped writing and read Mark Twain's autobiography instead.

Fortunately, this coincided with flying to Australia which gave me plenty of time to read a book or two. When I was out there I bumped into my old English teacher Mr Verney (exactly how this came about will require further reading), who was mightily impressed with me reading two hefty volumes of Mark Twain as he recalled the struggle to get me to read anything other than the *New Musical Express*.

When I returned to the UK, I moved the desk away from the window, and started to write. I followed the advice given by the master, and by the simple device of starting somewhere other than the *Doctor Who* years, the words began to flow. I know that isn't any guarantee the words are any good, and I'm aware of my limitations of grammar and vocabulary, but by now it was less a book for publication than it was a chance to re-assemble the jumbled events of my life and put them in some order. This also applied to the even more jumbled lives of my parents.

I was hanging out in my agent's office the other day, going through my job history on one of the old computers. It was late afternoon, and I was on my way to the Savoy Theatre where I'm appearing in *Gypsy* with Imelda Staunton (this is not a plug and by the time you read this the show will only be memories). I was sifting through my job notifications from 1990 through to 1999, a decade I always thought was a lean one for me, and was surprised by the number of jobs I'd done, not all of them good. I was giving a running commentary meant only for myself:

'What on earth was I thinking about when I said yes to this? The bloody script changed every day.'

I scrolled down to the next.

'Look at this one. It would have been nice to *have* a script to begin with . . .'

And another.

'This was a nightmare too. I asked for a moustache and glasses, hoping no one would recognise me.'

I looked up, suddenly aware I was going on a bit, and Neil, my agent's assistant, was grinning at me.

'How do you make an actor complain?'

'Go on then,' I said.

'Get him a job.'

There's another story that could be about me, or any of us in this business: An actor has been out of work for several months. He flops around the house day after day, bored, frustrated, and driving everyone around him crazy. He hates doing nothing, he says, he desperately wants to work. One day he gets an audition which goes well, and eventually he is offered the job. A week later, he goes off to the read-through, and returns with a spring in his step and a smile on his face. His wife asks him how his day went.

'It couldn't have gone better. The money's amazing, the part's fantastic, the director loves what I'm doing, and the cast couldn't be friendlier. But best of all – I've got tomorrow off.'

PROLOGUE

It's hard to keep your head down these days – and it isn't. I've been an actor for forty-four years and on the television for forty-two of them. There are bits of me all over the Internet (if you look for them and I'm begging you not to): clips from shows, public appearances I didn't know were being filmed. You can even see me singing if your inclination is to torture yourself. But the worst are the early interviews – and I've watched a lot of them over the last few months – with my public-school accent and sun-kissed hair. These were moments where I was supposed to be myself and yet as I looked at this soft-spoken, charming Englishman, I didn't recognise him at all.

When I went to drama school, I was a shambling, long-haired, weekend hippie with a South London accent. And now I think about it, I was pretty much the same when I left, except with a slightly shorter haircut. Then lucky accidents of casting meant I rapidly rose through the social classes and by the time I was regularly appearing on TV, I'd been moulded into something else entirely. That was fine if I was playing a part. The problem was, in my everyday life, in the face I presented on those interviews, I bought into this so completely, in accent and manner, that I was living as my alter ego. Even when I was offered a part that was a perfect fit for my background I found it hard to shed this new skin without the sense that I was not giving the public what they expected. This was almost certainly because, during this period, I lived my personal life in the public eye. Not in the extreme way that's possible nowadays – there was no reality show called *The Davisons* – but I lived in a well-tended goldfish bowl of my own making.

★   ★   ★

The editor looks suspiciously at me across the large table.

'*An Actor Despairs?*'

'That's right.'

There is silence. I try to sell the idea. 'It's a play on words, you see. It's a book. *An Actor Prepares*. By Stanislavski. Every drama student's bible. My parents bought me a copy when I started drama school.'

'And it's about . . . what?'

'Well, I don't know actually. I never got around to reading it.'

The other editor clears her throat.

'Obviously it's very important to us that you're happy.'

'Yes, very important.'

I know this is what people say when they mean the absolute opposite. But I admire the teamwork.

'And it's a funny idea . . .'

'Very funny.'

'But it sends the wrong message.'

I breathe out slowly. There's a sound like a death rattle in my throat.

' . . . What we don't understand is what you, that is Peter Davidson . . .'

'Davison.'

'What?'

PROLOGUE

'It's . . . Dav*ison*.'

'. . . that's right . . . what you, Peter Davidson, would be despairing about?'

Well, this conversation for a start. Fortunately, I haven't said this out loud.

I take a deep breath. 'Well, I'll explain this in the book, of course. Somewhere. But the idea is that actors despair. They despair no matter how well, or badly, they're doing. You might ask what I've got to despair about but I look back at my career, and think: OK, I've done series telly, but not the really prestigious stuff, and I've been in two feature films in my whole life, and one of those was a Michael Winner film so that doesn't count. In fact, it was enough to send me spiralling into despair all by itself. So the point is: whether you don't get the part with three lines in weekly rep in Skegness, or you just miss out getting the lead in the next multimillion-dollar Spider-Man reboot, your level of despair is fairly constant.'

The room is quiet. Are they wondering why they want to publish a book by such a loser?

They shift uneasily in their chairs.

'So you don't like *The Fifth(ish) Doctor: Peter Davison, The Autobiography?*'

'No.'

'We have a great pic of you smiling in the doorway of the TARDIS. Lots of blue.'

'Really shows off your charm, and energy.'

'I hate it.'

'What if it's not quite so blue?'

A week later, and I have compromised over the title, and the world is a cheerier place.

The editor looks smugly at me across the large table.

'Great, we really like *Life Outside the Box*.'

IS THERE LIFE OUTSIDE THE BOX?

'Is there life outside the box?'

'What?'

'That's the new title – *Is There Life Outside the Box?*'

'Oh. What does that mean?'

'Well it's a bit sci-fi-ish and faintly reminiscent of "Is There Life on Mars?" You know – the Bowie song? Also it's not saying definitively this *is* my life outside of the TARDIS or outside of the telly or however you interpret it. It's me asking wistfully . . . is there life outside the box?'

'I see.'

'And then the subtitle will be *An Actor Despairs*.'

The other editor clears her throat.

'Obviously it's very important to us that you're happy.'

'Yes, very important.'

'You don't like it?'

'We hate it.'

'How much do you hate it?'

'We won't publish you with that on the cover.'

I look at them, and slip my hand in my pocket, making sure I still have my Freedom pass.

'Of course, we're genuinely excited to be working with you.'

'We're doing our very best to accommodate your wishes.'

'And we're very enthusiastic about your autobiography.'

A gentle breeze blows through the room.

★ ★ ★

So the publishers and I have parted company. They refused to publish the book with the subtitle *An Actor Despairs* on the cover, the irony being that now I really am in despair, although cheered slightly by the despair providing me with easily enough justification for the title.

1

IN A GALAXY
FAR, FAR AWAY...

Thursday, 1 January 2015. In two weeks' time, I'm flying to Australia and New Zealand to host the *Doctor Who* Symphonic Spectaculars, a month-long commitment. A week after returning I start rehearsals for *Gypsy* with Imelda Staunton at the Savoy Theatre in the West End of London, a week out in May to do the Symphonic Spectacular tour of the UK, and then back into the show. When I agreed to write the autobiography there was nothing in my diary. A big fat empty yawning chasm of a year that suggested retirement was just around the corner. I had an empty year so why not have a go at a book? The day after I agreed, my agent rang, and the jobs started rolling in.

The TARDIS materialises at the entrance to a cul-de-sac of modern houses with a splash of the Georgian about them. We are on the outskirts of Woking, a commuter town thirty minutes from London. The main railway line runs along behind the houses. The daylight is fading quickly. The Doctor emerges, and looks through the window of the house on the corner.

IS THERE LIFE OUTSIDE THE BOX?

* * *

A Trimfone is ringing in the front room. No, not ringing. There is no way to describe the sound. Warbling perhaps? That'll do. It's a chilly evening in late March 1980. There is no one in the front room. Sandra, my wife (at the time), is upstairs, I am in the back garden, there is no answering machine attached yet, and so the phone sings plaintively.

It's hard to remember what life was like before this moment. I've got some time to think about it because another crap thing about Trimfones is you can't figure out where the sound is coming from, and the front room is still cluttered from our move of house. I rush in and start throwing boxes around, searching, before the caller can ring off.

I've been told the Trimfone warble was developed by the army for field telephone use on the battlefield. Its frequency makes it difficult for the ear to locate, and so the job of the sniper is that little bit tougher, which I imagine is a good thing. Apart from the confusing warble, the illuminated dials turned out to be radioactive, which is why millions of them were put into sealed containers and left in a car park in Wales. Good riddance. I nearly missed the call that changed my life.

Life before the phone call? It's all coming back to me now. One minute you're running in from the garden, frantically throwing things around, and the next . . .

'Peter? Hi. It's John Nathan-Turner. How would you like to be the next . . . ?'

Monday, 9 March 2015. Week two of *Gypsy* rehearsals, and I'm thinking I might be able to do this. Could be a bad sign as usually I'm at the despairing stage by now. Imelda is very generous and helpful but doesn't suffer fools gladly. Note to self: try not to be a fool. Yesterday I said a theoretical yes to Dan Harris and his Caribbean Sci-fi cruise, mainly because Elizabeth thinks it's a chance to visit the lands of my forefathers and because Dan says he will pay for the family to go as well. It's over a year away and is subject to work commitments, so is unlikely to happen. That was a dumb thing to write down and almost certainly means I'll never be offered another job. Singing practice with Nick Skilbeck went well.

★   ★   ★

My *Doctor Who* journey started many years before that evening. At the very beginning, on 23 November 1963. Actually, the day before, which brings me in a roundabout way to what happened two years before that.

In April 1961, we moved to the village of Knaphill, in deepest Surrey, to fulfil my father's sudden and unexpected ambition to run a local grocery store, a strange choice for a man trained as an electrical engineer, back home in his native British Guiana. Whatever roused him to this lofty ambition no one could imagine, but it left his family bewildered and was the closest my parents came to a marital crisis. The marital crisis bit we only discovered years later from my mother in a moment of age-related candour; all we children knew was that we were dragged away from our friends, from the cosy world we loved, and were plonked down in the middle of nowhere.

This sense of loss was felt by me more than my sisters. Shirley, being of a more gregarious disposition and, on the threshold of her teens, slotted into the local grammar school with ease and set about developing 'style'. She was the only one of us to pass the eleven plus, and even when her hemlines ascended and her necklines plunged, she remained the perfect role model, and in our parents' eyes, the touchstone for what we siblings would never achieve.

3

Pamela was nearly four when we moved, but was quiet and self-contained, and took everything in her stride. Barbara was only a year old and knew nothing about anything at all.

It turned out that Knaphill wasn't quite the middle of nowhere, it was a thriving little village bordering a tract of unspoiled common land that shouted out to be explored, and, best of all, my family was now living in what was essentially a sweet shop. Two weeks after we moved in, we all came down with a severe case of conjunctivitis, but that was as bad as it got.

At least for us.

My mother didn't get away so lightly. My father's dream of being a shopkeeper was a financial black hole, and after struggling to pay the bills for eighteen months, he went back to work in the service department of an electronics shop in nearby Woking, leaving my mother to run the grocery business, a job she was unsuited to in every way. She hated the shop as much as I loved it. It made no money, possibly because I spent a good deal of my time stealing sweets after we closed up for the evening.

Eventually my father put up a large padlocked door to keep me out, which deprived me of confectionary for a few months until the mice came to my aid by nibbling the ends of boxes packed with bars of chocolate and leaving them unfit for sale. I had no problem sharing with rodents if it meant free access to chocolate, and so was allowed to cut off the offending ends of the bars, leaving me with a good two-thirds of each one intact. How could life get better?

* * *

Tuesday, 24 November 2015. This is the point at which we tick off the days on *Gypsy*. No more Mondays. Last night's performance was interesting. Imelda did the whole of the first scene with a mouse wriggling its way up her sleeve and across her shoulders. It made its great escape as the children made their exit, and the chaperones saw it disappear into the darkness of the wings. Imelda, unsure of its whereabouts, spent most of the second scene shaking out her coat, to the bafflement of Patrick, who plays her father. Imelda, of course, was unfazed by the incident, being more concerned about whether the mouse might have been injured leaping from her sleeve. I would not have coped so well, having been traumatised as a teenager by mice running across my bed. A consequence of living above a grocery store.

* * *

One day my father, feeling the stabbing pains of guilt and taking advantage of a healthy discount at his new place of work, came home with a new television set. His children were tremendously excited – despite his distinguished history in electrical engineering, this was the first time we'd ever had a set that worked efficiently without a vigorous thumping. I'm not sure how the new set was supposed to placate my exhausted mother who had no time to watch anyway, what with washing and ironing and making dinner after the shop closed, but that didn't occur to me at the time, because the TV had a massive 23-inch screen, in crystal-clear black and white, but most importantly it came adapted with a UHF tuner, which was the future of television. For the first time, in technology terms, our family was ahead of the game.

Which brings me back to Friday, 22 November 1963, when I was helping my mother carry bags of discarded clothes to the school jumble sale being held the next day, and a woman at the bus stop asked if we'd been listening to the news. That's the moment I heard Kennedy had been shot. By eight o'clock that evening the television news that had replaced the scheduled programmes, confirmed that President Kennedy had been assassinated.

IS THERE LIFE OUTSIDE THE BOX?

For years I was sure I had the enduring memory of NBC's Walter Cronkite removing his glasses, looking at the studio clock, and with a heavy heart confirming the President's death, but that isn't possible, this was long before the age of geo-stationary satellites and instant transatlantic images. Maybe I saw it the following day, and slotted it into my memory's timeline. Anything is possible because I was in a state of shock, which is surprising because I hadn't much idea of who Kennedy was. The Cuban Missile Crisis had made an impression, but only photos of him and Khrushchev looking belligerent on the front pages of newspapers, and the rather exciting thought that there might be another big war like the one my parents spoke of so fondly, and we would all get to live in an underground station.

The conflagration didn't happen of course, which was just as well because the nearest tube station was Waterloo; and that meant catching the bus to Woking and getting the train, which was unreliable at the best of times, and total war would have played havoc with the timetables. The most unwelcome result of this momentous event in modern history, in so far as it affected my life, was that no one in our house took much notice the following day when the first episode of *Doctor Who* was broadcast.

Except for me.

I remember being eagerly perched on the sofa in our upstairs sitting room, watching on our new high-tech TV in the corner next to the fireplace. I found the first episode more mystery than sci-fi but still gripping. We had to wait a week for the TARDIS to time travel though, when the following Saturday the BBC ran the first two episodes together, and in my opinion, the greatest science fiction show of all time, hit its stride.

★ ★ ★

. . . 'Peter? Hi. It's John Nathan-Turner. How would you like to be the next . . . Doctor Who?'

I stand there with my mouth open. Is it a joke?

'Seriously?'

'Absolutely.'

Sandra is desperate to know what the call is about, and when I tell her she's waving her arms about excitedly: 'Is there a part for me?'

John invites me to lunch, and a couple of days later we meet at Julie's Wine Bar in Holland Park. (In those days Julie's was to the BBC what the Polo Lounge was to the Hollywood movers and shakers.) It's the first time this has happened to me: a producer shelling out for lunch before I've said yes to a job, and I joke that it's proof he is serious. He tells me that he never jokes, which I realise later might well have summed up his approach to the show. Over the prawn cocktail I did my best to behave as if I was undecided but in my heart I knew this was an offer I couldn't refuse. I had watched the show from the beginning through the first two doctors, only drifting away when other more physically appealing pursuits began to preoccupy my life. The idea of turning it down and never being able to announce loudly that I was offered it first, was unbearable. Not that I was without my doubts: I was by far the youngest to be offered the part, perhaps too young; my career was going pretty well without taking the risk of taking such an iconic role (the risk was real as was proved when I left the series).

It was the main course of chicken Kiev that was the turning point, or the white wine John was plying me with and which I didn't have the wit to refuse. I was being whipped into a frenzy of excitement about what I could bring to the series – a younger, leaner, more athletic Doctor, a more accessible role model; and I had my own ideas to throw in the mix, a more vulnerable Doctor, and the return of a sense of jeopardy I thought had gone missing. It was the first of many discussions that extended throughout the making of the series, and by the time the sticky toffee pudding turned up, I had as good as accepted the part.

2

A SHORT HISTORY OF THE WORLD BEFORE I ARRIVED IN IT

Monday, 12 January 2015. Went to see my uncle John, to record his memories of my mother, of growing up in the thirties and during the war. It's something I wish I'd done with my parents but never got around to it. I felt the camera might make him self-conscious so I turned on a sound recorder and discreetly placed it on the arm of the sofa. I always liked my uncle John. When I was young he would occasionally take me to see our local football club Crystal Palace playing a league match. In those days they were a Third Division side, and so bad that we would regularly start cheering the opposition. My mother used to say I took after him, and I wish it was true as he's extraordinary – always upbeat and without a bad word to say about anything or anyone. His approach to life could be summed up with the phrase my mother would often use but never quite mean: 'You've got to see the funny side of it.'

★ ★ ★

IS THERE LIFE OUTSIDE THE BOX?

I'd never really thought of my parents as being particularly interesting or unusual because what else did I know? I imagine this is true for everyone. A few years ago I was watching a cable channel when an old episode of *Campion* came on. I called my reluctant sons into the room, pointed at the screen and said, 'Look. Who's that?' They stared blank-faced at the TV, and said indifferently, 'You,' then turned around, and left.

My parents' lives became more interesting, the more I discovered. There is only one sibling left on either side now, and Olga, my father's sister, was absent for the first few years of his life. A few months ago I flew to see her in Florida, where she lives with my uncle Ben in a senior living development, and grilled her as discreetly as I could. This was not very discreetly at all, as she suffers from a combination of deafness, and tinnitus, which required me to over-enunciate each question at maximum volume, at least twice, before she understood. It didn't help that my uncle Ben would then shout the question again, frustrated that she couldn't understand. When we finally got through to her, the phone would ring and a concerned lady from reception would enquire whether everything was all right as the neighbours had heard shouting, and despite the amplified phone, my aunt couldn't understand her either, and it was down to me, the nephew (or possible assailant), to take the call and reassure them everything was fine.

* * *

Sunday, 12 April 2015. This evening I was sitting at the computer when my son came downstairs with an old school exercise book of mine, which he'd found on top of a bookshelf in our bedroom. It had no writing on the front, and was probably one I'd nicked from the school stockroom during Mr 'Ron' Davies's technical-drawing class. Joel wanted to know if I had been alive in 1940 and I told him, no, I wasn't that old, which confused him because there was writing in the exercise book that mentioned that year. I took it from him and discovered forty-two pages written by my father, detailing his arrival in Britain from the colonies during the war. The handwriting was in pencil, very small and neat, and some of the punctuation had been corrected by my mother. Elizabeth was doing something similar to my efforts only the other day, so it was familiar, a kind of shared experience between my father's memoir and my own.

My dad's literary ambition was to have a story published in the 'Humour in Uniform' section of the *Reader's Digest*, and it may be it was this that inspired him to sit down and write. I regarded it, with an unusual pang of sentiment, as his gift to me from the past. His opportunity, having been rejected by the *Reader's Digest*, to get his short memoir into print.

★   ★   ★

My father, Claude Neville Gordon Moffett, was born in Georgetown, British Guiana in 1918. He was the third of five children; the youngest child, Olga, was born in 1920, and by the end of 1921 both parents were dead. Donald, their father, died in a fire, and shortly after, Ivy, their mother, succumbed to pneumonia. She was twenty-seven. The newly orphaned children went to live with their maternal grandmother in a small two-bedroomed apartment in Rosemary Lane in the Tiger Bay district of the town. There was one bedroom for Claude and his elder brother Orville, and another for their three sisters, Trixie, Eileen and baby Olga, along with Granny and their mother's sisters, Aunt Lily and Aunt May.

Despite a fearsome physiognomy, Granny Louise was a cheery, big-hearted woman who could refuse no one in need. Mealtimes would present a challenge for the children as the extraneous and uninvited would turn up with uncannily good timing and necessitate cruel adjustments to the size of the children's portions. Before she was one, Olga was taken off to Brazil by a great-aunt who just happened to be visiting, presumably at lunchtime, and didn't see her siblings for almost twelve years.

Aunt Lily soon decided enough was enough, and escaped the turmoil by marrying a man rich enough to own his own house. Aunt May, however, decided to assist her mother in the role of surrogate parent. I remember her, in later years, as a slightly forbidding presence, but there's no doubt she gave up any ambitions she might have had in order to bring her sister's children up. She was a reasonably good pianist, and so decided each of the children should learn to play as well. Barely a day went by without them sitting down to a regimen of scales and simple classical pieces. Olga, who came late to the party, remembered it as torture. It turned out that only my father had a talent for it, and even he slowly rejected the classical in favour of the popular songs of the day, which he mastered by listening to the radio and playing along.

He grew up, like so many in the West Indies, playing cricket on the dirt squares of the local park, and also became accomplished at tennis, although *accomplished* may be a relative term, judging from the few times I played against him, but I suppose by then I was a competitive teen and he was getting older and a bit out of practice.

Olga remembers her return to British Guiana after the sudden death of the Brazilian aunt, and being met by my father as she disembarked. She was thirteen years old and spoke only Portuguese and had no memory of him, but she insists they knew each other instantly. She was pleased to be back with her family albeit in the increasingly cramped surroundings of Rosemary Lane, but she found my father a little over-protective and censorious. Orville was the more outgoing, while Claude, living in his elder brother's shadow, was quiet and watchful.

A SHORT HISTORY OF THE WORLD BEFORE I ARRIVED IN IT

For years we children tried to get him to tell us stories about his childhood, but he resisted so much that we imagined he was concealing a family secret. We had no grandparents from his side of the family, only a succession of colourful and confusing relatives turning up to visit. His reluctance to open up was frustrating because he had a compendium of humorous stories about the war, which he would tell whenever opportunity arose, often amusing himself so much that the punchline was lost in a fit of giggles. We wanted to know about life in a foreign land, and he wanted nothing more than to be drawn into the bosom of the motherland. Now I've come to realise it was a cultural quirk, common in the Caribbean: what's past is past. Or as Olga said to me when I asked her about their family history, 'Oh, what does it matter?'

But of course it did matter. What to us was a taste of the exotic was, to my father a bothersome distraction in his quest to be accepted as an exemplary British citizen. The fact that his only son was born with blond hair and blue eyes, courtesy of inheriting my mother's dominant Caucasian genes, unlike my sisters, made the transition complete. Over the years however, his West Indian heritage became more than a distraction, and while we never knew of it until later, there's no doubt he suffered discrimination and rejection at the hands of Mother England that he loved. When Enoch Powell gave his 'Rivers of Blood' speech and my father had to stand in line and register as an alien, having been eventually accepted by my mother's extended family and friends, probably did nothing to soften his feelings.

My mother's family was well adjusted and sensible. Or so I thought. Both my mother's parents were born and grew up in the thriving naval town of Portsmouth, and their parents in turn had settled there by making the long trek from Eastleigh, all of twenty-five miles away. I discovered, by browsing one of those 'find my ancestor' websites, that on my mother's side I come from an impressively long line of washerwomen and handymen, who managed to scrape a living along the very bottom of the Victorian social edifice. Because of this there is precious little information about any of them, except for brief mentions in various censuses, and the slightly scandalous inference that my grandfather and grandmother were second cousins, a fact that caused much disapproval within the family and among the more respectable washerwomen and handymen of the area.

The census of 1901 shows my three-year-old grandmother in a hospital in Portsmouth while her parents were logged pottering around somewhere in the north of England. Whether this was a prolonged separation from their daughter or a day excursion to Hartlepool the census doesn't reveal. I assume it was when she was hospitalised with scarlet fever, a dangerous and often fatal disease in those days. I know she caught it at some point in her childhood, and that she was given a new serum made from the blood of horses, which probably saved her life.

I remember my mother telling us the story of Nan's brush with death so clearly because it seemed almost magical. The illness, she told us, caused her thin and mousy locks to fall out, but eventually it grew back as beautiful thick and rich auburn hair. I never had an inkling she was only three and that her hair would have probably thickened up and changed colour without any life-threatening illness or controversial cure intervening, and now it's rather drained the magic from the story. At the time it was like a miracle and I took it to mean that every cloud had a silver lining, that adversity can be turned to advantage, and that ugly ducklings do turn into swans.

A year or so later, it came true for me. I went into hospital to have my tonsils out, and a few days later was discharged with a very sore throat and two large cardboard boxes of unread comics the nurses had collected for me. Every cloud did have a silver lining.

14

A SHORT HISTORY OF THE WORLD BEFORE I ARRIVED IN IT

* * *

Sunday, 15 March 2015. We're rehearsing on Sundays because two of the cast are appearing in *Singin' in the Rain* in Paris, and this is the only day they have off. They did the show in Chichester, so don't need much rehearsing. My voice is getting ropey after my bad cold, I've told them I never lose my voice, I just sound more and more like Lee Marvin. By the way, I wish people would stop telling me how nice Kevin Whately is (he played Herbie in Chichester), although I ought to thank him. Four years ago I was in his 'last ever' *Lewis*. He categorically told me that he'd had enough and was finished for good. Every year since then, he has filmed another series and couldn't do *Gypsy* in the West End because he starts again in a month's time. Jammy bastard. But thanks for the job anyway.

* * *

My maternal grandparents, Herbert and Isabel, met sometime before the Great War. They might have known each other while growing up, or could have met later at a family get-together because my great-grandmother clearly appears on both sides of the family tree. They must have got as far as courting before the war interrupted their lives, because when my grandfather returned in 1917 they married almost immediately.

When the Great War broke out Isabel had got a job sewing sail canvas for use on aircraft in the burgeoning Royal Flying Corps. Every Monday she would catch the Portsmouth Ferry to Ryde on the Isle of Wight, and travel to the sailmaking factory, most likely that of Ratsey and Lapthorn, where she would work, eat and sleep until Friday when she would return to Portsmouth. Meanwhile Herbert joined the army as an infantryman, and was immediately shipped to France.

IS THERE LIFE OUTSIDE THE BOX?

This was a dangerous time to be sent to the front line. In his book *A River Out of Eden*, Richard Dawkins makes the point that all of us living today have direct ancestors with one thing in common: they all survived long enough to produce offspring. How close I came to not being here, how it came down to matter of chance, was told to me by my Uncle John. My grandfather arrived in France with the rest of his regiment and was immediately marched towards the front line where the British losses were appalling. So great that the field hospitals were overwhelmed and chronically undermanned. He ventured briefly onto the front line, managed to survive, and as he was being marched off to an even more dangerous part of it, the regiment was halted as they passed the command headquarters. Officers emerged, and cast their eyes over the weary men. Thirty infantrymen including my grandfather were randomly picked out and told to report to the medical officer; the rest marched on toward the trenches.

He spent the first years of the war as a nurse tending to the wounded, the gassed and the dying, including those from his own regiment, and never saw front-line action. He did, however, take part in one of the stranger practices of battle. After the slaughter was done, and wearing their Red Cross armbands, the medics of both sides would roam the battlefield searching for those who had any chance of survival. They would only take their own, but if they came across a wounded German, they would call out, in the familiar vernacular of the day, 'Oi Fritz, couple of yours over here, still breathing.'

This was not the safest of work, there was no hard-and-fast rule that you couldn't be shot by a sniper. It was more a gentlemen's agreement, which fortunately for him, and all of us who came along afterwards, was adhered to at least until he left France. In 1917 he briefly returned to England, married Isobel, and left for India where he spent the rest of the war. They were garrisoned at the colonial hill station in Kasauli, in the Indian state of Himachal Pradesh. In 1922, after the birth of their first son, Herbert signed up for a further five years. It's not hard to understand why. While Britain was still recovering from the trauma of the Great War, the town of Kasauli, with its cobbled streets, colonial architecture and beautiful terraces, looking out over the blossomed mountains and valleys of the Solan district, was a place still living in the great days of the Raj.

My mother was born there in 1924, left when she was only three years old, and of course had no memory of it. Shortly before my grandfather's enlistment ended, they found out Isobel was pregnant again, nevertheless they left India in the early days of January 1927. The voyage to Britain was long and arduous, Ted was intolerably mischievous, and my mother spent her time reading books. My grandmother shouldn't have risked the journey, but Herbert brushed aside concerns, confident that his army medical training would prove sufficient. As it was, she held on until the boat docked in Woolwich, and then pretty much gave birth to my uncle John on the dockside. After a short stay recuperating in Woolwich barracks, where my grandfather was officially demobbed, they set about finding somewhere to live. My grandmother favoured returning to Portsmouth but Bert was having none of it, and was seriously considering getting a house close by in Woolwich, insisting the prices were reasonable and it was close enough to London to look for work there. His underlying plan was probably to keep as far away as possible from his mother-in-law with whom he had a testy and troublesome relationship. He was eventually dragged as far west as Mitcham in Surrey, where he finally dug his heels in and they bought a newly built house at number 38 Longthornton Road.

It was 1927. With impeccable timing they arrived in Britain the year after the general strike, martial law and wide-scale civil unrest. The workers and government alike were exhausted, and an uneasy truce had broken out. My grandfather, deciding not to continue with matters medical, landed a job at Robinson and Cleaver, a large department store in Regent Street, where he supervised the shop girls in the drapery department.

As the years went by, Ted developed his mischievous side, especially when faced with the stuffy and the pious; my mother remained diligent and serious, and while she 'wasn't a lot of fun', as John puts it, she was at least the academic light of the family.

How she must have despaired over me.

* * *

Sunday, 11 January 2015. My sister Pamela called to say she'd spoken to Olga in Florida. Uncle Ben went into hospital last week for a routine procedure, and has developed a form of mild medical dementia. It almost certainly means they will have to move from their own apartment in the assisted-living buildings to the more 'care' oriented part of the complex. They're both in their nineties, and have, until now, been remarkably healthy. Olga and Ben are first cousins, although they were past the age to have children when they married.

* * *

There are many reasons I admired my father, but the quality I most envied was his ability to fall asleep almost anywhere. On the bus, in the classroom, at mealtimes and, most impressively, while sitting on the lavatory. Olga and Trixie both recalled shouting and thumping on the bathroom door trying to wake the loudly snoozing Claude. (He once fell asleep painting the stairs in our house at Canmore Gardens; I was only a small baby and had been taken for a walk to get me to nap, and when my mother returned he was curled up on the dust sheet.) He would insist he was only resting his eyes, but everybody knew the truth. In later years he confined his naps to the evenings in his favourite chair, or the occasional trips to the theatre to see his son on stage. This would infuriate my mother so much she would elbow him firmly in the chest which would make him grunt loudly and rouse him long enough to catch a brief glimpse of me.

* * *

The return of his sister Olga to Georgetown brought life and colour back into the house. As a way of avoiding learning the piano herself, she encouraged my father to play, and inspired by her disingenuous flattery and requests to play popular songs, he even composed a couple of his own. These songs were his pride and joy and for the rest of his life whenever he saw a piano, he'd sit down and play his two-song set. In the late fifties he hired a cheap recording studio in London, and had a couple of discs pressed. Just him, playing the piano, with one song on either side of the fragile acetate record. I don't think he ever sent them to anybody; it was satisfying enough to make us sit and listen. The titles were 'Smash That Clock' (the A side I think) and 'Bonsoir', and, although we never told him at the time, they were pretty impressive.

Sadly, someone, probably me, smashed one of the records, and the other was lost in a fire at his place of work in 1966. He wasn't one for the old A-A-B-A style of song writing, but they were so familiar to me, so much a part of my life, that when he was seventy-five, I did my own version of 'Smash That Clock' in my home studio, adding a jazzy brass section, another verse, extra lyrics, and a middle-eight variation that introduced a tempo change. Full of pride I presented him with my version on his birthday. He thanked me, but was a little baffled as to why it was necessary to tamper with something that was already perfect. Later my mother told me that within a couple of days he was playing it to friends and family as if it was all his own work, and, really, it was.

* * *

The house at 38 Longthornton Road was a modest size and backed onto the Smith Meters factory. It was typical of three-bedroom houses being built across swathes of southern London, losing the villages and small towns beneath a blanket of suburbia. Every Saturday afternoon the family would go to the cinema, although Ted, being the eldest, often managed to wriggle out of these family outings. John had no choice, even though he would rather be watching Crystal Palace play with Mr Jones who lived two doors up. His reluctance was exacerbated by my mother's devotion to Deanna Durbin, whose films, usually playing the perfect all-singing all-dancing teenager, always took priority. My mother, singing and dancing excepted, was busy becoming the perfect teenager herself. She was bright, diligent and demure, by which I mean all the qualities a brother really hates.

Every summer their grandmother would come up from Portsmouth to stay for two or three weeks. This was torture for Herbert who never liked his mother-in-law, and she in turn never got over her resentment of the marriage. She would take up residence in the chair to the left of the fireplace, and he would park himself on the far side of the room at the dining room table, his thin fingers drumming on the maroon chenille tablecloth. This carried on into my own childhood, and although by that time she was much older, and her visits shorter, the standoff never faltered.

In those early days, the saving grace was Ted, who would mercilessly wind up his grandmother by interrupting and questioning everything she said with a saintly innocence that would have his younger brother laughing and even brought a hint of a smile to his father's grim face. John remembers Grandma admonishing them for their laziness, and recalling how it had taken them two days to walk into town when she was young. 'But where did you stay overnight? . . . In a pub? Which pub was it?' Grandma was appalled; she disapproved of pubs: 'Did you have a brandy before you went to bed, or did you stay up all night drinking?'

John idolised his elder brother, and wanted to be just like him. Sheila – my mother – stuck in the middle, looked disapprovingly in both directions. It was Sheila who read books, always helped out around the house, and while Ted and John went to the Rowan Road Secondary School for Boys, Sheila effortlessly got into Mitcham Grammar School.

After he left school Ted settled into a job at Liberty's in Regent Street, an employment opportunity that his father had worked hard to procure. He hated it. Each night he would lie in bed and regale John with tales of the awfulness of working there, about the snobs who worked on the shop floor, and always managing to make it amusing, until he drifted off to sleep, to the disappointment of his brother. By the end of 1938, he'd had enough, and gave in his notice. My grandfather was furious, he rarely involved himself with the lives of his children, but when he did, he expected them to go along with it, but Ted was over sixteen, and his own man.

* * *

My father, meanwhile, followed high school by attending George-town Technical Institute, and began his working life by joining the Argosy Company's Radio Service Department, a branch of the Argosy Company which employed pretty much everyone in Georgetown who wasn't already working in the sugar cane trade, planting rubber trees, or searching for gold. The Argosy Company also ran a daily newspaper (unsurprisingly called *The Argosy*), owned bookshops, was the official government printers and publishers, and was now expanding into radio. This was where young Claude went to learn his trade as an electrical engineer. The equipment he was servicing was almost exclusively Marconi-designed, and relied on shipments of Marconi-type valves, which were manufactured in London. With war looming supplies dried up and the only replacements possible were American standard, which had different connections and voltage requirements. With the flair of a Time Lord, he managed to cobble together makeshift connectors, and rewired base plates, and generally attached bits to other bits that never imagined being joined together, which resulted in many expired radios bursting back to life. He was slightly eccentric but he was indispensable, and within a couple of years he was in charge of the whole department. The Argosy Company of British Guiana knew a winner when they saw one, and my father was told, 'Claude, although you are young, have a gold tooth, and are rather too flirtatious with the young women who work here, you have breathed life into our service department. You are now the man in charge.'

The confidence that this promotion gave him affected him in other ways too: the departure of his older brother Orville to live in Trinidad left him as titular head of the family, and he emerged or (to keep the Time Lord metaphor going) regenerated into a self-assured young man. In the house on Barrack Street, Aunt May was the real power on the throne, but both there and away from it, my father found a gregarious, sociable and rather charming side to his nature that would serve him well. He had a couple of suits made, bought a few good shirts and some gold cufflinks (presumably to match his tooth).

In the wider world though, Britain was at war, and the

atmosphere in colonial British Guiana was gloomy. The disaster of Dunkirk was almost unfathomable for a country that believed in the unfailing strength of empire. There were even rumours of German battleships in the Caribbean. Then the Americans started arriving. By way of the 1940 Destroyers for Bases Agreement, in which the USA got land rights to put air or naval bases on British territory in exchange for fifty obsolete destroyers that were better than the non-obsolete destroyers the British navy already had, US navy personnel began appearing on the streets of Georgetown. Many found this discomfiting. There was a fundamental difference between the Caribbean colonial style, in which social position, not colour governed your place in society, and the American model of the natural subservience of the black population.

This resilience was something that was first observed with the abolition of slavery when former slaves doggedly refused to work for their former masters even for what was seen as generous wages. This may be the result of British slave owners being marginally less brutal and terrifying than their American counterparts, which in turn might be the result of having too much rum, and relaxing in the sunshine. Among the arriving Americans there was surprise and some indignation at the level of integration in the bars and places of entertainment, but the local population had no intention of deferring to anyone based on the colour of his skin.

Then in 1941, only a few months after he had taken charge, my father was listening to the radio (I like to think it was one he had resurrected) when he heard a broadcast from Britain about Winston Churchill's appeal to the colonies asking for skilled volunteers in all technical fields to join the war effort. The old Claude would probably have shrugged his shoulders and taken a short nap, but this was a man with special powers. He himself admitted it was his ego that made him do it but whatever the reason, he responded like a patriot and within a week was called in to the GPO engineering department for a test.

It may be considered fortunate to all concerned that the test was carried out by Mr Gagan, the chief engineer, whom my father knew socially, and who, obviously understanding the importance of my father to the war effort, ticked all the boxes and sent him on his way with his confidence even more reinforced. Much to the regret of the Argosy Company, not to mention all those in Georgetown who owned Marconi radios, my father left the firm in the summer of 1941 and prepared to leave 'the land of two summers' to help fight a war in a grey and cold country he had never seen but that was, in his heart, the motherland.

In Britain, my mother was growing up in the shadow of war. Ted had taken a job at Croydon airport, making propellers for Spitfires and Hurricanes, and was rarely at home after he joined the local Territorial Army. In 1940, a few months after war broke out, she evacuated to Weston-super-Mare. She missed London even though she was safe from German bombing, and my Uncle John who arrived a few weeks later, says he missed the German bombing even more than he missed his home. To him and probably to my mother, the possibility of a German landing on top of them was a risk worth taking to enjoy the excitement of the nightly raids. The seaside town was quiet and they never felt welcome at their overcrowded schools. John tried skipping school but Sheila would turn up at the house where he stayed and give him extra lessons to make for those he missed and to make sure any outstanding homework was done.

* * *

Thursday, 21 May 2015. My last show before I go off for a week on tour with the *Doctor Who* Symphonic Spectacular. I'm feeling bad because only last week Imelda told me she didn't like people going off for holidays. This is of course a prior commitment and doesn't come under the heading of holiday, but even so I won't be here for the next week. While searching the name 'Orville Moffett – Trinidad' on the Internet, I found his name mentioned as the grandfather of a murder victim in Canada, which would have made him my first cousin once removed. Admittedly, I would probably never have known he existed if he hadn't come to a violent end. This murder and conviction date back to 2007, and as far as I know, Orville had no contact with his brothers and sisters after he left for Trinidad. Except for my father's brief visit en route to Britain.

★ ★ ★

On 5 October 1941, after a slap-up party, as my father called it, saying goodbye to family and friends, he sailed to Trinidad to visit his brother Orville. He stayed there for three weeks, during which time he did some very basic training and was issued with his army paybook, officially changing his status to Signalman Moffett – Royal Signals. He was presented with a uniform which appealed to him so much that he handed over his suits, shirts and gold cufflinks to Orville, something he later regretted. This may have been the last time he ever saw his brother who never returned to British Guiana, and never visited England. Orville was seldom spoken of by any of the family during my lifetime. I've never even managed to find out if he had children, although Olga in her slightly woolly ninety-five-year way, says he may have had a few. My mother reckoned the family thought he'd married someone unsuitable, which probably meant a black girl as opposed to the olive-skinned jumble of his own family, and that in turn leads to the exciting prospect that I may have first cousins knocking about somewhere in Trinidad.

Signalman Moffett sailed on the *Viceroy of India*, now converted to a troop carrier, on 1 December 1941. The journey was a perilous one. The U-boat threat was reaching its peak with almost five hundred ships lost so far that year. To avoid adding to that number, the *Viceroy* charted a course hugging the American coast, going east just off the coast of Greenland and turning south as they neared Iceland. All this might have helped them avoid U-boats, but now there was the added risk of hitting an iceberg; they somehow avoided both.

The ship was largely empty and carried more crew than soldiers. Among them were Signalmen Jackson and Mortimer, two other newly recruited wireless operators from Trinidad, with whom my father made friends. If he knew the danger he was in, he was remarkably cool about it, though for the first week he was so seasick he wished for anything that might shorten the voyage. He lay in his bunk, a bucket beside him, and felt the ship zig-zag, a sure sign of avoiding submarines, and felt not an ounce of fear.

On 7 December, the news came through of the Japanese attack on Pearl Harbor, and America's immediate declaration of war. These events seemed to rally my father, and he rose from his sickbed determined to mend radio equipment until the enemy was defeated.

Five days later, the ship sailed up the Clyde, which was slightly unfortunate because he was supposed to be arriving in Portsmouth. He stood by the rail of the ship, overwhelmed by the scenery, the rich green of the grass, the unfamiliar beauty of the trees, and the majesty of the castle (he later admitted it may have been a largish house) that sat proudly where the verdant hillside met the crisp blue of the sky. Best of all, his journey was over, he was still breathing, and very nearly in Britain, albeit at the opposite end of the country from where he'd expected to be.

By the time they disembarked it was dark, bitterly cold, and the city was enveloped in a forbidding wreath of fog. Along with the two wireless operators he was put on a train to Portsmouth. This journey was as bad as any part of the sea voyage. The carriages were noisy, cold and dimly lit, and the train jerked to a halt every few minutes. In the early hours they had to get off the train at one large, grimy London terminus, and make their way across the smouldering city to an even larger and more grimy one. They finally arrived at the Portsmouth barracks on Saturday morning, exhausted and hungry, to be greeted by an air-raid siren, and a quick visit to the makeshift shelters. Eventually they were summoned to a room where the duty officer looked at their papers, looked at them, lit a cigarette, inhaled deeply, and said, 'We don't have Royal Signals here. Whoever sent you to Portsmouth is an idiot. Catterick Camp in Yorkshire is where you're meant to be.'

So Catterick Camp in Yorkshire is where they set off for, bright and early on Monday morning. That night, having settled in his twelve-man Nissen hut and feeling rather chilly, he asked the sergeant-major if he could have a couple of extra blankets. The sergeant-major's reply is unrecorded but he got his blankets and a whole lot of trouble besides.

★　★　★

After the intensive bombing of London eased, the children slowly returned home. My uncle's job at Croydon Airport had literally disappeared under the hammering of nightly bombing raids. He had been enjoying the Territorial Army, and now, barely realising what was happening, he joined the Army proper, and left for India. He was away for the rest of the war, and suffered badly from illness and disease while he was abroad. My mother said he was never the same again.

Shortly before he returned to London, John had seen John Grierson's *Night Mail*, set around a recitation of W. H. Auden's poem, at the cinema, and had his heart set on becoming a postman. As he sat on the train to London he faced the prospect of telling his father, a prospect so daunting that before he reached Paddington he'd decided to get a job in the city instead. My mother carried on and passed her exams at the grammar school in Weston-super-Mare, and was the last to return home. It was a very different home they returned to.

As she had in the Great War, my grandmother had returned to work, and was running the canteen at Smith Meters, the factory at the rear of their house. After years of managing the afternoon teas at St Olave's church, she was primed for action, and with the factory running twenty-four hours a day since war broke out, she worked a twelve-hour shift. In addition to his full-time job, my grandfather used his army medical experience to help care for the civilian injured. Sheila and John took it in their stride and were mostly perturbed by the destruction of the Rowan Road cricket pitch and recreation ground, not by bombs but by the parish council's decision to 'Dig for victory' by planting vegetables where they had once played.

* * *

The initial problem my father had, in his first weeks in Britain, apart from his extended rail travel, the bitter cold and the lashing Yorkshire rain, was that he had no concept of the requirements of British Army discipline. The request for extra blankets had started the rot, and without his understanding why on earth that had antagonised his superiors, things went from bad to worse. They didn't like his rather raffish and carefree way of wearing his uniform, and thought that marching up and down the parade ground for a few hours a day might improve his dress sense. He complained about the men being made to stand in the cold waiting for inspection while the officers finished their tea and chatted. He nearly poisoned his entire unit by parking the battery generator truck, engine running, next to the sleeping quarters on a particularly cold and windy night, the breeze blowing the carbon monoxide fumes through the gaps in the walls. The final straw was being yelled at by the regimental sergeant-major for standing with his hands in his pockets, not an unusual indignity for the common soldier, but the sergeant had crept up behind him, and my father was so incensed by the rudeness and the close proximity of the shouting that he demanded an apology and threatened to report the RSM to the British Guianan government.

This might have brought a world of pain down on his head but for an incident with the Major's American AC/DC radio, which having been deemed irreparable by the existing signals workshop, was made whole again by my father who, reversing the technique he had used in Guiana, adapted (bodged) Marconi valves to work in the American set, and thus endeared himself to the people who really mattered. Despite the RSM having walked away muttering, 'We'll send you all back', a few days later Signalman Moffett was called to the adjutant's office where he received an apology from him, albeit a reluctant one.

Christmas 1941 brought his very first sight of snow, an experience that excited him so much he forgot his aversion to cold as he and the other signalmen climbed out of the windows of the Nissen hut to dig the snow from the door. His social life improved markedly when he was called in at short notice to repair the dance band amplifier at the Christmas Dance in the main Catterick recreation hall. From being an oddity and feeling slightly excluded, he now found himself with a free pass to all the dances.

★ ★ ★

My mother got a job at Palmolive-Peet at their London head-quarters opposite Victoria station, a very good job according to my uncle and very well paid. He found himself the beneficiary of her new plenitude when she began to buy him gifts of beautiful books. He admits he didn't really know her that well until this period, and that it was this sudden generosity as well as the time she had taken helping him study, that made him re-assess her qualities as a sister. Leaving school had also made her more confident and at ease with the world – even, occasionally, fun.

The two of them would meet up every week on Fridays, Sheila having slipped in her lunch hour to the cheap ticket booth, and she would take him to the latest West End productions, a pleasure she had found herself increasingly drawn to. They always had seats up in the gods, and he never knew what he was going to see but he was mightily impressed with the number of stars on offer. Cicely Courtneidge, Jack Hulbert, Bebe Daniels, Evelyn Laye and Fay Compton, names almost forgotten but who were stars of successful shows that ran in the West End during and after the Blitz, or until the theatre was bombed.

My mother was also becoming more rebellious; my uncle remembered one night the air-raid wardens closed Waterloo Bridge as the two of them made their way home after a show, forcing a long diversion to London Bridge, which the wardens were also about to close at the moment they arrived. She suddenly took John's hand and they made a dash for it, crossing the river with the shouts of wardens in their ears and managing to avoid the police on the other side. The fact she took my uncle on these evenings out meant there was no boyfriend on the scene, and my uncle can remember no talk of boys.

Within a year she had left her job and enlisted in the army, to the dismay of her family who thought she would never get an opportunity like that again, and were concerned for her safety. She stayed in London, was given the rank of sergeant, and assigned to military intelligence. She worked at a base deep below ground in Goodge Street Underground station, where she would go each day, slipping unnoticed through a small door into the complex of rooms.

A SHORT HISTORY OF THE WORLD BEFORE I ARRIVED IN IT

A few months after D-Day, by different routes, and unaware of each other's existence, both my parents found themselves in the newly liberated Paris. Heavy fighting was still going on towards the east as the German army was forced into retreating well into its own borders, but Paris had been quiet since the end of August. They were both sent ahead of the transfer of SHAEF, the Supreme Headquarters Allied Expeditionary Force, to the Trianon Palace Hotel in Versailles. My mother, Sergeant Hallett, was helping to set up the intelligence section, while my father, Signalman Moffett, was presumably wiring the telephones. Somehow despite the difference in rank, they met and began a tentative romance. It was an unlikely alliance – my mother, born in colonial India the daughter of a British army man – and my father, born in the Caribbean and one of the colonised – both children of the British Empire, but worlds apart. Details are very sketchy about this period, all I have are photos. I think they must have been taken in the winter of 1945, pictures of my mother smiling happily in the snow, or leaning against a tree, her collar pulled up against the cold, even then her happiness is plain to see. No doubt they must have suffered discrimination at some point, she blonde-haired and blue-eyed, my father with his West Indian accent and dark skin, but there's certainly no evidence of it in these pictures. Indeed, if there ever was, it was something neither of my parents chose to share openly with me. There are some of my father posing on his motorbike or trying to fish, the photos demonstrating my mother's habit of not quite getting the whole of her subject matter in frame. There are also a couple of them together, their faces side by side. I'd seen these photos many times over the years, lying around in drawers or in old, crumbling albums, and never gave them a second thought. They're dog-eared now but looking at them after so many years, and with both of them gone, they assume a poignancy and importance they never had before.

IS THERE LIFE OUTSIDE THE BOX?

I know my mother returned to Britain before my father, because we have letters, written in Paris, wishing away the days until he saw her again. She was certainly home for VE Day, because years later she told us about going to Piccadilly Circus and the day of celebrations. When exactly she introduced her unlikely boyfriend Claude to the rest of her family no one knows but I would have loved to have been a fly on the wall.

★   ★   ★

Monday, 12 January 2015. I am with my uncle John, to record his memories of my mother and of the war. He tells me about night-time air raids and the chaos all around him. He might be describing a slapstick comedy he remembers seeing, and manages to make being bombed sound like fun. But I'm really there to ask what the family thought when his sister, this reserved and serious girl, returned after the war with a man from the Caribbean, complete with West Indian accent, tight black curls, a dark complexion and a gold tooth. He pauses and considers, 'I think she knew what she was doing,' he says.

The TARDIS materialises a few houses down from 38 Longthornton Road. It's a dull autumn day in 1945. There are no cars parked in the road, and the houses are uniformly pebble dashed. The Doctor emerges, and walks slowly past the number 38. He sees a couple standing in the porch.

★   ★   ★

My grandmother opens the door. On the step is her daughter Sheila, and, over her left shoulder, stands Claude, a gleaming smile showing off his impressive gold tooth, his short but untamed and tightly curled black hair. He is worryingly foreign. My grandmother is doing her best to hold on to her involuntary smile of welcome, but she is plainly disconcerted,

'Oh, and this is . . . ?'

'Claude,' interrupts my father, offering his hand in greeting.

'You'd better come in,' says my grandmother, resisting the temptation to add, 'quickly'. She shows them into the sitting room, and offers them a nice cup of tea.

'I'll go and see where Bert is.' And she hurriedly leaves. The couple look at each other. She is apprehensive, he is relaxed, and gives her a confident wink. Later, Bert follows my grandmother into the room; she puts the tea tray on the table.

My father smiles and rises from his chair.

'Claude,' he says.

'Yes,' says my grandfather. 'You must find it chilly here.'

Later still, Sheila takes her mother out to the kitchen, leaving the men alone. My father steadies himself and asks Mr Hallett for permission to marry his daughter.

My grandfather wasn't happy. He liked Claude but disapproved of the marriage, foreseeing many difficulties ahead of them. He was baffled, as were the rest of the family, as to how their daughter could have chosen this man to marry. However, as my uncle said, 'she knew what she was doing', and the growing up in wartime had made her resolute (something I would find out later, to my cost), and negativity in others only made her more determined.

Claude and Sheila were married on 20 April 1946 at St Olave's church, Mitcham. No one seems to know why they returned to British Guiana shortly after that, but presumably it was to settle there and bring up a family. My aunt says my father had always wanted to come to settle in Britain so the impetus for the move back must have come from my mother. What was she thinking? Perhaps she wanted a clean break from everything her life had been before.

IS THERE LIFE OUTSIDE THE BOX?

Whatever the reason, my mother couldn't get on with life in British Guiana. Aunt May's house on Barrack Street, although not large, had servants, which my mother found uncomfortable. In fact it wasn't unusual in Guiana for fairly modest households to have them but that did nothing to make her feel at ease. My aunt Olga tells the story that, as my mother stepped off the boat, my father ran ahead and whispered firmly to his siblings, 'No dirty jokes.' The irony being, according to Olga, that my father was the one who told them, a side of his personality my mother had not seen, or if she had, clearly disapproved of. In the end I imagine that it was motherhood that put an end to the idea of a life in the Caribbean, and a year after my sister Shirley was born, they made plans to return to Britain. My mother and sister returned first, leaving Claude to follow a few months later.

My father left British Guiana for the last time on 24 September 1949. He never returned, even to visit. Stranger still, he had no inclination to do so: he simply closed the door on that period of his life and never looked back.

★ ★ ★

Monday, 13 April 2015. This is the start of the week leading up to press night, and consequently we are still rehearsing bits and pieces that Jonathan isn't happy with. My voice is still sounding like gravel and I am getting advice from all directions; Imelda has suggested chewing gum before every entrance and it seems to help. I'd asked school-friend Dave to see if he could dig out all his old slides and photos and transfer them to a digital format. This is a big ask because Dave is a natural-born Luddite and has sent me an email expressing his concern about anything to do with these newfangled computer formats like FAT32 and JPEG. 'It's all getting too hard,' he says. He sent me birthday wishes as today is my birthday.

A SHORT HISTORY OF THE WORLD BEFORE I ARRIVED IN IT

★ ★ ★

I was born on Friday, 13 April 1951, which, let's face it, was not an auspicious start, and as soon as I was aware of the unease surrounding the combination of day and date, I decided it would be a good idea to make it my 'lucky' day. I still tell people this, proudly, although I cannot recall anything lucky ever befalling me on the day of my birth. For a start I wasn't born in the Caribbean like my sister, but in St James's hospital, Balham, in a less than exotic area of South London. After they returned from British Guiana, my parents bought a modest house in Streatham. Of the many immigrants arriving from the West Indies during those years, my father was more acceptable than most, but he still stood out from the pale and suspicious British native. He spoke with a definite Caribbean lilt and wore his hair slicked back with Brylcreem; then there was his stylish and rhythmic walk, as if he might at any moment break into a few steps of the rumba. His experience in the army had made him socially very confident, and if there was any local resistance to him, it was washed away by his charm and persistence. Yet this exterior masked a deep insecurity that I never realised was there. Years later, when we would argue about politics and particularly the Vietnam War, I would, like a typical teenager, dismiss his views as ridiculous and outdated and he would often end up alone in his views. I only found out long after he died, that he felt I was disrespectful because he was foreign and different, which was so far from the truth it makes me ache when I think of it. I'm sure there were only moments when he felt that way but I still wish I could reassure him I was only being an arse, because that is every teenager's job.

Later, stuff happened that may have increased his sense of not belonging, but in my childhood memories he remains a charmer. My mother on the other hand was made of sterner stuff, and because of that they were a perfect match.

* * *

Friday, 28 August 2015. Shirley has come up with some photos of our family in British Guiana. Reminds me of how they turn up unsuitably dressed for the British weather, but certainly bring some colour to Canmore Gardens.

* * *

The house at 5 Canmore Gardens was a small three-bedroom terraced house built in the thirties, and until I was five, the upstairs was rented out to a couple who are now only the faintest of shadows in my memory. I have a recollection of the husband wearing discomfitingly thick glasses, and sporting a pencil moustache, and his wife having an aloof and disapproving air. It's equally possible I've conjured this up from an amalgamation of B movies, involving Nazi war criminals on the run. They were probably a perfectly nice couple but by the time my synapses pulled themselves together sufficiently to form long-lasting memories, they were gone, made unnecessary, I suspect, by a modest increase in my father's wage. The slightly more spacious house meant my father's family could come to visit. The fearsome Aunt May, along with Olga and Trixie, his sisters, would arrive and seem to take over the house completely. They spoke in accents more pronounced than my father's and wore colourful and flimsy frocks, quite unlike anything I had ever seen, most probably made by Olga who had a talent for dressmaking. They must have been freezing in our house, which probably accounts for them curling up on our furniture and eating our food. They brought with them trinkets for my sister and mother but nothing much for me. Except (and this is an experience I have had many times in the last year) I woke up this morning and remembered a stuffed, real baby crocodile, which suddenly appeared in our house. It's a strange thing to suddenly remember but my memory of it is quite vivid, although who brought it, and who received it, I'm not so sure. Sometimes other slightly less related relations would arrive, people referred to as great-aunts or second cousins, and who my father could never adequately explain the reason for them being there. These visitors would disturb the tranquillity of our lives for a few days, then disappear just as suddenly.

In the few photographs I possess, my older sister Shirley and I seem inseparable. There were three years between us, and I think she saw me as something to dress up, instruct in the ways of the world, and be at her side whenever she wanted me there. Then one day Shirley started school. I was confused. Why I couldn't go at the same time? There were no playgroups to occupy me, and I was too young and inquisitive to be let out of sight. I had to sit patiently and watch as my mother did housework and listened to *Housewife's Choice* and *Mrs Dale's Diary* or any number of wifely-centric radio shows. We infants got fifteen minutes at 1.45. A brief story, a nursery rhyme, a bit of a song, and that was it.

It didn't help that I was shy. Stupidly shy. I was envious of my sister who could talk for Britain. She'd chat with strangers on the bus, on the street, and in every shop we visited, while I stood dumbly next to her and total strangers admired her precocious qualities and friendly smile, and my mother beamed proudly. When anyone spoke to me, I would blush and hide my face. Only at home would I feel safe from the attention of others.

My sister started piano lessons when she was five, so it wasn't long before I did too. She was older, of course, but also had a real talent for it; I began to lose heart when they tried teaching me to use my left hand. The idea that one was expected to use both hands at once was absurd. I battled on for a few months, and then asked my mother to let me give up, to which she agreed. It's something I never let her forget.

Despite this, my early years were turning out to be generally happy and full of providence, which for the purposes of gripping the reader's interest, is a little disappointing. Mind you, this was the mid-1950s, when the Prime Minister told us we'd 'never had it so good', and even a steady, bomb free, dullness was a great relief to everyone.

The best I can offer in compensation, is a few indelible memories involving modest levels of physical pain, a bit of destructive childish exuberance, and emotional scarring caused by the exclamation, 'Wait till your father gets home'. Like being chased up the garden path by my sister and slamming her fingers in the front door and the absurd overreaction of her and my parents over a minimal amount of blood and the loss of a couple of fingernails. It was one of the few times I remember being walloped my father.

Then there was falling over while running home from school, sprawling wildly and grazing my bare legs on the road and badly gashing my knee on the kerbstone. My mother insisting that I needed stitches which sounded impossibly barbaric and painful to me, and me begging her not to take me to hospital. I still have an unpleasant scar to remind me of my faintheartedness. I can't stop now.

Arriving home to discover my mother was out, and deciding to climb in through the small, but open, top window of our front room, watched by a horrified Mrs Gosling from across the road. And discovering I'd grown slightly larger than I thought, and in the struggle to free myself, my flailing feet shattering the glass of the larger window below, leaving me stuck fast and unable to extricate myself for fear of impaling myself on the remaining shards. Big trouble.

Jumping on the leaf of the dining table to impress my sister, and splintering it apart from the rest of the table, followed shortly after by inadvertently smashing several large bottles of my father's precious homemade ginger beer stored in the garden shed, when the flimsy roofing felt inexplicably gave way under my weight.

And finally, when I was nine years old, in an attempt to avoid the traumatic visits to the barber shop, going into the bathroom with a large pair of scissors and cutting my hair in a straight line just above my eyebrows, thus inventing the Beatle cut a good two years before they did.

Of course, there are the painless memories as well. Our first car was an Austin Ten, which must have been over twenty years old when we got it but was still one of the first cars in our road. The registration number was ABY165. I couldn't tell you the number of my present car, but in those days it was an important part of your car's personality. The Austin Ten (ABY165) was eventually followed by a Ford Prefect (PTG 539), and so on. My father had taken his driving test secretly, and so our first sight of the Austin was when he told us to go and take the L plates off the car parked outside.

Our car was brilliant.

Never mind that it was draughty, often wouldn't start, and slowed to a snail's pace at the slightest sniff of an incline. We'd never had it so good. Occasionally we would take a family trip to Box Hill or the even more occasional trip to the seaside at Littlehampton. We were lucky, there were children in our street who had never been to the seaside, never experienced the thrill of the mid-journey picnic lunch by the side of the A24. Not near the A24. Not down a small country road, or in a quiet village, just off the A24. Literally six feet from the main road we would happily sit, ingesting heavily leaded exhaust fumes, the odd egg sandwich and cup of tea and watching the traffic and the world go by. After all, the lay-by was so convenient, so easily accessible, so car friendly, why would anyone need to look further?

If it rained on the journey we would still do the picnic, sitting in the car, in the lay-by, windows steamed up, and listening to the swish of tyres on the wet road, the small car shuddering uncertainly with every passing lorry.

In the school holidays I would often be shipped off to my uncle Ted's house in Tatsfield. I had no idea where Tatsfield was (it was in a forgotten corner of Kent apparently), but I knew how to get there. I would walk up to Streatham Common, small suitcase in my hand, and wait for the 706 Green Line bus that took you into the heart of the village. If I was lucky my uncle Ted would be driving the bus and I'd get a free ride. From the middle of the village it was a long walk, past the church and the tiny school, along an unmade road until I reached their house. If it was dark or raining, my auntie Doris would be there to walk back with me, usually accompanied by her daughter Linda, or my cousin Ian. Linda, who was five years younger than me, had Down's syndrome in the days when no help or encouragement was given to the parents of children with the disability. Linda had been handed to Ted and Doris with nothing more than a cheery 'Do the best you can', which is exactly what they did. They had two other children. In those early years she was happy and affectionate, but there was no attempt at education, and she would entertain herself, playing in the garden, or around the house, always clutching two hand brushes which never left her sight. She was always pleased to see me and I suffered her hugs and affection as well as any young boy might. I rarely saw her wearing shoes, even in the wintertime and her speech never developed beyond something only those close to her could understand.

Years later she loved watching me on the television, and always knew, despite never being able to read, when any of my programmes were on. Later still, I became a patron of the Down's Syndrome Association, and was amazed at the progress children with the condition had made. At the annual achievement awards there would be artists, drama groups and gymnastic displays. I met one boy who gave me an impromptu performance of my last *Doctor Who* story, acting out all the parts and reciting the lines (as far as I could tell) perfectly. All this progress was too late for Linda, who in later years suffered depression, born of frustration, and eventually succumbed to heart disease at the age of forty. By then I was a patron, and was also making a radio series called *A Minor Adjustment*, about a couple bringing up a child with Down's. It was written by Eric Merriman and his son Andy, (he who eventually persuaded me to write this book), whose daughter Sarah starred alongside myself and Samantha Bond. She was, and is, a shining example of how attitudes have changed since my cousin Linda was born.

Back in the late fifties, my visits to Tatsfield were always longer than I would have liked, and sometimes, after a heavy snowfall, I would spend hours sobbing, because I couldn't get home. Ted and Doris were baffled: it should have been paradise for a growing boy, with fields and footpaths, and a wood, right there at the end of the garden, where we could play all day. But I had a yearning for the urban landscape of Streatham, and playing in the concrete culvert of the River Graveney beat the Kent countryside every time.

One autumn day in 1960, Uncle Pino turned up. I'd not been aware of the existence of Uncle Pino until I came home from school, and discovered him sitting on the sofa in our back room. A small man immaculately dressed, his olive skin and thin dark hair finished off with a moustache to match. I don't how accurate this description because he's assumed mythical proportions in my memory. Even if I was so badly done by.

The only certain fact, agreed by all parties, is that Uncle Pino was a millionaire. Not that I was aware of this at the time, I had no advanced warning, no little wink from my father, or discreet note handed to me by my mother. I was simply instructed to be nice to Uncle Pino, and to show him the places of interest around the neighbourhood. Showing someone the places of interest around Streatham Vale was a pretty tall order as far as I was concerned, but I showed him my school, the recreation ground, the railway line, and walked beside the fabulously unimpressive River Graveney until eventually we found ourselves in Streatham Vale and the long parade of shops.

My sister Shirley had passed her Eleven-Plus, and was in her first year at Rose Hill Grammar School, and so had escaped the exacting responsibility of tour guide. That said, Uncle Pino seemed an extremely pleasant man, relaxed and funny, asking me questions about my school, about my friends, and indeed by the time we reached high road shops we were getting on about as well as anyone can expect to get on with a nine-year-old boy who would rather be playing in the dirt. Later I found out that Uncle Pino, who was a distant relative, and therefore an uncle only in the honorary sense, had gone to Venezuela and made his fortune in something loosely connected to the oil business. It was all a far cry from Streatham Vale, where we walked slowly along the row of typically South London shops.

He was silent a moment, and then said decisively, 'I'd like to buy you something. A present. What would you like?' Had I been in possession of all the facts, had my mother slipped me that note or had I paid attention when my parents spoke of my father's complicated family history, my answer might have been very different. As it was, the best I dared come up with was a Matchbox toy car. I didn't even particularly like Matchbox cars, preferring the larger, and more substantial Dinky range but I was afraid of being too presumptuous. So, instead, I chose a very nice, matchbox size, light blue two-tone Hillman Minx. (Interestingly, many years later, a second-hand, two-tone Hillman Minx would be the first car I owned.)

Uncle Pino, encouraged by my display of gratitude, enquired what present my sister would like and I replied that I didn't know. At that moment we were passing the bike shop and what followed was one of the great injustices of the modern world. He bought her a bicycle. It had three gears, whitewall tyres, a matching white basket on the front and a fancy dynamo to power the lamps.

It cost £23. That's £481.21 in today's money. No one seemed to care. My parents were thrilled for their eldest and brightest child. My big sister beamed like a big dynamo-driven headlamp on a beautiful blue bicycle, and Uncle Pino shrugged as if to say 'Really, it's a small gift, nothing more.' I stood there, clutching my pathetic, tiny metal car, wanting to scream, 'No. This one is the small gift. It only cost you one shilling and sixpence,' but I don't think anyone would have heard me.

Uncle Pino, after dealing me such a cruel blow, didn't even stay a single night with us, preferring his luxury London hotel, and before I knew it, he'd buggered off back to Venezuela, never to return to Streatham Vale.

I'm comforted by the discovery that if we'd put away our respective presents on that day in 1960, and brought them back out today, my collectable matchbox toy would be worth more than my sister's bicycle. One in the eye for you, sis.

Because my father was an electrical engineer, we had a television set before most people in the street. I think it was a 1948 Bush TV12 and had one channel, the BBC. From about 1953 onwards, new sets came with a tuner upgrade which meant they were ready for new stations. When, in September 1955, ITV began broadcasting, we staggered on with our one-channel set, while all around us neighbours were buying receivers and getting the exciting new channel that came with the added extra of adverts. Rather than buy a new set, which wasn't cheap, my father used his engineering skills to install a two-channel tuner. It was mightily impressive, even if it only worked intermittently. The picture would flicker, and the frame would roll, something that could be temporarily cured by the expertly applied thump of the fist on the top of the set. It had a tiny 12-inch screen and the picture was washed out, but we knew nothing else. Even with the advent of ITV, we were BBC people, and *Dixon of Dock Green*, *Blue Peter* and *Crackerjack* were favourites.

I loved the radio and I still do. It was the soundtrack of everyday life. Whether it was *Children's Favourites* on Saturday mornings or *Beyond Our Ken*, *Round the Horne* and *Hancock's Half Hour* at Sunday lunchtimes. My mother still listened to *Mrs Dale's Diary*, who was still worrying about Jim, which had the rather useful side-effect of driving me out to the street to play. In the 1950s no one worried about the dangers, and once you reached the age of five you were pretty much free to do as you pleased. The street was our playground where I could climb the trees that lined the road, play hopscotch on the paving stones and ball games in the middle of the road. There were few cars in Canmore Gardens, and fewer still passing through.

I had a friend across the road, called Christopher Shevrill, two doors down were Robert and Margaret Gosling, and next door was a girl called Sandra. This group made up the core of our non-school friends. Christopher Shevrill and I made Canmore Gardens communication history, by running a piece of string diagonally across the road, between our two bedrooms. With a cocoa tin can at either end we could hear each other talk clearly, although it turned out we didn't have much to say to each other at the end of a long piece of string.

If we got tired of playing in the street we would go round the corner to the River Graveney, the sad remains of a river which had been culverted where it passed through the vale, enabling the building of new houses. We'd squeeze through the bent railings, climb down, and dam the river with bricks and wood until it regained a little of its dignity. After heavy rainfall, without any assistance from us, it could get as much as two feet deep, and even look quite threatening as it raced along its concrete conduit on a wild ride to Tooting. Today it's heavily fenced off, another victory for health and safety over practical engineering.

Over the years, I had acquired a rather impressive collection of Dinky cars, and I decided it was time to make the most of them. I also had a few Matchbox cars, including the infamous Hillman Minx, but as I grew older I became more particular about matters of scale, and they were set aside. I undertook major construction work in the front garden, and using my mother's best spoons, which I'd found tied with a bow in the kitchen cupboard, I excavated a network of tunnels under the crazy paving garden path and through the flowerbeds, enabling my Dinky Toys, including the impressive Tank Transporter, to cross from one side of the small garden to the other. Surprisingly, my parents viewed my destruction of their garden and flowerbeds with something akin to pride. Perhaps my father foresaw a son's glorious future in engineering. If so it was one of many career choices he envisaged for me as the years passed, and in every one I let him down.

Most Sunday afternoons we would walk over to my Nan and Grandad's house in Longthornton Road. Probably no more than a fifteen-minute walk, it seemed a vast distance to my young legs. My sister Pamela arrived in 1957 and after that, the walk with a pram or pushchair, seemed even longer. When we got there, we would have tea and crumpets, and afterwards play card games, usually Whot!. These were the only times I felt close to my grandfather, or at least caught a glimpse of another side of him. Playing cards with him was fun. He would cheat, and do it quite openly, so when we accused him giggling uncontrollably lively, he would fix us with a stare, looking wounded we would laugh even more.

When I was younger, my great-grandmother would occasionally

be there, sitting by the fireplace, dressed in black, her hair tied tightly in a bun – a cross between Whistler's mother and Granny Clampett. I thought my memory of her might have been garnished but I have the pictures to prove it. She died when I was about seven years old, leaving little more than her empty chair. The house smelled musty and slightly damp, and was always much colder than our own. Upstairs in the box room, inside a tin chest of my grandfather's were things of wonder; a brass telescope (which I eventually inherited), a letter signed by Winston Churchill, various bits of army paraphernalia, and a number of medals and coins. In the small back garden were gooseberry and blackberry bushes, and an apple and a plum tree, from which, if the season was right, I would stuff myself until my stomach growled in protest. In the late fifties she still had no fridge, and the milk was kept in a bucket of water outside the back door. This is the house my mother was born and grew up in, before the war, before she met my father, and where they lived after they married in 1947, before they went back to his birthplace in British Guiana.

Every Sunday we attended the Holy Redeemer church in the vale. At least my mother, sister and I would, I don't remember my father being with us, except when the children were reluctantly participants in the service, so it's safe to assume he spent his Sunday mornings getting on with a bit of DIY, by which I mean he put his feet up and read the *News of the World*. Midway through the church service the children would peel off into side rooms for Sunday school. I loved Sunday school. We would sit in groups around kindly but ineffectual teachers, who told us stories that made no sense at all and were riddled with plot holes you could shove an average-sized *Doctor Who* producer through. The main thrust was 'Be good or else, because God is watching you,' which I thought was pretty unlikely and only made me want to misbehave to see what he would do about it. When I was bad, which I managed to be without much effort, he simply ignored me. This has always seemed to me a formula that has worked for both of us and I'm happy to continue with it, even if he doesn't exist.

On the other hand, it could be that God, working in his mysterious way, took his revenge in 1960 by putting a really dumb idea into my father's head. He woke up one morning and announced to my mother that he'd always wanted to run a village shop. This was so much to the left of left field that she was speechless; he had a relatively good job, we lived in a nice little house in a street where we knew our neighbours, and now he wanted to move away to the country to become a shopkeeper.

3

THE ELITE
OF CLODS

Saturday, 31 January 2015. The *Doctor Who* Symphonic Spectacular Tour. After much discussion and negotiation, I have just arrived in Perth, Australia on a first-class ticket on Emirates Airlines. It was a bit like flying in your own apartment but so much better appointed. It's a hell of a long journey, and involved a change of apartment in Dubai, but as far as I can tell I spent most of the flight either asleep or eating everything that was offered to me. Perth is hot. It's not even our first venue but I'm here for pre-publicity which involves criss-crossing Australia and New Zealand, stopping occasionally to actually do the show.

The following morning, we meet early to drive to a TV interview happening just up the road, and I'm thinking about making it back to the hotel in time for breakfast. I'm forgetting that this is Australia, a big country, and just up the road is actually a two-and-a-half-hour drive in the heat to the Pinnacles, admittedly a beautiful alien landscape, where they have put a three-quarter-size TARDIS which I can't stand too close to for fear of exposing its lack of stature. The next day I fly to Adelaide for more interviews, and then our first show in the Entertainment Centre.

The production team are ahead of me, working hard, and I arrive only two days before the show, in time to meet with Paul Bullock who's directing the Spectacular, to see if he'll agree to my Adelaide 'jokes'. We did the Symphonic Spectacular tour last year, and I think we make a pretty good team.

Ben Foster, our conductor and arranger, has been persuaded to join us again despite recently becoming a father, and he's brought his new family with him. The first two shows go very well, and then I'm off to Auckland for press stuff while the team moves on to Perth. Auckland is also hot and celebrating Myers Park Centennial. The following morning between interviews I notice an email from the production office in Perth. At first I don't read it properly, but it seems to say someone's daughters were at Winston Churchill School with me and now live in Perth. Later I sit down, and look at it properly. It's not about the daughters at all. It's from Mr Verney, my old English teacher, although he refers to himself somewhat disturbingly as Mick. He's in Perth for the Cricket World Cup and to visit his daughters, and has noticed an advertisement for the show. Three days later I fly back to Perth, and on the Thursday morning I meet him in the lobby of the hotel for coffee, nearly fifty years after he changed my life.

★ ★ ★

They say all you need is one good teacher, and if that's true, Mr Verney was the man. I had struggled with Mr Schlotel, a softly spoken, dapper man who was fond of his red biro when marking my work. With the arrival of Mr Verney, and the coinciding decline in my circumstances, everything changed. He loved cricket, unlike the games teacher himself, who had no interest in you unless you could kick a ball accurately. Mr Verney resurrected the cricket team, organised fixtures, and enthused all of us. He arranged school camping trips to the New Forest that were chaotic but, I suspect, brilliantly character-forming at the same time. His classes were lively, slightly offbeat, and always interesting. More importantly, he seemed to see something in me. For the first time I would write an essay and he would write, 'Imaginative! Well done!' He encouraged me, where no one had before.

Mr Verney initiated the tape-recording club, where a group of us would do interviews, and write skits, recording them on a large reel-to-reel Grundig machine. We called ourselves The 'Elite of Clods' (a name nicked from a long-forgotten *Mad Magazine* comic strip), and we'd got together in 1964 at the beginning of my third year in senior school. For the first two years I'd clung by my fingertips to a place in the A form, repeatedly finishing near to last in the class, and living with the constant threat of a demotion. At the beginning of my third year the inevitable happened. Even so, I was outraged that they could do such a thing to me, and asked to see the headmaster to demand one last chance (actually a fair amount of pleading was involved), after all I had potential. I knew I did. I knew about my potential because my reports had so often pointed out my disastrous failure to live up to it. Mr Barnes, a headmaster with a kindly and ponderous nature, was not quite the pushover I'd hoped, and would only promise to review his decision if my work showed a marked improvement. Even so I went away confident that within a few weeks I would be restored to my former glory, and for this reason I decided not to tell my parents about going down.

This was a very big mistake.

I never got around to improving my work, mostly because I was 'a lazy good for nothing layabout who would never amount to anything', as Mr Lee, who taught us religious instruction, told me (maybe misinterpreting one of the more important tenets of the good book), but at least in part because everyone in 3b turned out to be much more appealing than the classmates I'd left behind. The rather formidable and bookish girls of the 'A' stream were replaced by the likes of Sally Garbutt and her best friend Linda Russell, who once turned round in class and opened her blouse to show me the love bite on her heart-stopping cleavage. The boys were a less impressive bunch of misfits, clearly bright(ish) but lacking the commitment to better ourselves, made all the worse by the tremendous effort we put into disrupting attempts to educate us without ever doing anything that could be properly classed as misbehaving.

In audible whispers we would count the number of times our geography teacher used the words 'in actual fact' in a single lesson; forty-one was the most recorded I think. We would try to prevent the fragile Miss Taylor from teaching us music by asking her opinion about any subject at all as long as it wasn't music, and leave our games teacher fuming at our inspired attempts to avoid physical effort. I garnered modest praise for 'a horse trod on my foot, sir', an excuse so ludicrous and unlikely that Mr Dable still mentioned it the day he took his leave of the school. More serious cases of unruliness were dealt with by the aforementioned Mr Lee, an indiscriminate and enthusiastic exponent of corporal punishment.

He was the lord and master of the Stasi-like band of prefects and the man who presided over the weekly 'Prefects' meeting'. This select bunch had the power to mark your card and compel you to appear at the Friday lunchtime cane-fest where Mr Lee would be itching to whack the aforementioned with his trusty stick. Yes, I'm bitter and twisted because I seemed to end up in these kangaroo courts more often than I deserved. I once stuck a silly *Mad Magazine* sticker of Alfred E Newman on the windscreen of Mr Schotel's car, a crime which was, apparently, akin to an act of terror. It's a matter of some pride that I made it all the way to the Sixth Form as the only one in my year never to be made a prefect.

THE ELITE OF CLODS

I missed Keith Kimnell who had been my best friend in the first two years of school, and who was a bit of square peg himself, having already made the decision not to consider further education but to be a policeman instead. (Incidentally, he later became a High Court Judge.) Our friendship stuck for a year or so, until the many distractions of Form 3b inevitably came between us.

In my fourth year a new school was built. We left the old Victorian building near my house, and moved to a bigger, bells-and-whistles building on the site of the old Inkerman barracks and firing range. In the first few years of the school this caused problems from time to time as it turned out that not quite all the explosive ordinance had been removed from the grounds. The school was renamed the Winston Churchill Comprehensive after one bright spark of a pupil wrote to his widow to ask her permission. Baroness Spencer-Churchill even popped down to open it, the whole school crowding into the shiny new assembly hall to see her declare us officially open, although as she was lacking the powerful lungs of a teacher, no one could hear a word she said.

The tape-recording club benefited from the new school by getting a Grundig portable tape recorder to add to its armoury, which in turn led to our imaginations pushing the boundaries further from the original concept. From the beginning we were heavily influenced by *I'm Sorry I'll Read That Again*, a radio show that featured John Cleese (and others who were the building blocks of so many other shows such as *Monty Python, At Last the 1948 Show*, and *The Goodies*), and by this time we had managed to drive away the more sensible members of the club and were reduced to myself, Dave Boylett, Matthew Schrock and Ric Dunning. We became the Elite of Clods. Among our more memorable productions were 'The Lone Stranger', 'The Lost Kingdom of Knaphilla', 'Tales of the River Post Office' and 'Thunderferrets have went'.

IS THERE LIFE OUTSIDE THE BOX?

We did mock interviews where we were constantly interrupted by the discovery of unexploded shells. We pretty much did what we wanted. At the end of the fourth year Mr Verney decided the school should enter the Rotary Club public-speaking competition. This was an absurd idea. Everybody who was anybody in Woking knew that every year the winner was either the girls' or the boys' grammar school. We knew that no newfangled comprehensive school would be allowed to breach the bastions of the Rotary Club, but nothing would deter our heroic English teacher. He even chose me to give the main speech alongside an unsuitable colleague to introduce me and someone even worse to propose a vote of thanks. Shamefully I've forgotten their names, but surely there must be a monument commemorating the event somewhere.

This was a formal affair, which meant scraping the dried food off my blazer, and borrowing Keith Kimnell's school tie, and was held at the Rotary Club in York Road. I had decided to give my speech about philosophy, something that I knew absolutely nothing about, and assumed, almost certainly erroneously, that no one else did either. It was entitled, 'The Cat Sat on the Mat', for reasons I can't recall, but were so vivid at the time. I remember the main thrust: nowadays (those days) we spend too much time analysing everything we do, and waste our whole lives doing it. The underlying message was likely to have been *leave me alone, and let me watch more telly*, but when I practised it in the shed in our garden it sounded moving and profound.

In the Rotary Club tradition of courtesy, the girls' grammar school spoke first. Their speech might have been brilliant but I was busy having a panic attack wondering how on earth I'd got myself into this and at the same time trying to remove the last of the food marks from my trousers. The boys' grammar school team applauded their counterparts politely, and shuffled in their chairs, impatient for the chance to cover themselves in glory. Then there were other schools, lesser schools, like ours, who got up, and droned on about this and that, and sat down again. Finally it was our turn. We got up, and climbed on stage like dead men walking, and it occurred to me that I couldn't imagine any three people less suitable for the job.

I was introduced by my inaudible proposer, and nervously rose to my feet.

'The Cat Sat on the Mat. The question is whose cat? Whose mat? And why . . . ?'

It was nonsense, of course. But in place of coherence, I found passion rising in my voice, my lips quivered with conviction, my arms gesticulated wildly and my fist clenched with self-righteous fury. A bit like Mussolini, a bit like a bad Charlton Heston performance.

When I finished there was silence, and then the applause started. A trickle at first, but rising to a tumult (it's possible time passing has exaggerated this bit ever so slightly), and we sat down exhausted. The evening finished with the boys' grammar school, but they were beaten men, and in their hearts they knew it. We had won, and quite how the Rotary Club allowed it to happen no one knew.

I'd like to think of the grammar school girls and boys sitting there, their mouths hanging open in disbelief, but I never really looked. I got £5 as a prize, and the following morning Mr Barnes the headmaster wrote to my parents to suggesting that I should immediately apply to Italia Conti Stage School where he knew of someone who knew someone who might put in a good word. Well-meaning as I'm sure he was, I was not blind to the subtext: 'I've found a way to be rid of your son.'

* * *

Wednesday, 28 January 2015. To be honest I am slightly surprised that Mr Verney is still with us. When you're young, I guess all teachers seem old even if they're in their twenties – forty years younger than I am now. When we were in the second year a student teacher called Miss Staples turned up at teaching practice and offered to take some of us for extra English. It was an after-school lesson, and therefore voluntary. Miss Staples was stunningly beautiful with long brown hair almost to her waist; in consequence she had the biggest extra English class in the school's history. Pupils with top marks would claim a virulent attack of stupidity, and would squeeze into the small room set aside for her lessons. I remember thinking how tragic it was that she was so much older than me, that fate had dealt us such a cruel blow. She was probably about nineteen at the time.

Mr Verney is now a sprightly eighty-five. I had the coffee, he drank only water. He insisted I call him Mick, which was the only difficult part of our meeting. We talked of cricket, of his frustration at my not fulfilling my potential, but also his pleasure at my success. He'd stopped teaching shortly after I left, and had made quite a name for himself in youth cricket both in Britain, and in Sri Lanka. He still lives in the same house close to our school.

★ ★ ★

I didn't leave the Winston Churchill School. Italia Conti had a horrible uniform, and cost loads of money. Mr Barnes, with my best interests in mind, suggested I might get a bursary, but it was unlikely on the back of five-quid prize from the Rotary Club, and he saw his dream of a school without me fading. I decided to carry on where I was, promoting my own mildly anarchic agenda in the school. There was no doubt my credit rating had been revised upwards, and I joined the drama club run by Miss Lightfoot. Jane Lightfoot was fairly new to the job, and one of the new breed of attractive teachers arriving at our school, and this may have been the reason I turned up regularly for this after-school club. We would improvise scenes in small groups, and then perform them for each other. I thought I was amazingly good at this – my confidence was sky high after my Rotary Club triumph – and I'd usually grab centre stage in the scenes. I was loud and resonant, where others mumbled. I demonstrated where others shuffled aimlessly, their arms swinging limply at their sides.

After one of these sessions Miss Lightfoot, or Jane as she liked us to call her, summing up the afternoon's work, announced that she thought I'd been overacting. I was stung. It still stings a bit when I think about it now, and I resolved that I would never be guilty of overacting again. I even joined the Byfleet Players, a local amateur acting society to which she belonged, just to prove how understated I could be. Fuelled by the encouragement I received, this was probably the first time I considered the possibility of acting as a career, but even then it was only for a brief moment – acting wasn't something that seemed within the grasp of someone like me. Despite the school's rather impressive name, beneath its new skin it was still a secondary modern, dreaming of a comprehensive utopia. The grammar school system was alive and well in Woking. No one in my school had ever gone to university, and its success was measured by how many of us went to teacher training college. That was my destiny, and even that looked a slim possibility after my slip into the B stream.

It was 1966, and after a dismal history of not quite and almost but . . . I had a girlfriend. Diane was in the year below me and lived a bus ride away, and soon she acquired honorary member status in the Elite of Clods. She was my calm plateau of patience and understanding after earlier mismatches, and before the hiccups of later life.

IS THERE LIFE OUTSIDE THE BOX?

A SHORT INDISCREET HISTORY OF GIRLFRIENDS

In 1962 on a school day trip to Boulogne. Vicky Cordery grabbed my hand, and didn't let go of it for six hours. I think that makes her my first girlfriend, at least that's what she told me at the time. The exact length of the relationship I've forgotten, but I never let my hand dangle invitingly in her company again. Then there was Shirley. She was an 'almost' girlfriend, that is to say, we hung out together but never so much as kissed. Once I'd got over the fact she had the same name as my sister and was two years younger than me, I was besotted. She was pretty with elfin blonde hair. Her friend Jane once fell over backwards outside the prefabricated classroom block, displaying a wondrous view of stockings and suspenders, an image burned forever into the cerebral cortex of every boy who witnessed it. In the Easter holidays in 1965 I summoned the courage to ask Shirley out and we went to the Odeon cinema to see *The Intelligence Men* with Eric Morecombe and Ernie Wise, which I didn't even want to see, but I didn't care because during the trailers I managed to snake my arm around her shoulder. It was uncomfortable but tremendous progress, I thought, even though now it was there I was too afraid to move and after two hours everything from my fingertips to my shoulder-blade was a lump of dead meat. As the credits rolled she jumped up from her seat and my arm dropped lifelessly into it. I got a kiss on the cheek as we parted at the bus stop and three days later she dumped me. She was my first love and a little of me died inside, I had a gnawing sense of loss and several times took the bus to Woking to stand at the end of her road looking up at her house. I never saw her. A few weeks later, while Shirley steadfastly avoided me, her friend Jane told me she was going out with a bus driver, and the following year she fell pregnant and left school. Once again I was crushed, but my reputation amongst my peers was much enhanced by the assumption I'd been up to a hell of a lot more than I had.

Then there was Jocelyn, who was a bit posh, and went to church every Sunday, and whose mother thoroughly disapproved of me. She would have disapproved even more if she knew her daughter let me put my hand up her jumper. The milestone event happened when I was fifteen, on a school skiing trip to Blair Gowrie in Scotland and more than made up for the almost total absence of snow. Most of us spent the week in the hotel bar in a state of phantom drunkenness, consuming multiple bottles of something called 'Chandy' which we thought was shandy but turned out to have such a tiny amount of alcohol we'd have had to down a Scottish loch full of the stuff to get genuinely drunk. In the end I wasn't suitable boyfriend material for Jocelyn, or her mother, especially as my dress sense was becoming increasingly influenced by the colourful excesses of Carnaby Street. A few weeks after her mother dumped me, I saw Jocelyn with another boy, outside Woking swimming pool. He was smartly dressed and neatly groomed and while I'd decided I hadn't liked Jocelyn that much anyway, I was still torn up by the cruel betrayal. Even though I was now going out with Diane.

Diane was a year younger than me and I first noticed her because she was Sandra Luxford's best friend. None of the boys liked Sandra Luxford for the simple reason she had too much taste to like us. Then one night I had a dream in which she was sobbing uncontrollably and I was there to give her a hug and comfort her. From that day forward it was much harder to dislike Sandra Luxford, which in my book, meant it was acceptable to go out with Diane, who was very sweet and pretty and smiled a lot and was easy to like. It was a shame about her friend.

IS THERE LIFE OUTSIDE THE BOX?

★ ★ ★

Sunday, 15 May 2015. My eldest son Louis is about to take his GCSE exams, and, like every righteous middle-class parent with a licence to live in Twickenham, I miss no opportunity to remind him of the importance of exams, and how vital the revision process is to gaining decent grades, if you want to be an investment banker.

Worryingly, I've not actually seen him do a lot of homework in the five years since he started senior school, although school exams seemed to have been passed, and passed with flying colours, so homework does seem to have been done, presumably while balancing his books on his knees as the District Line train trundles slowly into London. I admit it's my problem. Despite all the evidence to the contrary I look at him, and I see me. Me, the disaster, me, who has no right to tell him to revise, except in so far as I'm an example of what happens if you don't, although I'm not a very good example of that, actually, because things have turned out rather well. I try to explain to him that I understand what it's like to be going through the exam 'thing', and as he's leaving for school (he always seems to be leaving these days), he gives me a gently withering look. Gently, because, as he keeps telling us, he is the nicest person in the world. I think about arguing with this declaration of 'niceness' because way back in 1967, I'm pretty sure that was me.

4

THE SUMMER
OF LOVE

Monday, 19 October 2015. Tonight Lauren Hall, playing baby June, managed to smack herself in the face with one of the black batons. She wobbled briefly, obviously in great pain, and with tears (from the whack on the nose, not from emotion) rolling down her cheeks. This distracted stage management, who didn't know the extent of the injury, so that the phone ring was cued too early, causing confusion on stage as to the possibility of it ringing in the correct place as well or whether Julie should answer it anyway even if it didn't. They were also the quietest audience imaginable, leading us to believe they were all sitting there grimly wondering when something vaguely entertaining would happen. Although I know from personal experience that's unlikely. Many years ago after a matinee attended by my mother, I complained to her that the audience hadn't laughed much. She said, as if to reassure me, 'Oh I never laugh out loud, dear, but I smile an awful lot.'

★ ★ ★

The Summer of Love started on 12 May 1967. That was the day 'A Whiter Shade of Pale' was released. I'd already heard it on the radio a few times, and something about it connected with me so strongly that even today it remains my favourite song. For me, the timing was perfect or, looking at it another way, an absolute disaster. Gary Brooker (formerly of the Paramounts) was the lead singer of Procol Harum. Keith Reid wrote all their compelling, if bizarre, lyrics.

This was the brief but beautiful era of pirate radio. The happy days before the awful jingle-jangle of Radios One and Two ruined our fun by claiming to have invented it. The days when you could listen to Tony Blackburn without wanting to strangle him. The days when Kenny Everett would play the new Beatles single two weeks before anyone else. The days when John Peel would play an entire album because he thought we would be better people afterwards. The days when everybody cool listened to Radio London – the Big L, a pirate radio station broadcasting twenty-four hours a day from an old US Navy minesweeper, parked precariously three miles off the coast of Frinton-on-Sea. Despite this unpromising location it was the best of the floating pirate broadcasters. Along with Blackburn, Peel, and Everett, there was Dave Cash, Ed Stewart, Tommy Vance and a host of others. So I sat around in my kaftan and beads, browsing through *New Musical Express*, and listening to the music.

What I was supposed to have been doing was revising. The release of 'A Whiter Shade of Pale' coincided almost exactly with the start of my GCE and CSE exams. I'd like to claim it was the conjunction of those two events that was responsible for the ensuing disaster, but that would be unfair on Gary Brooker and the boys. The truth is that I'd somehow forgotten to learn anything in the previous two years or at least forgotten to learn anything that might help me pass exams. For example, it might have helped if I'd read the set books for English Literature, but *The Cruel Sea* by Nicholas Monsarrat, while being an excellent book, (as I discovered years later) is, in its 'cadet' edition form (with the action and sex scenes edited out), a pile of poo.

Perhaps Geography might have gone better had Mr Giovanni, a large pompous man with a wheedling, and irritating nasal voice, taught us something other than stories about his mother hiding under tables to escape earthquakes. Had Mr Freestone in his cool 'I'm not that interested in this myself' way, not rendered us almost catatonic in history. Had I bothered to pay slightest attention to the patient Mrs Norris in maths. Had music with Mrs Hennessy-Brown not been so much damn fun. The list goes on. About two weeks into the exam process I had become sufficiently worried by the ongoing debacle to occasionally turn up early at school for a bit of last-minute revision. One particular morning, knowing I had an exam in the afternoon, I sat in the school library, laid my textbooks carefully out in front of me, several pencils, and an exercise book for revision notes at the ready, almost as if the act of such precise organisation would make up for the fact I wasn't going to get around to any revising. So the morning passed pleasantly enough. I can't remember how it passed, only that I was having a fine old time chatting enthusiastically with various friends about nothing in particular when a teacher ran in to tell me my GCE exam had been that morning and had started an hour and three quarters ago, and there was only fifteen minutes left.

In the end I came out with one O level – in English Language, and even that was the lowest pass grade possible. In CSEs I fared rather better. It would be difficult not to. There was a pass mark in CSE exams, but it was little more than writing your name at the top of the paper. Perhaps my greatest triumph was managing to fail CSE woodwork. As my teacher, Mr Bidgood, said in his state of shock: 'All you have to do is recognise wood.'

My parents were angry with me. My teachers collectively shook their heads, and I was a bit miffed about it too. My primary offence, as far as I could tell, was having potential, which I thought should have been seen as a virtue. I was responsible for my own potential, after all, so why shouldn't I fail to live up to it? If I was as dumb as a brick I suppose they would all have patted me on the back, and given me a new bicycle, and told me I was amazing for getting grade six in English. But the fact that I had unfulfilled potential seemed to be far worse to them than having any sort of aptitude or promise in the first place. And so I was a complete failure, a loser of epic proportions. It was goodbye to any possibility of going to teacher training college. Oh my God. No teacher training college. What would I do? Even my father's idea of a job in a building society was out of the window.

My girlfriend Diane was called in to prevent me doing something silly. I can't imagine what they thought I'd do, because I wasn't really that depressed, just feeling a bit sorry for myself. I spent a few minutes communing with our cat, and then started tapping out forlorn notes on the piano. That's when they called Diane, who came round and discovered the truth. This was the summer of love, and I was sitting at the piano, not because I was depressed, but because I'd come up with a really great wistful melody line. In my mind's eye it was soaring into the charts, eclipsing Scott McKenzie and pushing aside the Beatles – the boy with one 'O' level makes good. There's nothing like a bit of A minor to E minor when you're feeling down. Throw in a relative major to perk things up, and you're on your way to San Francisco.

These are the questions I long to go back and ask that boy. What was I thinking? Why, except in my fantasies, did I not think about what came next? Why was I so utterly free from realistic ambition? Or did I know that beyond the brick wall I was heading uncontrollably towards, everything would be beautiful, everything would fall into place?

* * *

Thursday, 15 September 2015. Getting ready for the show and listening to an interview with Carol Burnett on the *Howard Stern Show*, I looked up clips of her show on the Internet. Even though they are almost fifty years old they are still really funny.

In the interview she attributed her success, at least in part, to 'seeing' herself as a success. It was the same for me but I 'saw' myself as a song-writing sensation, and that never happened. That's the truth for most positive thinking.

* * *

Despite the fact that Gary Brooker played the piano, the guitar was the instrument of the moment. I went to London, and stayed a night in a flat my sister shared near Alexandra Palace, where she was training to be a teacher at Trent Park College. In the evening we sat around, and I had a feeling she might be about to give me a rehearsed telling off for my lack of application, or worse still a 'pep' talk, so I put an album on the record player. The cover was a photo of a man with long hair and a bowler hat, and it was called *Alice's Restaurant*. I nearly turned it off after a couple of minutes, but my sister was hovering, waiting to pounce, so I stuck with it. My sister could write a note and leave it on my pillow. The title song was a revelation. It was 18 minutes long, Arlo Guthrie playing his acoustic guitar live, and the funniest thing I had heard. It brought a sense of humour and the summer of love together in a complete package.

So in the midst of this very personal disaster, with my father's dream of me working in a building society fading, I determined to get hold of a guitar, and more importantly, the Bert Weedon *Play in a Day* guitar tutor. I found out later that this was the book which gave the (guitar-playing) Beatles their start. It was also the only guitar book they stocked in the local music shop. My poor father's patience was sorely tested. We both knew if I'd applied myself in my exams, the way I applied myself to every page of Bert's *Play in a Day* songbook, I'd have passed them with flying colours and could at that moment be handing out mortgage applications at the Abbey National. Instead, I had a dodgy nylon-string guitar from the local junk shop, which sounded fine, but was impossible to keep in tune, and which I soon replaced with a steel string 'Aria', with the help of a small parental loan. Not that the Aria was any great shakes either, and my fingertips were raw with practising chord changes. As I learned, I made up little songs and wrote weird psychedelic or Dylanesque lyrics, and consequently never got around to learning songs people wanted to hear.

I was a great disappointment at parties.

'Hey, Pete, play something we can sing along with.'

'I can't.'

'Play a Beatles song.'

'I don't know any.'

'How about Donovan or Dylan?'

'Sorry.'

My parents' grocery store had run out of steam the year before. The profit margin in groceries was slim to non-existent, and my mother was worn out running it. My father had a new job at Pye TVT in Weybridge, and while it wasn't highly paid, it was enough to see us through. The shop closed down in 1966, which relieved my parents of the worry of me stealing sweets, and opened up new exciting possibilities for us all. The Elite of Clods now had a clubroom, and a pretty cool one at that. We painted the walls, threw old cushions on the floor, and generally decorated the place in our unique style. We planned to party, party, party. We'd invite girls, who'd sit around knocking back Babycham, while we played three-chord masterpieces and they gazed up at us as if we were gods. We never quite got around to it. Only Ric and I had girlfriends, and the chances of getting other attractive girls to turn up to a slightly damp derelict shop and hang out with a bunch of nerdy boys was a bit slim. If there was free love around it wasn't hanging out around Knaphill High Street.

Our idea of a great night out was going down to the St John's church youth club on a Friday night, where the vicar would often turn up for a chat, sipping a glass of lemonade and looking about as cool as we did. It was a very pleasant angst-free life, mostly because I was free from ambition and gave no thought to life beyond my teenage years.

That summer we wanted to head for St Ives in Cornwall, by this time designated hippie capital of the UK. We didn't really count ourselves as hippies, nor did we aspire to be. We were more like the friendly weekend version. It was great to be something other than a Mod or a Rocker, and we managed to fit our slightly geeky, provincial version of flower power under the beautiful hippie banner.

We were, of course, fascinated by the hippie revolution that happened in San Francisco, but as I had not so much as smelled marijuana, let alone inhaled it, all that seemed a long way away. Our own provincial hippie revolution was more sedate. My mother made me a kaftan out of old curtain material, and brass curtain hooks sewn down the front, and my friends and I bought colourful wooden beads from Carnaby Street. We were a diverse bunch. Raymond, probably the wackiest of us, had discovered Frank Zappa, and Velvet Underground. We would spend a Saturday evening listening to 'Freak Out' or the expressionless vocals of Lou Reed and Nico on the Velvet Underground album in Raymond's mum's house, their traumatised budgerigar flying frantically around the room, while his mum supplied tea and biscuits. Dave was, in his own dry style, the funniest of us. Fond of genuine folk music, rather than the current fads, he nevertheless took to wearing an orange kaftan, even more obviously made of curtain material than mine. He had taken an interest in film, and photography, and had bought an old Leica camera, and began, in his rather slow and careful way, to document our lives.

In the autumn I returned to school to retake my exams. I was determined to stay on for the sixth year almost as much as the teachers were determined that I should leave. I re-sat the English Literature exam despite still not having read *The Cruel Sea*, which I suppose played a considerable part in me failing for a second time. The headmaster, confident that I would run screaming from the school insisted that if I was staying on to re-take for a third time, I would have to start an A level course. I was far more stupid than he imagined, and announced my intention to do A level maths.

All the more impressive because I hadn't even done it at O level.

Teachers and headmasters alike, not to mention my mother, were speechless. In fact, I'd been quite good at mental arithmetic at junior school and reckoned I could busk it long enough to see me through to the exams in the summer. I might even turn out to be something of a prodigy. Mrs Norris, the maths teacher, smiled patiently, and waited for me to fall flat on my face. At Christmas, as a newly elected and populist house captain I wrote and directed the house pantomime. It pushed the boundaries (and the headmaster's temper) almost to the limit. We poked fun at the teachers who disapproved, and threw custard pies in the faces of those who agreed to make guest appearances.

I knew the fun couldn't last. There was no point staying on for the second year of the Sixth Form. Maths was ridiculously hard, and would never be of any use to me anyway. If I didn't pass the exams at the third attempt, I knew I'd be helped on my way. I announced that come what may, I'd be leaving in the summer. I'd had a bit of luck because the set book had been changed to *The Lord of the Flies*, which happened to be one of the few novels I'd read.

THE SUMMER OF LOVE

Before I left, I had a careers meeting with Mr Freestone, our Sixth Form head. I told him I'd thought about applying for drama school, and he looked at me in the way you might look at someone who's expressed a desire to grow wings and fly. He suggested I looked at stage management, or something behind the scenes instead. This was surprising, because the last time I'd done something behind the scenes was on the school production of *Song of Simeon*. It had gone splendidly well until the last performance, when, whilst closing the curtains after the final scene, I wound the handle the wrong way, revealing to the audience the entire backstage area including myself, the actors changing for the curtain call, and the deputy headmistress with a bunch of flowers at the ready.

* * *

Monday, 13 July 2015. Arrived at the theatre tonight, and there's a letter from Wally Walters who tells me he saw the show a couple of nights ago. Wally was the star of many productions at the Byfleet Players, and later, after I had left school, married Jane Lightfoot. Jane Walters died in 2011 and I didn't find out until I read her obituary. She'd gone on to run several drama groups for young people in Surrey, and she always had a soft spot for me, following my career, and turning up to say hello whenever I was at the Yvonne Arnaud Theatre in Guildford. She certainly deserved credit from me, although I'm not sure she wanted it.

After coming to see me in *The Owl and the Pussycat* with Stephanie Lawrence, she asked me when I was going to do something serious, which I might have found quite hurtful had I not, at the time, been asking myself the same question.

* * *

By now, I was a regular member of the Byfleet Players, the amateur drama group Miss Lightfoot had introduced me to. My first appearance was at the age of sixteen, in Jean Anouilh's *Antigone,* playing Haemon, Antigone's lover. At one point in the play, I lose my temper with my father, Creon. It's a very dramatic scene, and one that gave no end of amusement to my mother, who told me she'd seen that look so many times before. I had the same experience recently, when I saw my son Louis in a play, shouting and swearing and threatening people with a baseball bat. We smiled because the anger was so familiar, and then we found it a little unsettling and I determined to keep my honorary Fifth Doctor engraved cricket bat well out of sight.

In the summer I re-sat two exams and took my leave of school forever. My final anarchic act was reversing the signs on the girls' and boys' loos, in the hope of causing a little disruption the next term. It was a strange feeling to walk out of school for the last time, and I surprised myself by feeling emotional about it. I'd had a love–hate relationship with this place and those who worked in it, and now I was leaving for good. As I walked out of the building, I joked that one day they would ask me back for prize day. It was my way of saying I'd prove them wrong, and I never for a moment thought it would happen.

I had to get a job. My dad said he would ask at Pye TVT, but I didn't fancy that. Working at the same place as your dad? No, I decided to wait a bit, and look around.

That summer we made it to St Ives. We'd missed the initial flurry of hippiedom but we still camped on the side of a hill, sat on the rocks by the sea, playing cheap wooden pipes, and strumming guitars, and completely failing to pick up any easy free lovin' girls, until, as the sun went down, and the tide crept in, an unexpectedly large wave would soak us to the skin. Dave took pictures.

THE SUMMER OF LOVE

*   *   *

Sunday, 19 April 2015. I met up with Matthew (who used to be Raymond) and Dave (and his brother Phil), and the other Dave who's not Dave (maybe we should call one of them David?); Ric couldn't make it in the end. After his mum's death he's returned to Bristol from San Diego, but is spending most of his time looking after his dad. We sat by the river, and talked about the good old days in the same way I used to listen to old blokes sitting around talking all those years ago. I asked Dave if I could have copies of some of the old photos he'd taken over the years. I'm thinking if I don't come up with enough words for the book, I could put in lots and lots of pictures, and have the first coffee-table autobiography.

'Well the thing is, Pete, they're all on slides.'

'Can't you get something to convert them?'

'Well, you can, yes, and a bloke I know was going to give me his, but his wife won't let him cos it cost too much money in the first place.'

'I'll buy you one.'

'Well, the thing is, you have to plug it into a computer.'

'You want me to buy you a computer?'

'I have a computer . . . it's just I don't understand them.'

*   *   *

I returned to discover I had increased my GCE tally by three hundred per cent. I had finally passed English literature, and rejoiced in the idea I would never have to read a book again. I had also passed music, which made me feel slightly arty, if nothing else. I obtained a job as porter at Brookwood mental hospital which was only half a mile from our house. I also got down to researching drama schools, and generally felt a surge of energy and optimism about my future. So full of life and enthusiasm that I even managed to persuade my mother that drama school was the way to go. The truth is there wasn't any other way to go. Three O levels would get you nowhere. But at drama school you didn't need exams, you only needed talent, which at this point was a rather important 'only', and one that I had no idea if I could fulfil. Also my love of life received a small setback when I turned up for my first day of work at Brookwood hospital.

I was attached to the matron's office, and discovered my duties included collecting bodies from the wards and taking them to the mortuary. This is not what I'd signed up for. Disposing of dangerous surgical waste was one thing, even rounding up patients for electric-shock therapy, but I had never seen a dead body. That first day nobody died. For the first four days nobody died. Roger (I'm not sure if that was his name but he reminded me of a bloke at school called Roger so that's what I'll call him) looked more disappointed as each day went by. Roger was the other, more experienced, porter with matron's office, and a year or two older than me. I assumed he'd done the dead body thing many times, and was keen to show it was no big deal. I was beginning to think I might get through the first week, until I walked into the office on Friday morning. Roger was standing there smirking, and trying to look serious at the same time which gave the impression he might at any moment spontaneously combust. 'Body in Florence ward,' he said and walked past me out of the door, and I was left looking at matron who smiled sweetly, and returned to her work.

So you go to the mortuary, and take the metal coffin that has no lid, and always struck me would be perfect for a multiple person sledge in winter, and you put it in the van, and drive down to Florence ward (Brookwood was a big place), round to the rear entrance, where you get a stretcher trolley, and discreetly place the metal coffin on the lower level. Then you get a sheet, and put it over the upper level, hanging neatly over the sides, creating the impression of an empty trolley which you then wheel along the corridor smiling at people until you reach the ward.

There's a screen around the bed, and the body is lying there peacefully, and you fold the bottom sheet over the body so you can lift it up by the sheet itself, and place the deceased in the metal box. You make sure someone has attached a label to the toe, mistakes can happen, bodies can get mixed up. Sheet over the top of the trolley, and off you go. On the way out the nurse will probably say, 'If she starts moving bring her back.' You may have to stop at the sister's office for paperwork, as life goes on around the newly departed waiting in the corridor. Roger and I drove the body to the mortuary, and carried the coffin in. I knew this would probably be the worst part, and so did everyone else. As we entered there was a body laid out on a slab, the feet sticking out forming a V-shape towards me, the label neatly attached to the big toe.

The assistant pathologist was sitting on an empty slab eating a sandwich, swinging his legs, and generally looking as happy as sixpence. Roger stopped a moment so I could take in the scene, then as we moved past him, he grinned a mouthful of teeth and sandwich, and offered me a bite. This, of course, was a set-up, a sort of porter's initiation ceremony, and one that I was delighted to repeat a few months later when a new recruit joined us. The other main job for your skilled porter was the delivery of medicines. They seemed to get through a shedload of medicines at Brookwood, which we would collect from matron's office in baskets, and deliver to the individual wards. This was usually straightforward except with Alex Ward, which was a secure facility, separate from the others. They often had twice the quantity of drugs compared to the other more informal areas of the hospital. There always had to be two of us to enter Alex, which operated a kind of airlock procedure. You opened the first door, and brought the baskets in, locked it, and then opened the second door.

The reason became obvious the moment you opened that second door, as the patients who were mobile, turned and were drawn towards us . . . and the way out. It's not a pleasant similarity but I'm reminded of it every time there's a zombie sequence on TV.

A couple of months into my time there I was sent to clean the windows in one of the wards. I realised this would take all day but there were only about five or six elderly patients there, all bedridden. I started at a modest pace, moving along the windows, towards an old lady who, as I got nearer to her, I realised was breathing with great difficulty. A nurse would check her every few minutes, and by lunchtime it was obvious she wasn't going to hold on much longer. It took her most of the day, her breathing becoming more laboured as I worked my way towards her. She died at about ten past four in the afternoon, the nurse checking for signs of life, and pulling the screen around her. I finished my last window, put away the stepladder and buckets, and went home. I didn't know her, and no one except me was there at the end, and I think it troubled me for no more than a day or two but the memory has stayed with me always.

5

AN ACTOR PREPARES

Monday, 27 April 2015. Imelda Staunton has invited the cast to Smollensky's bar a few doors from the theatre. A group of potential sponsors for RADA scholarship places came to see the show tonight, and we're meeting them afterwards for drinks that might lubricate their wallets. I'm happy to do this. Anything that helps to alter the sad truth that drama schools are now for rich kids is fine by me, but I still enjoy pointing out to anyone who'll listen, especially the principal of the school itself, that I didn't get into RADA.

★ ★ ★

I started auditioning for drama school in January of 1969. I chose two: RADA, mostly because everyone's heard of RADA, and the Central School of Speech and Drama, because it sounded friendlier than the others. For my speeches I'd chosen Prince Hal's from *Henry IV Part One* as my Shakespeare, and Alan Bennett's vicar speech from *Beyond the Fringe,* for my modern.

The latter was an odd choice, but I'd been a big fan of Peter Cook and Dudley Moore, and having listened to all their comedy records, I came across *Beyond the Fringe*, which was where their partnership started. Jonathan Miller and Alan Bennett had been a revelation.

I auditioned for RADA first, and things didn't go well. We auditioned in a large room with the panel in the darkness at the far end of the room. I was probably rubbish, but twelve hopefuls an hour – on the stage – off the stage – and out the door? How could they tell? According to the student showing us in (and briskly out), this went on day after day, for two or three weeks at a time, several times each year.

I never heard any more from them.

The Central audition was a different matter. After my two speeches, which I doubt were any better than at RADA, I was called down from the stage to talk to the auditioning panel. They asked me what I'd done in the way of extracurricular drama, and were interested in why I'd left school after only a year of Sixth Form. How could I avoid the saga of exam disasters?

'I left school to experience life.' I couldn't think what else to say.

'What did you do to experience life?' said a sceptical voice.

'I got a job in a mortuary,' I said.

It sounded like a set-up, but I wasn't that clever.

I got a call back for the following Saturday, an all-day workshop during which they gradually whittled down the size of the group. We started with forty of us and by lunchtime we were reduced to twenty-five. A bit of improv, a bit of movement, after which we would be left to stew for a few nervous minutes before a stony-faced bearer of bad news returned and read out a few names and informed the aforementioned they could leave. That was the pattern, if your name was on the list – you were for the chop. By the afternoon, there were ten of us sitting in the green room waiting. Five of us would go forward, if we were lucky. Everyone else seemed relaxed and confident. Then stony face walked slowly into the room and read out five names – and mine was one of them. I was so crushed by disappointment that I almost missed him say, 'Those people, please stay, the rest can leave.'

A week later, I received a letter telling me I had made it to the shortlist. This seemed like an achievement even if I hadn't actually got in. That's what people told me anyway. It wasn't an impossible dream anymore, merely one that dangled just out of reach, and now I would have to wait the whole summer before I heard anything definite. Always assuming I survived the Isle of Wight pop festival.

★ ★ ★

Friday, 26 June 2015. Digging around in old boxes that haven't been disturbed since we moved to this house nearly fourteen years ago, I find the A4 books in which I wrote my song lyrics. Opening boxes and old suitcases is all part of my research to assemble the jigsaw of memories in near enough the correct order. Somewhere in my head, in an obscure synaptic dead end, are the tunes for all these lyrics, but at first sight, there's only about half I'm able to remember. Probably just as well as many of the words make no sense at all, or they're a bit cheesy. But there are some that are as familiar as the day I wrote them. 'Seventeen' is one. My twenty-one-year-old self documenting the growing pains of the previous five years. The second verse begins:

I took the boat, in my Air Force coat, to the festival.
And took my place beside my friends
in fields of grinning geeks
and paid-up weekend freaks
But by the time I left them I was ready to move on.

★   ★   ★

Four of us stepped off the ferry in Ryde harbour on the Isle of Wight, following signs to the buses taking us to the festival site. There were hundreds of us, joining thousands more in the slow-moving queue. Not too far ahead of us, there was loud music playing. The buses were a long walk, and we never reached the music playing ahead of us because it turned out it was coming from the main stage of the festival, four miles away. That Friday every ferry was packed with the faithful, some like us with tents, some with only sleeping bags, and many with only the clothes they stood up in. A hundred and fifty thousand turned up to see a line-up of rock stars culminating with Bob Dylan and the Band, late on Sunday night. We pitched our tents on the edge of the central area, from where we had a good view of the stage. On the Sunday morning someone showed us a copy of the *News of the World* reporting the scandalous goings-on at the festival. Naked girls frolicking in foam, free love, and drugs for everyone. We never saw any of it.

On Sunday afternoon Julie Felix appeared on stage to play a set. No one could understand why Julie Felix was even on the bill? She was a pleasant, middle-of-the road folk singer, but we were here to see rock bands and music legends, not Julie Felix and her happy-clappy folk music. Our ears were ringing from the compounded decibels of two days of rock, when Julie started singing, 'We're all going to the zoo tomorrow.' The crowd listened, dumbfounded, and Julie, blissfully unaware, encouraged the exhausted crowd to join in. Against the odds a few of the audience, in front of the main stage, started to sing along, which pepped Julie up no end and she started clapping her hands above her head and playing the guitar at the same time, which sounds impossible but I swear it was happening, and then more people were joining in and the ripple, more of a wave now, spread outwards and enveloped us all. A hundred and fifty thousand happy hippies singing, 'You can come too, too, too, we're going to the zoo, zoo, zoo.'

A few days after I got home I had a letter asking me to come back to Central. I repeated my audition speeches, was called down from the stage, told how much better I was, and offered a place. It was over in fifteen minutes. Coming back on the train from Waterloo, I bumped into someone who'd been at my first audition. He was a year or so older than me, and was now dressed in a suit, and I suggested he should try again next year. He said he was very pleased for me, but thought he probably wouldn't. Raymond gave me a lift from the station on the back of his Honda 90. I knew everybody would be looking out of the window, so I tried to look depressed so that when I came into the house and they looked at me sympathetically and I could be really cool and say,

'What's the matter? Of course I got in.'

★   ★   ★

You could see Central the moment you came out of Swiss Cottage Tube station. The entire back wall of the Embassy Theatre was held up with scaffolding: a necessity that prevented the building from collapsing into the waste ground next door. There was a newer office-like building on the other side, and a prefabricated studio across the road.

Stage 72, as our graduation year was called, assembled in Room D in early October. George Hall was the head of the drama course. He was a charming and engaging man, whom we all came to love and admire. There were about thirty students in our year, most straight out of Sixth Form, but a few were older. At twenty-seven, Saul was the eldest. He was a white Jewish South African, a trained lawyer and vehement anti-apartheid campaigner. After my father came to see one of our shows, Saul told me if he'd been in South Africa, he wouldn't have been allowed into the auditorium. It was the first time I'd thought about it. We only had one black student in our year. More shocking was that although for us it was a three-year course, black students were told there was no guarantee of getting parts in the final year, so they could leave if they wished. Even more shocking than that is that none of us, not me, not the anti-apartheid campaigner, not even the student herself, complained about it.

That morning we had a tour of the ramshackle buildings, rooms A through to E, the drama/dance studio across the road, and finally the Embassy Theatre itself, the heart of the school, which for my time there, and for years to come, was held up by scaffolding. Of course everyone seemed more outgoing and more talented than me, but by the end of the day I had started to make friends, and had even found a place to stay in a rooming house in Belsize Park. I'd intended to commute from my parents' house for the first few weeks but three days later I was ensconced in my small room and spending the evenings with this new cosmopolitan mix of friends. I even developed a strange northern(ish) accent, which I brought home with me on my next visit, baffling my sisters. I must have thought I was so cool, but on reflection was acutely embarrassing. Not that my new friends and colleagues noticed – we were high on being drama students and, hanging out on the front steps of the Embassy Theatre, our scripts held casually at our sides, we felt we had arrived. Voice lessons, movement lessons, animal studies (this activity involved going down to London Zoo once a week, and choosing an animal to present as a performance at the end of term) – it was all go. Play studies with visiting writers and directors, like the volatile Eric Thompson, father of Emma Thompson, who narrated *The Magic Roundabout* on children's television, a clever, and acerbic man, who would often chuck you out of the class if you were so much as a minute late. For movement we had the legendary Litz Pisk, who told us, in her strong Austrian accent, of her mother who had thrown herself off a cliff many years before.

'She died, but for a moment . . . she flew.'

After a few weeks of the rooming-house life, students began dispersing to flat shares. I could easily have done the same, but partly because I still yearned for home at the weekends, and had a certain horror at the idea of sharing a space, I was left outside the loop. Eventually, I took a room in a flat in St John's Wood that was being vacated by a third-year student. It was a big mistake. It was well appointed, very expensive and the other occupants had proper jobs, wore suits, and spoke with loud posh voices. I was like a lost child, and would only venture out of my room after I was sure they'd all left for the day. The more I avoided them, the more the dread of seeing them grew. It was two months of hell before I emerged one evening for long enough to tell them I was moving out. I'm not sure they even knew I'd moved in.

At the end of the first term they gathered us together in Room D to tell us that Dave Clark (of the Dave Clark Five), would be joining our year. He was looking to the future and wanted to build an acting career, after the popularity of the band had declined. Rather than give him individual tuition, the faculty decided they would have him join our year. Looking at the rag-tag bunch that made up Stage 72, they were being optimistic.

'Glad All Over' was the second single I ever bought. I never told Dave because it would have sounded like a lie, and also I'd have to admit I never liked them much after that. But Dave himself we all liked. He looked like a pop star, tanned, leather-trimmed and gold-medallioned; he was unassuming and friendly. Of course, he did live in a penthouse apartment in Mayfair but that aside, he was just one of the guys. He did have a circular bed, but I suppose that's only to be expected. And an E-type jag – but who didn't have one of those?

* * *

Friday, 3 July 2015. Went on Twitter, intending to tweet but was distracted by a post from Colin Baker. I like to follow Colin because I think it's important to keep abreast of how Wycombe Wanderers are doing, and how Colin's getting on with his Sky TV package. Under the tag Freddy and Jane at Baker Towers, there is a photo of my friend Fred Marks from drama school, I had no idea Colin knew him. I hope they aren't planning to join forces and start a singing duo.

* * *

After Christmas I moved into a house on Falloden Way, just off the North Circular Road. After the intimidating atmosphere of the St John's Wood flat, this was the coolest house in town. Everyone else was in the year above me, and a couple of them even had live-in girlfriends. There was not a suit in sight and Liverpool accents abounded. I had my own room upstairs, next to Fred Marks, who played the guitar and sang far better than me, and years later, became one of the *Rainbow* team of Rod, Jane, and Freddy. Eventually we started playing together and started dreaming of bigger things.

Falloden Way was a fair distance from Swiss Cottage, and while it was possible to get there on the bus, a quicker way was to get a lift from Rog, another Stage 71 student, who drove a grey mini-van, and lived up the road. As many as five of us would pile into the back and hang on for dear life as he drove down through the side roads of Golders Green and Hampstead. At some point we had to join a busy road but that didn't stop Roger, and in the back we would close our eyes and hope for the best. It wasn't so much the speed of the driving, more the length of time we spent either on the pavement or on the wrong side of the road. Roger was on a mission, and with little traffic driving out of London why not use the oncoming lane? Pedestrians were perfectly capable of throwing themselves into a hedge if the situation demanded it.

Oh what fun we had.

Highlight of our second term was Dave Clark recording a new single and wanting the entire year to appear in the video. 'Everybody Get Together' was, in fact, an old Kingston Trio number. The Dave Clark version turned it into a pop anthem slightly reminiscent of 'All You Need is Love', and, in the end, the whole of Central were invited to take part. We filmed it on the Embassy Theatre stage, one weekend in February, and had a great time. I think we even got paid a supporting artiste rate, which we probably spent in the Swiss Cottage pub on Sunday night. We appeared on *Top of the Pops* a few weeks later, and it wasn't nearly as much fun as it looked on TV; we left the studio bruised from being shoved out of the way as cameras moved about the studio floor, and disappointed at the number of videos we watched on studio monitors.

It wasn't all bad; we got to see John Lennon playing a pretend piano and Yoko Ono wearing a sanitary pad as a blindfold, and miming to 'Instant Karma'.

Being on *Top of the Pops* stirred my song-writing ambitions again, and I could often be found playing my guitar in the changing rooms downstairs, singing my songs or trying to master a new bar chord technique Fred had taught me. One of the other actors in our year persuaded me to sing a couple of my songs at a musical evening he was organising at the foreign student halls on Haverstock Hill. I needed a song for a live audience, I thought, momentarily forgetting the 'foreign' aspect of the venue, so I wrote an Arlo Guthrie-influenced song called 'Officer McKirk', complete with a sing-along chorus. I thought it was a bit of fun and nowhere near as good as the serious songs I was writing, but less than a year later it would be the first to be recorded.

* * *

In the summer the Elite of Clods hit St Ives again. This time we drove down in Ric's Morris Minor, and camped in two tents overlooking Mother Ivy's Bay. We cooked on a methylated-spirit cooker, sat on the rocks playing guitars and wooden pipes, and looked soulful. Then, late one evening, there was the mother of all storms, which washed away our tents, and the four of us spent the rest of the night in the Morris Minor. I was by far the biggest but in a moment of madness I volunteered to sit in the driver's seat and was awake all night. In the morning, as we looked about at the campsite carnage, we decided it was a rubbish holiday and we never wanted to see St Ives again.

I had intended to go back to the house on Falloden Way the night before the autumn term started, but as usual I was behind schedule and so caught the morning train, dragging my suitcases up the steps to the foyer. There was a commotion in the coffee bar and people turned around looking surprised to see me.

At 4 a.m. that morning the house in Falloden Way had been raided by the police and all five occupants arrested and taken to the police station. The house had been searched and small quantities of illegal substances had been found and removed. I sat with a cup of coffee in a state of shock and listened to the news as far as anyone knew it. I was blessing myself for my tardiness and good fortune, but I had honestly never seen any illegal substances and probably wouldn't have known if I had. Later, I learned the police would have found a heck of a lot more had they inexplicably not searched those arrested until they got to the police station. The larger amounts had been shoved down the back of the seats in the police car along with a quantity of pornographic photos that no one knew existed until one of the girls had been told to hide them under her top.

It had been fun while it lasted but now I had to look for somewhere else to live, and a week later I moved into a basement flat at 198 Goldhurst Terrace on the other side of Finchley Road. I shared a large room with another student on my course, John Curless, while the other was shared by two more of our year who had shacked up together. John was a perfectly normal chap apart from an obsession with Frank Sinatra albums, which he'd play until I was driven crazy enough to love them too. We shared the flat with a considerable amount of rising damp, colonies of ants, and occasional small rodents who would wander in from time to time, take a look around, and decide they could do better. The big news was that Vladek Sheybal lived two doors away, an actor often seen playing Eastern Europeans on TV and film, in the sixties and seventies. We would smile and nod when we saw him, and he would tip his hat in return.

I hadn't shared a room with anyone since the age of nine, and while it was large, and our beds were placed at the greatest possible distance from each other it obviously wasn't conducive to girlfriends, or invitations to 'come back to my place' after a wild night in Swiss Cottage, something that was only a theoretical possibility in my case. Fortunately, John had started going out with a girl who was the daughter of a master at Harrow school, where he would visit at weekends and where he was allowed to sleep in her bed, something I found unimaginable. At least it left me with the room to myself, and my on/off relationship with Diane moved firmly to the on position.

I was almost twenty-one, and for my birthday my parents gave me (a few months early because I told them I was desperate) a Philips tape recorder with sound on sound. This meant I could bounce guitar or keyboard tracks back and forwards on the same machine and build up a multiple track song. It was a bit like the way they made *Sgt. Pepper's Lonely Hearts Club Band* – but really, really crappy quality. Still I was a happy man and it spurred me on to more song-writing.

I was also booked for a return engagement at the foreign student halls on Haverstock Hill, where 'Officer McKirk' had gone down so well, despite the probability they had not understood a word. At some point Dave Clark must have heard me rehearsing in the changing room, because he took me aside soon after and asked to hear the whole song, after which he said he'd like to put it on his next album. I was stunned. He might not have been my first choice of recording artist, but bloody hell, I was going to be a proper song-writer. Certain I was embarking on a second and hugely successful career, I blew sixty quid on a car from *Exchange and Mart*. A beautiful two-tone grey Hillman Minx that turned out to have more filler in the bodywork than metal, and made a dreadful whining sound once you managed to get it into fourth gear, and not to mention that any key, even the one to our front door, could be used to unlock it.

A few days later, Dave Clark handed me a large envelope of contracts, and explained that he could have just bought the song outright, and though I might be £500 richer that way, I would no longer own the rights. He didn't think that was fair, so instead he gave me a standard fifty-fifty publishing deal, meaning I would earn royalties until my death and even seventy years after that. Which I agreed was very fair.

I'm sixty-four now, and so far I've earned about seventy-five quid from the song.

* * *

At the end of the second year some of us of got the chance to escape the confines of Central, and play to an audience that wasn't made up of other students and tutors. The trip was hosted by a small theatre just outside Grantham in Lincolnshire. There were about ten actors in all, and we stayed on site in dormitory rooms, one for boys, and another for the girls, although that wasn't so clearly defined by the end of the week. It reminded me of the good old days of school camping, where a degree of tent hopping was not uncommon.

I can't remember much about the play, only that it featured a dog, and at some point John Curless was supposed to walk in and comment on what a fine dog it was. Unfortunately, due to the hot weather, the door at the back of the theatre had been left open and the dog had left the set and wandered off into the car park. As John made his entrance, I tried desperately to indicate the lack of a canine presence, and that maybe we should skip that part of the script. John, apparently mistaking my raised eyebrows frantic head tilting and circular arm movements, as unexpected additions to my lexicon of acting, looked at me quizzically, and ploughed on.

'Fine-looking dog. What breed is it?'

Later, John insisted that he didn't have his contacts in and was confused by the shape of the large cushion on the sofa, not to mention my new and eccentric acting tics. Sadly, my response to his on-stage enquiry about the breed of the large cushion on the sofa, has been lost in the mists of time. But with hindsight, it's bloody obvious he knew the dog wasn't there, and realising that cutting his lines would considerably reduce the size of his part, decided a page and a half of conversation about an imaginary dog was far preferable.

That summer we Clods broadened our horizons, and drove down to Pembrokeshire in my dodgy Hillman Minx. The long expanses of beach made a change from the rocks, and small coves of Cornwall. We met up with Diane and her friend Benny (who got the nickname because she reminded us of the character in the Top Cat cartoons). The holiday itself was uneventful, the only real excitement was on the journey home when the hydraulic brake fluid leaked out of my car somewhere between Porthgain, and Carmarthen, and we drove the next two hundred and fifty miles with only a clapped-out handbrake to slow us down.

Sunday 5 July 2015. Met up with my sisters Pamela and Barbara. They are very keen I should make it clear that I was a complete bastard to them, and would carry out many cruel and un-necessary tortures whenever possible. It's a bit of a shock because I always thought they quite liked me, and even though I explain that I was their big brother and that was my job, they remain unconvinced. On a positive note, I ask them for details, and they're a little short on substance, m'lud.

My parents had moved house, from the crumbling and boarded up old shop, to a pleasant mock Georgian terraced house nearer Woking. I went home most weekends, to keep warm, do my washing, eat properly, and torment my younger sisters. Every Sunday Pamela and Barbara would sit around until lunchtime, not bothering to get dressed, which would infuriate my father, and annoy me enough to threaten to throw them out of the front door, if they didn't do something about it – which they wouldn't – so out the door they went. This meant walking down the close around the back of the garages and in the back door, in only nightdresses and dressing gowns. It became a kind of Sunday ritual, and something I thought was all in fun. It turns out I may have been the only one who got the joke.

Less forgivable was the photograph of Pamela I'd taken a few years before, after she'd been given a grass skirt as a present from a visiting relative. I persuaded her to pose at the end of the garden, next to our monkey tree, and when she wasn't looking had stuck up a sign behind her saying, 'London Zoo: Wild Beasts Section.' I still feel bad about it, and far worse about how funny I thought it was at the time.

That's it. Apart from that I've been thoroughly nice my whole life. Let's move quickly on.

★ ★ ★

The third year in a drama school is usually about simulating an actor's life in repertory theatre. Lessons were kept to a minimum, and instead we did four shows a term for which the public could buy tickets. I was given a leading role in the first show: Pinero's *The Magistrate*. Clearly they realised I was one of the few students that had the range to play a man of his age, and I felt sorry for Chris Blake who only had a few lines as a young man. It wasn't until the week before we opened, and I thought about which agents and casting people I might invite, that I realised no agent wanted to see a twenty-one-year-old actor pretending to be a sixty-year-old, unless it was for the comic effect of the clouds of talcum powder billowing around my head as I walked across the stage or turned my head too quickly. Chris with his small but perfectly cast part got an agent. I was left high and dry. For the rest of the year I only played minor roles.

★ ★ ★

Dave Clark had promised to invite me along to the studio for the final mix of his album and in February I went along to the Landsdowne studios in Holland Park. Everybody from Acker Bilk to the Sex Pistols had recorded there, and it's where, a few years later, Johnny Pearson would record the theme to *All Creatures Great and Small*. Deep in the basement of a block of flats, it was state-of-the-art, with a sixteen-track Studer tape deck and a Cadac mixing desk that had been newly transistorised. I wondered how it would feel going back to my little Philips two-track machine after this. They had added a banjo part to my song, which Dave was very excited about, but I was immersed in the history of the place, and while the track sounded great, it didn't raise my spirits as much as I'd hoped. There was something going on in my head that I couldn't figure out. Did I want to be an actor or a songwriter? As both had got a step closer I was beginning to doubt I could make a success of either. Maybe I should have gone for the building society job my father had wished for me. There were many better actors in my year alone, and thousands of hopeful songwriters. I had two chances of making a success of my life, and both were insane longshots.

Life has a way of rolling along even if you just stand and wait for it, and in the absence of a better idea, I waited for fate to show its hand.

The last opportunity to get an agent was the speech presentations at the end of the year. Central hired the Criterion Theatre in London's Piccadilly Circus, with a view to filling it with agents eager to see the latest talent. We were limited to a three minute speech, and I for one kept well within it. Some were more ambitious. One student chose a six-minute speech from *Hamlet* and when told to cut it down, refused, announcing that he would simply do it quicker. On a nerve-racking afternoon, it was a little light relief to hear him racing incomprehensibly through one of Shakespeare's finest speeches. I received two letters: one from ICM and another from a small agent called John Mahoney Management. ICM stood for International Creative Management, and was the obvious choice and I made an appointment to meet them. The impressive building was in Mayfair, and the offices were well appointed. Unfortunately, the agent seemed to have no idea who I was, what speech I had done, or if the letter had perhaps been sent in error.

I met with John Mahoney a few days later at his office, a large apartment near Baker Street tube station that doubled as his home. He was short and round, very camp, and wore the world's worst toupee, but I got the impression he remembered who I was, and I warmed to his slightly nervous enthusiasm. He told me how busy he was handling Robin Nedwell's career. Robin had been playing a supporting role in a comedy series called *Doctor in the House,* but had graduated to the lead after Barry Evans, the original star, decided a career in films was beckoning. With the real world now less than three months away, I accepted his offer of representation.

All that remained at Central was the final evaluation. This was done individually in a small office on the second floor, I have no idea of the reason for it. Apart from making the confident more so, and depressing the hell out of the rest of us, these assessments were only memorable for being entirely wrong. I can think of three or four students who emerged convinced they were going to take the profession by storm, whom I've never heard of since. I was told I wouldn't have much of a career until I was forty years old, but after that had a reasonable chance making a living. I wondered if they had any thoughts on how I might fill in the next nineteen years.

I wasn't unduly concerned by their presages of doom. I had a plan.

Fred Marks was back after almost a year in Dundee, and with the help of a student on the stage management course who would lend us the money, we planned to record our songs in a proper studio.

A couple of days later the school secretary showed me a letter from Nottingham Playhouse asking if Central could send along two or three students to audition for an Acting ASM position in the upcoming season, opening with *Love's Labour's Lost.* I was uncomfortable with Shakespeare, especially since my nightmare experience at the read-through for our second-year production of *A Winter's Tale.* I was content to be cast as third gentleman, with only a handful of lines, but on the day, our Leontes was under the weather (bit of a bender the night before) and didn't turn up. The director looked around the room, his finger wavering in the air, until it came to rest, pointing firmly in my direction. Two and a half hours of gibberish later, I crawled away, having mangled the play to within an inch of its life.

Now here I was again. After I had read a scene, the director, David William, an intimidating presence with his long blond hair and black cape, gave me a couple of pointers and asked me to try it again. After which he gave me more notes and one last try. It was relentless, but despite my sense of failure, the following day they called and offered me the job. Later on the director told me, that while the others had been good, I was the only one who'd taken his notes. It's one of the few nuggets of information I like to pass on to aspiring actors, not as important as making friends with the caterers, but useful nonetheless.

It was my first professional engagement – £18 a week, starting at the beginning of July, and rehearsing in London – and meant I had my provisional Equity card. In those days there were only two ways to get your hands on one of those: a job in repertory theatre, or a TV commercial. Other than that it was catch 22. You couldn't get a job without an Equity card – you couldn't get an Equity card unless you had a job.

My new agent had been working hard to get me an advertisement and sent me along to meet a casting agent. I sat in the waiting room filling in a form that listed special skills. I could drive (even without brakes), I could swim (with my head above water), but there were so many others. I asked the assistant if it mattered how many I filled in. She looked up from her desk and said, 'Tick everything except horse-riding.'

That's how I came to be cast in an Army recruitment commercial that involved riding a 750cc Triumph motorcycle despite having never so much as been in control of a moped in my life. I tried to explain my concerns to my agent, but agents have a way of sitting in their comfortable offices in Baker Street and brushing away your concerns with a cheery, 'It'll be fine.'

It wasn't fine. First there was the row of powerful and beautifully kept British motorbikes, and facing them were the young actors hired to play the motorbike riders. All of us had lied about being able to ride. The director was furious, he flailed his arms about and threatened to fire us, but this was an Army recruitment commercial, and time is money and it wasn't as if I hadn't tried. Over the weekend, my friend Raymond had let me have a go on his Honda 90, and then changed his mind again when I missed riding into a ditch by six inches.

This was the pitch. Six guys cruise down Primrose Hill on their bikes, and stop outside a café. Their friend arrives, having just signed up to join the Army. We mock him mercilessly, until he tells us what brilliant career opportunities are available, and one by one we decide to sign up as well. The final shot is kick-starting our bikes and riding off up the hill looking for the nearest Army recruitment centre. Well, the last shot was a no-no because kick-starting 750 cubic centimetres of British motorcycle engine is quite difficult, and well-nigh impossible for a drama student who's spent the last three years looking cool and carrying nothing more than a script and a battered copy of Stanislavski's *An Actor Prepares*. And without the engines running, riding uphill wasn't going to happen either. But for the opening shot, Primrose Hill was perfect. We were given a decent shove-off by some proper men on the crew and coasted silently downhill, coming to a stop outside the café. Add genuine Triumph engine noise in the edit, and you'd never know. Until now.

Suddenly drama school was all over. There was no official party and no hats were thrown into the air. There was a speech of encouragement from George Hall, handshakes from all the gang at the Embassy Theatre, and after that, we drifted quietly away. I was sent my diploma in the post a few weeks later. One moment I was a top dog, third-year drama student, the next, I was on the very lowest rung of the business. Except that I had a job. Even if Acting ASM (assistant stage manager) could mean I'd be asked to sweep the stage.

A week before rehearsals started, Fred and I went into a small studio in North London and recorded our songs. Our benefactor, Mark Cunningham, sat in with the engineer, and gave us encouragement. There was nothing fancy, just us and our guitars, but the difference of a proper studio with simple reverb was startling. We came away believing we had something worth pushing on with. Then I remembered I had a job.

* * *

Thursday, 9 July 2015. A few weeks ago Becky, who's head of sound on *Gypsy*, told me, in passing, that her dad was an actor who worked on TV during the seventies and eighties, and had been in two *Doctor Who* stories with Jon Pertwee. His name is Terence Lodge. I'd looked him up and his face was very familiar. Then today I was trying to find out information about my first professional job at Nottingham Playhouse, and tracked down a cast list for *Love's Labour's Lost.* Along with Brian Cox, Amanda Grinling, John Horsley, Robin Bailey and several others, there was Terence Lodge's name. I had spent four months or so working with him, and that familiar face fell into place and triggered memories of my own inauspicious start.

* * *

We started rehearsing in Earl's Court in late July and moved up to Nottingham four weeks later. Predictably, I missed out on flat-share opportunities and ended up renting a room in the small village of West Bridgeford, with its glorious views over the river Trent to the

Wilford Road power station belching steam and smoke into the Nottinghamshire countryside. I was an idiot. Once again I'd chosen to be reclusive rather than sociable, diffident rather than congenial. It was a decision I regretted almost immediately. For one thing it was a twenty-five-minute walk to the theatre; for another, my landlady was a tiny, fearsome woman who left notes on my door complaining about my untidiness and the playing of loud music. I had nothing to play loud music on, so I assume she meant me playing the guitar.

At the theatre there were costume and wig fittings. I was playing Mercade, who turns up towards the end of the play and tells the princess her father is dead and that she is queen. It flips the play from comedy to something more serious, and to highlight the moment David William insisted I was dressed in black, with a ghostly face and white wig. I'd rehearsed for weeks, making my entrance at the back of the stage, waiting until the frolicking couples noticed me, and delivering the short and sombre speech. It was in fact my only line in the play, but it was a bloody important one. Which is why it was surprising I was so calm as I sat in the dressing room on opening night, listening to the play ticking by on the tannoy. When my call came I made my way up the stairs to the stage and calmly waited for my cue. I ran the line in my head, one last time. At least I tried. For weeks I'd rehearsed without a hitch and now I couldn't remember how my speech started. I couldn't picture it on the page. I knew the gist, of course but in my rising panic, words and lines started swimming around in my head and then – I heard my cue to start the long walk onstage.

The actors turned and looked at me. I looked at them, and out at the audience beyond. I have no idea what I said in that terrible moment, but it wasn't what they were expecting. I think I threw in a verily and a many-a-day and possibly some other Shakespearian sounding stuff that all in all amounted to 'Hi, Princess, your dad's dead', and then I thought it was best to stop.

IS THERE LIFE OUTSIDE THE BOX?

Brian Cox was shaking with laughter, his mouth firmly shut in an attempt to control himself which only made it look as if, at any moment, his head might explode. Amanda Grinling, to whom my line had been addressed, looked as if she had no intention of continuing with her career let alone with the play. Even Robin Bailey, an actor of remarkable composure, had the broadest of grins on his face. The audience, as is often the case, didn't notice at all. I accepted my career was over, that was what the hand of fate was telling me. How could I carry on after this? It was my first night as a professional actor, and it was a disaster.

In the end, it was the best thing that could've happened. After the curtain call, my fellow actors whooped, slapped me on the back and hugged me. I was, within the small world of the Nottingham Playhouse, a legend. The moment so imprinted itself in the mind of Brian Cox that when I bumped into him thirty years later, he still remembered me by my old name, and the character actor John Horsley, and made a point of congratulating me on getting a smile out of Robin Bailey.

It made me feel an integral part of the company, and while I never got around to moving out of my depressing room in West Bridgeford, I engaged in the social life of the theatre more than I ever thought I would.

During the second production Peter Moffett disappeared and was replaced by the more streamlined Peter Davison. It turned out there was already a Peter Moffatt, spelt differently, but for Equity, it was too close for comfort. Not that he was acting any more, having successfully established himself as a director, but by way of the Equity option called 'honourable withdrawal' he had kept first dibs on his name. The name Davison had come out of a long discussion in the green room, where everyone had chipped in and no one could agree. 'Davison' happened to be the name under discussion when the deadline was reached. (Equity omitted to tell me there was a Peter Davidson already working as an actor, something that would come back to bite both of us a few years later.)

The name problem is something that my sons, who are budding actors, have also inherited – and through an equally similar but unexpected set of circumstances. *Doctor Who* show runner and writer, Steven Moffat and *Sherlock* producer, Sue Vertue, have two boys the same age as ours, called Louis and Josh, while ours are Louis and Joel, and to add to the confusion, they are friends. Moffett and Moffat are almost identical in pronunciation, so when my son played Prince Edward in *Richard III* at Trafalgar Studios, he used the name Davison as Louis Moffat had already acted professionally. Not wanting to be outdone, my other son Joel, in his first job in *The Widowing of Mrs Holroyd* at the Orange Tree Theatre in Richmond, also took the name Davison as there is another Joel Moffett working in the USA. The boy is thinking big.

* * *

Sunday, 17 May 2015. While searching for a tie to wear with my suit for when I begin the *Doctor Who* Symphonic Spectacular tour next week, I discovered a diary from 1973 that I started as a bet with my friend Dave. By chance, it covers a period that was and was not a momentous time in my life. I won the bet when Dave gave up around the end of May, and I stopped a few weeks later when he finally admitted his failure. I remember being annoyed I'd carried on so long after winning. Now I think it's a shame I stopped.

* * *

I was having an easy time at Nottingham Playhouse. I had a couple of lines as a grovelling villager in Ibsen's *Brand*, which starred Brian Cox on full throttle and was a sight to behold, especially from three or four feet away. It wasn't without its drawbacks, however, because along with the brilliant and powerful acting, came enormous quantities of spittle, that in moments of Coxian passion, would fire upwards and outwards, sparkling in the stage lighting before raining down on the villagers, whose de facto grovelling attitude was looking upwards with our mouths open in wonder. During the day we could get chits from the theatre box office that would get us into the city's cinemas free of charge. I had also discovered reading, something I had left unchartered throughout my time at school. Now, I'd rummage through second-hand bookshops for the classics and the modern. I discovered Dickens and Thackeray, Stevenson and Conrad. I even read the unexpurgated edition of *The Cruel Sea* (see GCE set book – failed). Sometimes the company would meet in small groups for afternoon tea or visits to country houses, it was very civilised.

I borrowed enough money to buy a car – a second-hand, pale green VW beetle. The next Sunday I drove it home to show my friends, and on the way back up the M1, I was involved in one of those multiple-car pile-ups that were so popular in that era. I'd been waiting in stationary traffic because of a crash a few cars in front, when a squeal of tyres, heralded the arrival of several more vehicles that wanted to join in the fun. I ended up in the back seat, the force of the impact having ripped the driver's seat out of the floor, and with the rear of the car (where the engine sits) badly damaged, not to mention a twenty-five per cent deficit in the wheel department.

Christmas season at Nottingham Playhouse. I was cast as a lute-playing Robin Hood in the children's show and the murderous John Felton in *The Three Musketeers,* as well as being a musketeer/Cardinal's guard in the rest of the show. Suddenly, I was doing eighteen shows a week and my wages hitting a high of £36 a week. I was having a great time, but I was knackered.

The beginning of 1973 brought an end-of-term atmosphere to the company. The very first performance of the year was attended by our director Colin Graham and was one of the rare occasions we reverted to the original script. By Tuesday we were back to our increasingly informal ways. We would change our lines for our own amusement (and sometimes for the better, I thought), and comedy business continued unbounded. These are bad habits, but when you're exhausted and nearing the end of a long run, it sometimes inadvertently revitalises the show.

In the tavern scene where the musketeers taunt the Cardinal's guards, a musketeer cries, 'Long live the King!', to which the guard replies, 'I recognise no King but the Cardinal!', and a swordfight begins. On the night after the director's visit, the musketeer unexpectedly cried, 'Long live the Queen!', and the guard, realising he had no option, replied with a thunderous, 'I recognise no Queen but the Cardinal!' There followed a wonderfully energetic if slightly comic swordfight, as if, by whacking each other viciously with bendy steel rapiers, we could banish the giggles.

Richard Eyre, who was taking over as artistic director, arrived to meet any actors hoping to stay on in the company. I met with him briefly, after which, to his everlasting regret, he let me go. A week later, we did our last show and early the following morning I caught the train back to London.

* * *

Monday, 31 August 2015. Imelda returns after missing only three shows due to exhaustion, the result of a week of not sleeping. She insists she is fully recovered but we are all on tenterhooks, at least for the first ten minutes after which we forget she was ever off, and have a good show. On my way through the pass door I come face to face with Maggie Smith who tells me I was splendid. I tell her I try to hide behind Imelda so I get a taste of the glory. She replied that hiding behind Imelda was quite an achievement in itself.

* * *

The following day I was signing on in Woking for the first time. I don't know how many actors signed on in Woking in 1973 but at a guess, it was none at all. Even so the morning started off quite pleasantly. When I told the first lady I was an actor, she sent me to see a second lady who told me to go and look at the 'Jobs Available' carousel while I waited for a third lady to interview me (I suppose it was on the off-chance that Olivier had nipped down on the train from Waterloo, and pinned up an 'Actor required for vacancy at National Theatre', card, having heard there was one arriving in Woking that morning). I explained to the third lady, who was less friendly than the previous two, that I was an actor, and we usually had to wait around until jobs turned up, which she didn't like the sound of at all, and demonstrated this by ignoring me. She started flicking through the rolodex in front of her, and while I was telling her I was sure there'd soon be an offer, she stopped me with a look and held up one of the cards.

'Until that happens, we have an opening for a butcher's boy.'

That's what she said. It's written in my diary, so it must be true. I didn't even know what a butcher's boy was, or what qualifications you needed (it was doubtful I had them anyway), or why she thought it was the ideal job for me, but that evening, my mother put forward the notion that she'd confused the wearing of straw hats, formerly popular with butchers and entertainers alike (the Black and White

Minstrels came to mind), and calculated being a butcher's boy would make me feel at home.

It was true when I'd told the third lady there might be an offer. Peter Farago, who'd directed us at Central, had joined the Young Lyceum company in Edinburgh, and was enquiring about my availability to play Speed in *Two Gentlemen of Verona*. William Shakespeare was out to get me again, I thought, and while I wasn't keen, it sounded marginally more appealing than a career in butchery.

In the meantime I met up with Fred, who was concerned our rise to pop stardom was stalling, and encouraged me to call Dave Clark, who'd promised to put us in touch with an A&R man. It took me a week to pluck up the courage to call him, much of which I spent sitting in my friend Dave's front room (he had a proper job), waiting for the Granada TV repair man to turn up. When I finally steeled myself to call, Dave C was incredibly friendly and sounded fairly pleased to hear from me. I cursed myself for being so timid.

He promised he would be in touch, and the call galvanised me into another burst of song-writing. At the weekends Diane came back from college, and together with Raymond, Dave and Ric, we would go down to the pub, play a game or two of bar billiards, then go back to Dave's house for a late-night episode of *The Avengers* or *Department S*. There's evidence to suggest that Diane found all this a very tedious way to spend our lives, and even more evidence to suggest I couldn't understand what she was going on about.

I was waiting for Dave C to call back, and eventually he did. I had an appointment with Adrian Rudge, who ran Intersong, the following week. Neither of the names meant anything to me, but I sounded impressed when he told me that Rudge had recently signed the publishing rights to Bruce Springsteen's songs, even though I didn't know who he was either. I was glad Fred was leaving it to me because I had a problem: Dave Clark was doing it because he liked my songs; I thought my best chance of success was playing with Fred. I felt sneaky going along to the meeting with two tapes: one containing my own songs, and the other the studio recordings we'd made the year before.

On Friday, 16 February 1973, I went to London to meet Adrian Rudge. The Intersong Music office in New Bond Street was buzzing, and Adrian was a busy man. He was speaking on the phone as he threaded my tape onto his machine, and it rang again as his finger hovered over the play button. Finally, he buzzed his secretary, instructing her to hold his calls, and swung his feet up onto the desk and started the tape.

Two days later I took the sleeper train to Edinburgh with two large suitcases, and a guitar strapped to my back. I was reluctant to go, ever since Adrian Rudge had flipped his feet off his desk, stopped the tape 15 minutes in, and said, 'I'd like to publish your songs.'

I was convinced my life had changed, and said so in large block capitals in my diary on the Friday night. Acting was a job that had to be worked around, whenever it got in the way, and it was definitely in the way now. What if Adrian called and said he needed us in the studio immediately? He'd mentioned a recording contract in a roundabout and slightly vague way, but it was good enough for me, except I was now four hundred miles away, in a land several degrees colder than was healthy. I had never smelled anywhere like Edinburgh. My landlady Mrs Murray said it was the hops mixing with the heather and the wind blowing in from the North Sea. On my first night there, I went to see *The Bevellers*, written by and starring Roddy McMillan, one of the heavyweights of Scottish theatre. It was brilliantly acted, gritty and funny, and I didn't understand a word anybody said.

The Young Lyceum company was altogether more eclectic, with a number of actors from south of the border; however Kenny Ireland and Alec Heggie more than made up for any Scottish shortfall. I enjoyed myself, both with the company and in the play. Peter Farago was trying to persuade me to come back in the summer to do a part in *Hamlet*, and then stay on for the festival. I called Adrian Rudge from a call box outside the theatre, who told me not to worry, he was still really keen. But there was something about the way he said it. The truth is, I was getting to like acting, and I seemed to be better at getting acting jobs than I was at being a pop star. I spoke to Diane, who said Edinburgh in the summer sounded fun, and I knew that would present a dilemma. At the beginning of March, I wrote a letter to Diane asking her to marry me. I don't think it was a very romantic proposal, a fault I was to repeat many years later with Elizabeth. Instead I wrote her a letter about how the play was going, and what films I'd seen and which books I'd read, signed it, and at the very bottom put:

'PS Oh, I nearly forgot. Will you marry me?'

There's no excuse for this affected casualness. It's purely selfish. I'm uncomfortable with in-your-face declarations of sincerity, because I think I sound stupid, and it makes me want to laugh, but I'm aware that by avoiding them I'm not communicating how I really feel. It's taken me forty years to figure this out and I've no intention of proposing to anybody else, just so I can get it right. Maybe in another life.

Diane wouldn't get the letter until Monday morning, and on Sunday a few of us climbed up to Arthur's Seat, a hill of considerable magnitude a mile east of Edinburgh, walking past Salisbury Crags, where the previous October, a few hours after their wedding, a husband had famously pushed his wife over the edge and tried to claim the insurance money. That night, I mentioned it in a letter I was writing to Diane, thought about it, and decided I should tear it up and start again.

6

EXIT, PURSUED
BY SHAKESPEARE

Friday, 10 July 2015. Out of the blue (she used those very words herself), I got a letter, sent to the theatre, from Diane, my first wife, whom I haven't seen for twenty-five years. It was another fifteen before that when we split up. She's coming to see *Gypsy* in a few weeks, and thought she should let me know in case I wanted to meet for a coffee. After what I put her through, she is remarkably sanguine.

* * *

On 9 June 1973, Diane and I were married in the registry office in Woking. I was about to go off to Edinburgh again, and I knew she would come to visit. These were the days when living together was 'living in sin', when couples checked into hotels under the name Smith. When Diane had come to stay in Nottingham, I'd told my landlady she was my sister, and had spent the weekend expecting her to burst in with a fiery crucifix. That doesn't mean I didn't love Diane, because I did. But I knew the reasons for the marriage were messed up. And that was before you considered my velvet suit, flowery shirt and white loafers.

I returned to Scotland for Ledlanet Nights, an arts festival organised by the publisher John Calder. We were putting on *Hamlet* and *Rosencrantz and Guildenstern are Dead* on alternate days. John McHenry was Hamlet, with Roy Marsden as Claudius. I was playing Osric and Alfred. There was no theatre as such in Ledlanet House; instead the audience sat in the large hallway on either side of the central staircase which became the stage. Ledlanet was Calder's country estate, and an hour and a half north of Edinburgh. There was no accommodation, and we drove there and back each day, it was a gruelling few weeks. Diane had got a summer job as our wardrobe supervisor and when we finished she retired to Edinburgh while I did the festival. The Young Lyceum's contribution was *Woyzeck*, directed by Radu Penciulescu, an intense and bearded Romanian who spoke little English. Peter Farago admired him, and considered it a coup to have him direct us. The rest of us were not so sure.

* * *

Monday, 20 July 2015. The cast all came in early today for a photo shoot for West End Bares, a late-night charity show put on by the casts of various West End musicals to raise money for MAD (Making A Difference Trust), an HIV and AIDS charity. The show is made up of musical numbers performed by actors wearing very few, if any, clothes. Tickets are like gold dust, and only for those working in the West End. I've been before, and it was great night out. I don't know what the *Gypsy* contribution will be this year, but I doubt I'll be asked – my nudity days are best left behind. The photo is also for the calendar. For the photo, the body-beautiful boys were keen to strip down to strategically placed hats, the girls, including Lara and Imelda, were only slightly more modest, with Imelda making excellent use of the cow's head from the show. I wore my coat, and shoes and socks, and, photographed from behind with my trousers rolled up, it gave the impression I was flashing everyone. I asked the photographer if it was funnier with, or without my glasses on, and Imelda pointed out that given the various states of undress of the others in the photo, no one would be looking at me, or my fucking glasses.

* * *

The trouble with *Woyzeck* was that Büchner, the playwright, had left it unfinished, so it had fallen victim to many interpretations. Radu had a script, but he was dangerously keen on improvisation. One afternoon after running the village scene, Radu had an idea. In his charming broken English, and never quite looking us in the eye, he explained his revelatory vision, that all the villagers should be naked from the waist up, including the lady villagers. Opinion about Radu's brilliant concept was divided. On the whole the boys didn't see much of a problem with it, while the girls were generally harder to convince. But there's something persuasive about bearded Romanians and their broken English, so that when we ran it again, we were all compliant, and topless. When we finished, the girls crossed their arms to cover their nakedness, and Radu looked at them thoughtfully and said, 'Yes, thank you, I have changed my thoughts. This will not work.'

The company was also involved in the main Lyceum production of *The Thrie Estaitis* ('The Three Estates') starring Scottish theatre heavyweights, Fulton McKay, John Grieve and Tom Fleming. I never really got to the bottom of what the play was about, as it was performed with authentic lowland Scots, and dialect designed to confuse the English. McKay strode about the stage, delivering imperious showers of spittle over everyone in his path, while Fleming's rich timbre made the piece a joy to listen to without making it any easier to understand. The male members of the Young Lyceum company, together with fifteen or so walk-ons, made up the army. I think we were the baddies, but it's only a guess. Every so often we would appear on stage, rough someone up a bit, then retreat to our distant dressing room, up four flights of stairs and along several corridors. All this went along without a hitch for several performances, and we had a fine old time between muggings, playing cards, slapping each other on the back and generally doing all the things that pretend soldiers do in their down time. Until the day it went horribly wrong.

The Assembly Halls had no call system as such, just a tannoy on which you could hear the show in progress; it was up to us to get down to the stage when required. There was usually someone paying enough attention to call out something like, 'Come on, lads, time to don our fibreglass helmets, and pikestaffs, and get moving.'

No one specifically had been given the job, and I suppose it was inevitable that, one day, the fun and games in the dressing rooms would prove too distracting. This particular night my landlady was watching the show, eager to see my several brief appearances. Four flights up, we were being unusually rowdy until someone waved their arms urgently and shouted.

'Wait, listen . . .'

The room went quiet, and we held our breath.

What we heard next, was our cue. Not our cue to put on our helmets and leave the room, not our cue to make our way along the corridors and down four flights of stairs. What we heard next, was our cue to appear on the stage. There was a moment of disbelief, followed by more moments of blind panic. Down in the auditorium, legend has it, the effect was mesmerising.

'Yonder cometh the army' (or words to that effect), said Fulton

McKay, raising his arm and pointing at the door through which we should have been entering. Absolutely nothing happened. Fulton wagged his finger meaningfully, as if this in itself might make us magically appear. Then a distant rumble started high up in the Assembly Rooms, increasing in intensity, as it moved slowly around the auditorium, getting louder and closer, people turning their heads to follow the sound (an audio effect worthy of Pink Floyd in their heyday), until finally, after what seemed an eternity, the entire Scottish army, sweaty and exhausted, toppled onto the stage, to be greeted by the snarling fury of Fulton McKay.

I enjoyed working in Edinburgh but I was starting to think I'd never work anywhere else. When I finished, Diane and I returned to warmer climes and moved into a small flat, not far from her parents, in the theatrically named village of West End, in Surrey. I'd heard nothing from Adrian Rudge for nearly six months and didn't bother calling him. For all I cared he could bugger off and publish that Bruce Springsteen bloke and see how far that got him. Besides, I had no sooner settled into our new home and wired up my tape recorder, than my agent called and said I had an audition.

I met Thelma Holt at her flat in London for what I assumed was an interview. She started by explaining about the play, *The Taming of the Shrew*, and the date we were starting and where we were opening, and it slowly dawned on me that this wasn't an audition at all, and that, in her view, I'd already accepted the job, just by turning up on her doorstep. This would be my fourth Shakespeare play since swearing I'd never do another one, and was as serious a case of being 'stalked by a Bard' as I'd ever come across.

I was powerless to explain the misunderstanding to Thelma and when I left the apartment an hour later, I thanked her and told her I'd see her at the read-through. Among the things I didn't know at the time was that for the next two months I'd be ripping Thelma's clothes off every night, while Nikolas Simmonds (Petruchio) took her from behind. Another was that I'd walked into a major panic. The planned production had fallen through, and the Open Space was committed to premiering a show in the Netherlands. As I was meeting with Thelma, Charles Marowitz was frantically working on a previously unfinished adaptation of *The Shrew*. They only had three days to cast it before rehearsals started, and as I was physically right – the part was mine.

Marowitz and Holt ran the Open Space Theatre together, and it had already gained a reputation for edgy theatre. His adaptation of *The Taming of the Shrew* stripped away the comedy, turning it into a shorter, sadomasochistic play that highlighted the subjugation of women. He interspersed it with devised scenes with Bianca and Lucentio in modern dress.

The Open Space Theatre was located on the western side of Tottenham Court Road, squeezed between an adult cinema club, and a dodgy electronics shop. You took the steps down into the basement auditorium, painted black, with rudimentary seating, and a communal dressing room at the back. Thelma Holt herself was playing Kate, and my own part was a nasty amalgam of Tranio and Grumio. There never was a read-through, because the script was a work in progress, and working with Marowitz was not what I'd expected. He was tall and charismatic, with a dry Mephistophelean sense of humour. On the opening-night press call he told the journalists I was Charles Marowitz and amused himself, watching me try to answer their probing questions. In fine restaurants he would ask for a slab of dead cow, rather than steak, then look at us, shrug, and say,

'That's what it is.'

We opened at the Hot Theatre in Den Haag, and went on to the Mickery in Amsterdam, where, after the last-night party, I had my first puff of a joint. The blood drained from my face and I staggered back to my room to lie down. It was pathetic. The next day we brought the play back to the Open Space.

The first night in London was held up for fifteen minutes because the *Sunday Times* critic, Harold Hobson, was late arriving and getting carried down the stairs to his usual front row position, where his wheelchair protruded well into the acting space. It was the first show I appeared in that was reviewed by a critic from a national newspaper, and I was acting an arm's length away from one of the most famous of all. By the end of 1973 the world as we knew it was falling apart. The coal miners were threatening to strike, and the oil-rich Middle Eastern countries had cut back production to a minimum. As a result, black-outs were common and queues for petrol stations grew longer. It didn't affect me much, because my VW Beetle still only had three wheels and sat lopsidedly at the end of my parents' garden.

In early February the miners' strike became official. The oil crisis was still in full swing, and Britain was already reduced to a three-day week, and now petrol-rations books were issued. It was a really stupid moment to think about buying a car, so that's what I did.

My logic went like this: car salesmen would be desperate to shift their inventory, and with the insurance money from my last motoring disaster in my pocket, I could snap up a bargain.

Instead I bought a Renault 4 van, complete with a lift-up flap above the rear door that, I was informed, allowed the goats to stick out their heads out on the way to market. This was a deal clincher for me. I'd been offered another job in Edinburgh and, subject to the availability of fuel, I planned to drive up. Now I could bring my goats.

On the 27 February, the Prime Minister Edward Heath called a general election with the slogan 'Who Governs Britain?'

To which the electorate replied with an emphatic, 'We're not sure, but it definitely isn't you.'

All of which meant that by the middle of March, queues at petrol stations had shortened and I packed my van to the brim with stuff I couldn't live without, excluding goats (which it turned out I didn't have), and set off up the A1.

I was back in Edinburgh to do *A Narrow Road to the Deep North* by Edward Bond. There were some new faces in the company, one of whom looked a square peg, wearing sensible grey trousers and a shirt and tie. There might have been a blazer involved too, because the overall effect was of an overgrown schoolboy. His name was Simon Callow and he was quiet, very bright, and would give me books to read by the likes of Evelyn Waugh and Aldous Huxley. Years later, after he was the Simon Callow we're all familiar with, I went to a party I knew he'd be attending. As we knocked on the door, I said to my friend that I wondered if the flamboyant Simon Callow would remember someone from his quieter days. Suddenly, a voice boomed from across the road echoing up and down the street.

'PETEEERR!' cried Simon, which kind of answered my question.

My repeated visits to Edinburgh meant my collaboration with Fred Marks had taken a back seat, and after I returned at the end of April, it ceased altogether. There was no definitive end; we just drifted in different directions. I was still recording my own songs, but the idea of performing them was less appealing. Diane was teaching, and so I had the flat to myself during the day and I made the most of it. I didn't have long because I'd been asked back to the Young Lyceum company yet again. This time it was a rock musical version of *A Midsummer Night's Dream* for the Leith Festival (a fringe festival of the Edinburgh fringe), and Farago had offered me Lysander, a leading part. Playing opposite me was an actress from the year below me at Central, Sandra Dickinson. I hadn't exchanged a word with her while we were students but I remembered her – it would be hard not to. She would perch on the foyer rail at the top of the stairs, holding court with a voice she might have borrowed from Judy Holliday, surrounded by acolytes and the casually fascinated. I think the first words she ever said to me were expressing disappointment that I was playing Lysander, rather than another actor in my year that she much preferred. Later she would laugh about her bluntness, and there's no doubt it made me determined to change her mind. That was how it all began.

We started rehearsals in the large room at the top of the King's Theatre, and Sandra proved difficult to impress. At the end of the first week she told me she wasn't sure how good an actor I was. She was a familiar face (and voice) at the time because of a Bird's Eye beefburger commercial in which she delivered the iconic line 'Gee, they got a band,' and though the public wouldn't always recognise her face, the moment she opened her mouth the reaction was instant. Our rock musical was free and performed in the open on Leith Links, the stage constructed from salvaged scaffolding with a raised platform for a four-piece rock band (on drums we had a young musician called John McGlynn, who later turned up in my life as an actor, playing the vet Calum Buchanan in *All Creatures Great and Small*).

These were the days before radio mics, or at least they were beyond the Leith Festival budget, so we used four hand mics connected to the PA system with long heavy-duty cables. The four mics had to serve all the characters, which often meant passing them to another actor, either at the end of the scene or sometimes between speeches. There was no quarter given to simplifying the action, and the combination was a recipe for cable tangles of spectacular proportions. On Friday and Saturday nights the audiences, fuelled by a few drinks, showed their 'appreciation' by throwing empty cans on stage. If we were really lucky, fights would break out and the police would turn up, make a few arrests and leave, while on the stage we carried on regardless.

There's no way round saying that Sandra and I were involved. We were both married and neither of us was looking for it to happen, but it did. I was intoxicated by the fact I'd won her approval, but it was our version of the same old story: we were away from home, performing in a rock musical and playing lovers. There was a reckless inevitability about it. As I get older I'm a little more honest with myself about the hurt I caused Diane, and at the same time, a little more forgiving of my folly. I can't say I regret it because that would include regretting Georgia, her children, and every other footstep, reckless or otherwise, along the path that led me to my current state of happiness. If having the affair with Sandra wasn't bad enough, what I did after that was unforgivable. When I returned to London I persuaded Diane we should move to Richmond, and we found a place on Richmond Hill only half a mile from where Sandra lived with her husband. In the following months Diane grew increasingly unhappy and eventually moved out and returned to her parents. Even though I was entirely to blame, it was still a bruising few months, I suppose because everybody except Diane was in a state of denial about what was going on.

By coincidence, that might not have been coincidence at all, we both went up for a TV series called *The Tomorrow People*, a children's science fiction series that was, ironically, intended as ITV's answer to *Doctor Who*. Based around four kids with telepathic and telekinetic powers, who wore 'jaunting' belts to move around, and lived in a disused underground station equipped with a computer called TIM, it nevertheless took itself rather seriously. Until we came along.

We were booked for three episodes, playing brother and sister. It was my first TV (if you disregard the army recruitment commercial, and I wish you would), and I was excited and terrified. At drama school there'd been no training for a medium most likely to provide employment for actors. I was learning as I went. We started with single-camera filming, where the importance of continuity and hitting your mark were lessons soon learned. Into the studio, where it was about finding your key light, avoiding masking yourself, and others, and learning which camera was on shot without actually looking for the red light.

By the end of the first week, I felt at home. I could hit a mark without looking, I could feel the key light, sense the red light on the camera, and if I was lucky, I could do all that and act at the same time. There was a faintly ridiculous side to my newfound skills: I was dressed as a space cowboy, with a dead fish in my holster, a blonde curly wig on my head and an accent out of the Beverly Hillbillies. The American accent wasn't so bad either, which I put down to many hours watching cowboy shows in my youth, and relentless coaching from Sandra.

Unfortunately, this was *The Tomorrow People*, and not *Armchair Theatre,* and the programme had a small budget, inevitable in a show aimed at children. Roger Price, who created the series, hadn't seen it going that way. His concept, like those of much later series like *Heroes,* and *Misfits*, was the next evolution of Homo sapiens, which he called Homo superiors. There's a story that *The Tomorrow People* became the inspiration for David Bowie's 'Oh, You Pretty Things', which features the line 'better make way for the homo-superiors'. The two had met and bonded in the canteen at Granada TV in Manchester, when Price was formulating his series.

Our story was a departure. This was series three, and Price decided to add a little humour for a change. The story had its tongue firmly in its cheek, and the regular cast loved the idea of sending themselves up. Afterwards there was talk of us returning in a later adventure. Stan Woodward even invited us round for dinner to discuss it. Everyone from the execs to the actors loved the idea.

The episodes were finally broadcast in April of 1975, and the young audience was both unanimous and unequivocal. They hated us. All plans for the return of Elmer, Emily and Momma were dropped, and the children of Britain breathed a sigh of relief. Despite the crushing blow of a future without *The Tomorrow People*, I'd made my decision. I'd rung my agent a few months earlier and told him I thought my future was in television.

It was the start of eighteen months out of work.

★ ★ ★

Wednesday, 12 August 2015. Diane came to see the matinee show to-day with two friends. We met up in the American Bar between shows, and they had a glass of champagne while I sipped a cup of coffee. She looked well, and seemed a lot happier than the last time I saw her. She has had some tough times, and while I wasn't directly responsible I realise the failure of the marriage was at the root of it. I warned her about the book, although I don't have anything bad to say about her, so hopefully it won't upset her. She has a good enough memory to correct me on some details of those early years, and she seemed dismayed I had forgotten she had worked on some of the shows in Edinburgh. Of course once she reminded me the synapses reconnect, and memories slowly repair themselves.

★ ★ ★

My marriage to Diane was over, and at the beginning of the year I'd moved from Richmond back into my parents' house in Woking, for what I expected to be a brief period. I was optimistic: *The Tomorrow People* was yet to be broadcast, and I was sure more offers would come my way when it was. Even the emotional pummelling of the marriage breakdown seemed to feed into writing songs, and in February I sent a tape off to EMI.

I'd also come up with a song for Sandra, called 'A Big Star in Hollywood'. It was what might be politely called a novelty song, but it was tailored to her talent for comedy. By now, Sandra was a well-known face on television. We recorded a demo at my parents' house, and sent it to a record producer called Peter Sames, who had produced Peter Skellern's hit 'You're a Lady', and he, in turn, persuaded Polydor to sign Sandra for a three-single deal. We went into the studios at Polydor in March. Sandra was not a natural singer despite possessing an interesting and characterful voice. After years of being told she couldn't sing, the recording process was long and difficult. The better song was on the B side, 'Never Get Over You'. Twenty years later, while I was hanging out in the Soho House in London, a club singer told me she sang my song in her set, and it was one of her favourites.

In mid-1975 'A Big Star in Hollywood' was released. Polydor believed in it enough to print a special sleeve with Sandra's picture on the front, but even so it received a truly awful review in *Melody Maker* and sold only a few thousand copies (although it went down surprisingly well in Japan). The follow-up single was 'Let the Love Get In', a song I'd written with a simple 'Walk on the Wild Side'-style bass line; this time we got a rave review in *Melody Maker* but still only managed a few thousand sales (and slightly less in Japan). Proving nothing except that no one really gives a toss about reviews in the *Melody Maker*. I was dropped as songwriter for the third single, and instead Sandra covered a song from Alan Parker's film *Bugsy Malone*. *Melody Maker* didn't care enough to review this release and I heard the sales were negligible (no one bothered to find out about Japan).

Out of the blue, I had a call to meet a man at EMI who really liked the tape I'd sent him. We met and discussed the possibility of a song-writing deal. It all sounded great but I was growing cynical, and a few days later, when they sent the contract through, I could see the catch. For a guaranteed £500 a year, I had to give them fifteen songs, five of which had to be acceptable to them, the others I could have back. There was no obligation on their part to get the acceptable songs recorded. They could, I thought, sit in a box for the next fifty years. And what if I didn't give them five that were acceptable? On the other hand, I was unemployed, and what else was I going to do? I stared at the papers, with my name typed in, and then put the contract in a box for the next fifty years.

Wednesday, 20 May 2015. Sitting at my computer this morning, I mentioned to my children that many years ago I was offered a songwriting contract with EMI, which I turned down. They were appalled that I might have compromised their financial future by doing something so stupid, so I told them about a similar opportunity years later – and how I'd turned that down too. They were apoplectic, which quite pleased me. It's nice to be appreciated by your children, even if they only appreciate what an idiot you are. Of course, I had perfectly good reasons for both decisions, if only I could remember what they were.

The second time it happened, I remember being driven around Wembley in a Rolls-Royce by a man who insisted he could sell my song to Frank Sinatra, and I sat there thinking that Frank wasn't quite the right man for the job. I suppose it's a bit late now.

* * *

By this time Sandra, having moved to Berkshire with her husband, had moved back to Richmond, without him. Our relationship had faltered, and I was finding it hard to deal with unemployment and my failure to make any headway into television. I was forced to take a serious look at what I was doing, and the dismal future in store for me. I was twenty-four and had already made a mess of one marriage, and career opportunities had stalled. I decided I wasn't particularly driven to be an actor, and had ended up in the profession courtesy of bad results at school and an unintentionally good joke at my drama-school audition. I enjoyed writing songs but spent more time imagining my success, rather than working towards it. Where other actors would be off blagging cheap tickets for West End shows, or writing to casting directors and repertory theatres, I would watch black and white films on BBC2 in the afternoon, and strum my guitar. Where other songwriters would be out there playing their songs to anybody who'd listen, I locked myself in my room and recorded them for my own enjoyment.

In September the friendly folk at the labour exchange lost patience with me too. I was called into the interview room and the usual stern lady showed me a vacancy for a filing clerk at the Inland Revenue office in Twickenham, where they worked what they called flexi-time, and that meant I could be available for auditions at any time, as long as I put in the required hours a week. She had a self-satisfied smirk on her face. She knew she'd finally got me.

I started work a week later in the filing room on the fourth floor of Regal House, and soon discovered that I liked the job and the people. At the time I was reading a book every few days, and I discovered a cluttered second-hand bookshop only five minutes from the office. After I'd done the morning filing I could hide myself at the end of one of the aisles, on top of the stepladder and read, with the chance to hide my book in a handy tax folder, should anyone unexpectedly appear. I did everything I was asked to do, but discovered that with planning I could do it in half the time. Tom, who was in charge of the file room, a kind and quietly spoken man, was impressed with my filing skills and turned a blind eye to my reading sojourns. Later he was the first to suggest I should join the Civil Service full time.

In December, my agent sent me for a commercial to play a trawlerman, I sat in the waiting room, feeling out of place and depressed; and I realised I had reached the end of the road. Afterwards I called my agent, my heart thumping, and told him I was giving up acting – if I got my head down, I told him, I could work my up the Revenue ladder and be a technical inspector by the time I was thirty. I was hoping he might try to dissuade me but he listened and said he understood, which made me more certain I'd made the right decision. I walked back to Waterloo over Hungerford Bridge with the trains rattling the footpath that clung to the side of the railway line. It was all a bit tragic and filmic; my acting career was over, I was just a civil servant at the Inland Revenue and the nearest I would get to show-business was filing Leslie Crowther's tax return. In a way it was a relief. I'd have a bit of money and while the year had been a rotten one, at least I was ending it by making a positive decision. That Christmas I attended my first ever office party and it's all true about what goes on in stationary cupboards.

Early in January, I told Tom and Ivy I was seriously considering applying for a permanent position. They thought it was a great idea, and were keen to help in any way they could, and suddenly I was set on a course that I knew would be hard to pull back from.

On 21 January 1976, for a brief moment, our little corner of the tax office was a popular place to be. It was the day of Concorde's inaugural commercial flight and at 11 o'clock anyone interested lined up along the long window of the filing room, which afforded an unrestricted view of Heathrow some six miles in the distance. A plane took off, and a small cheer went up, until we realised it was just a regular aircraft. Then another . . . was that it? No, that was only a jumbo jet. I thought we'd never be able to tell for sure from this distance but I had not reckoned on the most distinctive feature of the supersonic plane. At about ten past eleven, a low rumble seemed to spread through the building, the sound growing louder until we finally saw Concorde rising majestically into the sky at an impossibly steep angle. I never thought for a moment that I would get the chance to fly in it, let alone in the way I eventually did.

In February, Ivy handed me an envelope containing the application forms. I took them home, and kept them in my room, I remember not looking at them for several days, perhaps there was a part of me that still wasn't quite sure. Eventually Ivy asked if I needed any help filling in the application, and that evening I sat down with a pen in my hand, and the form on the dining table in front of me. After my name, and address, and date of birth, which presented no major problem for me, calamity struck. When I had applied for the temporary job, listing my five GCE's had presented no difficulty – I had written down the exams I had taken, rather than those I had actually passed.

On this application there was a note in italics that said 'Please produce certificates'.

That was pretty much the end of my career as a tax inspector. The following morning I went to Ivy, and reluctantly said I'd decided I really wanted to be an actor, and not a civil servant in the Inland Revenue. They took the news rather well considering the loss I would be to the service, and I was left only with the minor problem that I wasn't actually an actor either.

Then a week later an extraordinary thing happened. My former agent rang to say that although he no longer represented me, there was a part that he thought I might be right for me if I could tear myself away from the tax office.

The phone call was a message left on my parents' answer machine, and the following day I returned the call. It was a part in a TV serial of *Love for Lydia*, from a book by H. E. Bates. That lunchtime I made my way to the second-hand bookshop in Twickenham to see if they had a copy – they practically had an H. E. Bates department. I chose one in the best condition, and bought it for a few pence. The part of Tom was one of the male leads, all of whom are in love with Lydia. I auditioned at London Weekend Television, a franchise that used to broadcast as its name describes, starting on Friday nights through to

Sunday evening. I'd been reading the book on the train, and noticed it was first published in 1952; as there was no reprint listed it was fair to assume I had a first edition.

I was taken in to meet the producer, and director by Diana Parry, the fearsome head of casting for LWT (later as, I got to know her better she became less scary, and positively lovable if you got her talking about her cats). Richard Bates was the producer, and the son of H. E. Bates, and would later go on to produce *The Darling Buds of May*. Alan Clarke was the director – he would later become legendary for the banned *Scum*, and for *Made in Britain* and *Rita, Sue, and Bob Too*. Richard had a friendly face framed by a neatly trimmed beard, but Alan Clarke, unshaven, and wearing a cloth cap sat expressionless and said nothing. Dressed in jeans, work boots, and half turned away, he looked at me with an unnervingly sideways stare that De Niro later perfected. Meanwhile, Richard didn't ask me to read, which was a great relief, instead asking me if I'd managed to get a copy of the book. I held up my copy, and told him where I'd found it, and that it was a first edition, which made him gasp, and it soon became obvious his interest in the book was considerably greater than his interest in me. He asked me where the bookshop was, and how I'd found it, and if there were any more first editions, which led in a roundabout way to the subject of my place of work, which finally elicited a reaction from Alan Clarke along the lines of 'Fuck me, you poor fucking bastard'.

As I left with my book, I asked Richard if he would like my copy as I could easily get another; he hesitated, obviously aware of feeling beholden to an actor he might not want to cast. Instead I told him where the bookshop was, and left it at that. It was another three weeks before I was offered the part. Leaving the tax office was an emotional farewell. They presented me with a pen which, amazingly, I'd managed not to lose by the time Tom, Ivy and Eleanor appeared on my *This is Your Life* some sixteen years later.

Left: My Auntie Olga with Granny Louise in British Guiana, 1937.

Below: My parents' wedding day, April 1947.

Left: My father about to perform – this got him many invitations to Sunday lunches.

Left: On my christening day. I look quite happy in a dress.

Below: In the back garden of Longthornton Road, in my great grandmother's vice-like grip. Grandad looks a bit disgruntled, but he is in the line of fire from Uncle John's pipe. My nan is second from the left, on the same row.

Me and my sister Shirley. All dressed up and nowhere to go.

Above left: Mr Verney at his desk, in our spanking new school.

Above right: Diane and me, sweet and innocent in the classroom store cupboard.

Below: Masters Stores, High Street, Knaphill. The shop had closed down, but we still lived there. This place was party central – in our dreams. Raymond, Dave, and myself are trying to look inviting.

The young composer, with his Woolworths keyboard. Fortunately, the fan was so loud that you couldn't hear how out of tune it was.

Above: Diane and me on the bus at the Isle of Wight festival, 1969.

Below: Jocelyn, my first proper girlfriend, on the almost completely snow-free school skiing trip to Blairgowrie, Scotland. We barely noticed.

Left: My first *Doctor Who* press call. Out of view are sixty, or so, photographers. No celery because the producer wanted it to be a surprise. Either that, or he hadn't thought of a convincing enough explanation for it. Incidentally, that took him three years. © *Getty*

Right: Serenading a cow in 1970. A sign of things to come.

© *David Williamson*

Below: The Elite of Clods, in the days when you could sit on bits of Stonehenge. © *David Williamson*

Dave Clark and the best of Central School of Speech and Drama, at the recording of 'Everybody Get Together'. Fred Marks, later of 'Rod, Jane, and Freddy', is third from the left on the front row.

EXIT, PURSUED BY SHAKESPEARE

We began filming *Love for Lydia* early in the long hot summer of 1976. The series starred Mel Martin as Lydia, and Christopher Blake who had been in my year at drama school. Also in the cast were Jeremy Irons, Sherrie Hewson and David Ryall, along with old-school heavyweights like Rachel Kempson, Michael Aldridge, and Beatrix Lehmann. There seemed to be no expense spared, our costumes were beautiful, the sets were elaborate, and we filmed in many beautiful locations. The whole thirteen-part series was made on location, and unusually for that time, it was shot on video, which caused major problems technically, especially in that summer of hot bright sunlight as well as difficulties getting large outside broadcast trucks to locations.

The first two episodes featured a long ice-skating sequence which was shot on the disused Wisley airfield in Surrey. A large area of the old runway was covered with Perspex sheeting, and special skates were made with tiny wheels instead of blades, and we were sent off to Richmond ice rink to practise basic skills. Unfortunately practising on ice with tiny grooves being made by the blades in no way prepares you for the impossible job of skating on hard Perspex. When we started filming none of us could stay upright for more than a few seconds. It wasn't helped by Alan Clarke's desire to film everything in wide shots so our feet were always in vision. The winter effect was completed by tons of salt, and gallons of foam liberally spread over the landscape. The actors, and supporting artistes, all dressed for the winter weather, struggled slightly as the temperature that summer hit the high nineties, but as our director said, when he was appraised of our difficulties, 'It looks fucking great, though.'

They set up a video feed into a cabin so we could watch the scenes being shot, and I had to admit it looked beautiful. Day after day, the sky was a brilliant shade of blue, and the sun burned down on us. Chris Blake and I were sitting in the video cabin early one morning while Jeremy Irons was filming on the plastic ice. In the cabin with us were several chaperones and parents of the children who were skating in the background of the scene. Between takes Jeremy, forgetting his radio mic was still on, let loose a tirade about the 'little shits' who kept getting in his way and trying to get into shot. Chris leapt to his feet and in a heartfelt display of phony outrage, declared he had never heard anything so shameful and appalling in his life, and grinning broadly in my direction, he left the cabin.

By the third week of filming, the tons of salt, and the foam, were beginning to take their toll on the equipment. Salt is not ideal if you want to preserve electronics, and everything started to fail. The cameras, the lighting, the sound equipment, and everybody's patience, were being severely tested. The cost of these problems was described to me as 'huge'. We had a few days off until more cameras and equipment turned up, and we could continue filming. Two days later the filming stopped again. This time it wasn't the equipment. I had a call to say that filming had been cancelled with no explanation, and after a few more days off, we were summoned to a meeting at LWT. I called Chris but he knew no more than me. All we could do was wait. I expected to find myself re-applying to the tax office for that temporary job, or perhaps the last three months had been a dream, and I was about to wake up, sitting up on top of the stepladder at the end of aisle three.

The following week, about fifty of us gathered in the boardroom at LWT and a few minutes later Cyril Bennett, the controller of programmes, came in flanked by more men in grey suits. I had never met him before and he looked an uncompromising figure with slicked back hair, and large tinted spectacles. He explained that while LWT was still committed to making the series (a sigh of relief), they could no longer allow it to continue in its present form. Was he talking about recasting? It was surely more likely to be about the cost of lost equipment.

I was wrong – it was all about close-ups – and the fact there weren't any.

'It might be all right for BBC2,' said Cyril, 'but this is London Weekend Television.'

He was on thin ice with that remark, but I let it pass. We were told that we were going to reshoot the first two episodes again so the audiences could see our faces, and that Alan Clarke had been asked to stay on, but had rejected the offer. I imagined Alan's rejection was a little fruitier than Cyril Bennett was letting on. It was a major upheaval. Rather than the wide and evocative shots of the landscape, and lovingly detailed interiors, our faces now filled so much of the frame you could see nothing else.

The whole affair took another twist, when in September of that year Cyril Bennett managed to fall to his death from his third-floor apartment in Kingston. No one knows if it was suicide from stress caused by his failure to win the Saturday night battle with BBC1, or if, as was speculated, he'd slipped while leaning out of his window to see if his chauffeur-driven limo had arrived.

Filming the series took almost a year, and even though I blew my brains out in episode eight, I had to come back for numerous pick-ups. I was sure the series would be my big break. I couldn't see myself getting an opportunity like that again.

7

MY ARM UP
A COW

Monday, 27 July 2015. A mini media frenzy blew up yesterday over rumoured plans to bring *All Creatures Great and Small* to the big screen. By today, expectations were scaled down to a series remake by HBO. The story was fuelled by the *Daily Mail Online* yesterday morning and today they requested an interview. Then I had Radio Middlesbrough on the phone. The *Daily Mail* is one thing but if Radio Middlesbrough calls, you know the story must be big. Stars rumoured to be lined up include Sarah Jessica Parker as Helen, Hugh Laurie as Siegfried. I don't care one way or the other but the press want to hear that I either love it or hate it.

Mind you, I wouldn't mind a cameo as a grumpy farmer.

★ ★ ★

I auditioned for other jobs, while I eagerly awaited the release of *Love for Lydia*. Including a new series for the BBC based on the books by James Herriot about a veterinary practice in Yorkshire. I ran out and bought a copy of the first book, called *It Shouldn't Happen to a Vet*. On page 2 the character I was up for is described as being short and dark which seemed the absolute antithesis of me, and I began to wonder if my agent had stopped reading the breakdowns again. I went along to the audition even though my real focus was on the following September when *Lydia* would be broadcast. The signs were not promising, there was a room full of Tristan hopefuls, not all of them short and dark, but most looking more Tristanish than me.

We were given a few pages of script, and waited our turn. When I finally got in there I met Bill Sellars, the producer, and Ted Rhodes. They asked a few questions, and still sticking to the horse-riding rule, I answered them all in the affirmative. Do you smoke? Yes, I do (no, I didn't). Are you at ease with animals? – I've spent my life around animals (we had a cat). Have you read the books? Yes, I have (as far as page 2). I was surprised to find myself more at ease than I was auditioning for *Lydia* a year before. Ted asked if I would like a cup of coffee which, as things were going quite well, I accepted. Bill Sellars suggested a gentle read of the script, and with the arrival of the coffee, a small cloud appeared on the horizon. It isn't easy to read a script while holding a polystyrene cup of hot BBC coffee. Indeed, it proved so difficult that I didn't quite manage to do it. It started with a small sip before I turned over the page of the script balanced on my lap. The page caught the bottom of the cup, spilling a small amount of coffee but it was my attempt to avoid spilling more, and jerking the cup upwards that resulted in my spilling most of the rest of it over my shirt and the script. It was, as Ted told me later, comedy gold. I can't even remember if I finished the reading, I only remember sitting on the train home, my stomach still lurching when I thought about it.

Incredibly, I was still working on *Lydia*, doing some sound looping to replace lines that were indistinct on the original takes. This was something new to me, standing in front of a microphone in a dubbing theatre in Soho looking at myself and hearing the original track in one ear while re-uttering the line with some semblance of performance. It's never as good as the original sound, even with that unseen jet overhead, but sometimes it has to be done. I had heard nothing from the BBC for several weeks, and had all but forgotten about the vet series. My agent was more attentive now, calling me every few days about nothing in particular. One afternoon he rang to ask how I felt about doing a small part at Birmingham repertory theatre, where Peter Farago, whom I'd worked with in Edinburgh, had taken over as artistic director. I asked how long it ran for, which was only a few weeks. This was a difficult one, I wasn't doing anything else but a few lines in Birmingham didn't sound particularly appetising.

'What do you think?' I asked.

'Well, it's work, I suppose.'

I thought that was an odd thing to say, and was about to ask for the weekend to think it over, when he went on. 'The trouble is if you did it, you wouldn't be available for the BBC series they've just offered you.'

I imagined his thick glasses steaming up with the excitement of it all, and at that moment I was more excited for him than I was for me. He'd dragged me back from a career as a filing clerk and I was happy to have rewarded him. Despite the terrible toupee, he had a good sense of humour. He must have done, to wear the toupee in the first place.

I was to be what was described as a semi-regular. Tristan didn't appear in the opening show, and I was only booked for five episodes out of the thirteen, as the character was meant to be away at veterinary college. In early June of 1977 I attended a meet-and-greet at Television Centre. Chris Timothy, who was playing James Herriot, was slightly late, so I was introduced to Robert Hardy who was playing Siegfried. He was charming and eloquent, taking my hand in his and slapping it gently with the other and saying what fun it was all going to be. I thought how on earth am I going to play his brother when I'm from Streatham? It's a common problem with actors. The fear of being found out. I wonder if Colin Firth and Daniel Craig, both Secondary Modern boys like me, might have had similar thoughts when cast as Mr D'Arcy and James Bond? I remembered my mother had taken a shine to Robert Hardy when he played Prince Hal in the TV series *The Age of Kings* and I couldn't wait to tell her. I met Carol Drinkwater who was playing Helen, daughter of a local farmer and eventual wife of James Herriot. And Mary Hignett who played Mrs Hall. It was all going quite well until Chris Timothy walked into the room, took one look at me and said flatly, 'Too tall, recast.'

Everybody laughed. Everybody knew it was a joke. But it didn't stop me worrying that Bill Sellars might look at me again and think, Actually, now I look at him, he is.

In a quiet moment Ted Rhodes sidled over and asked how I was getting on with Robert. I said we were getting on fine. Ted leant over and whispered in my ear, 'Landed gentry, you know. Can be very difficult,' and raised an eyebrow. A look I would come to know well.

So I convinced myself they'd made a terrible mistake in casting me. I wasn't a reprobate, I wasn't outgoing, and outside of my comfort zone, I still suffered from acute shyness. I'd only asked a girl out once in my life and that was a disaster. On top of that, there was the blushing (something which, after years of embarrassment, I've finally conquered, though that might be down to the poorer circulation of middle age.

Playing Tom in *Lydia* had been easy compared to the task ahead. How long would the goodwill of Robert Hardy last when he discovered the dashing lady's man was a product of the lower middle classes with a barely average education?

In the next few weeks there were costume fittings at which the

Tristan character emerged dressed in fair-isle sweaters and cord trousers. It became an iconic image of my character and eventually led me to the dizzying heights of a knitting pattern brochure. They also highlighted my hair to match Robert Hardy's and over the next three years I'd regularly be seen sitting in a high-end hairdressing salon in a fashionable part of London, with bits of tin foil covering my head. Shortly before we started shooting I was taken to Television Centre for a final look at my costume. Bill Sellars and the production team stared at me and nodded happily. Polaroids were taken, with the Tristan look finished off by a Woodbine cigarette hanging out of my mouth.

In those days, filming expenses were given in cash and for a few weeks' filming, this would add up to a significant amount. You took your form to the cashiers' office that was located by the exclusive horseshoe car park in front of Television Centre, and they would ask you if you wanted cash or cheque. Almost everybody chose cash. I walked away with several hundred pounds in a discreet envelope, more money than I'd had in my life.

Filming began in July of 1977 in the Yorkshire Dales which, until the moment I turned left off the A1 at Bedale, I never knew existed. The road from the A1 winds through Little Crakehall, past Patrick Brompton, and swings left after Constable Burton. I had never seen anything like it, and apart from the curse of the TV aerials, I couldn't imagine it had changed that much since the thirties when the series was set. We were based in and around Leyburn, but the actors and production team took over a hotel in a small village of West Whitton – and I do mean took over. At the Wensleydale Heifer, we would serve drinks to ourselves, late into the night, and in the morning go into the hotel kitchen, and make ourselves breakfast.

* * *

IS THERE LIFE OUTSIDE THE BOX?

Friday, 19 June 2015. Tonight before the show Lara Pulver knocked on my dressing room door dressed only in a bath towel, and asked if she could heat up her coffee in my microwave (a likely story). It reminded me of an incident from my wild and carefree youth. In the early days of filming *All Creatures* we were based in a small hotel in West Whitton called the Wensleydale Heifer. I had sat in the bar most of the evening trying to catch the eye of a young actress playing a guest part. At about eleven she announced she was going to bed, I said loudly that I would be going up soon as well but she left before I could contrive to leave at the same time.

I sat there with the others for a few minutes before sadly deciding I should get some sleep. I had been in my room for about five minutes when there was a knock on the door. The girl stood there in nothing much more than a hand towel, and asked if I knew how to work the shower. By an extraordinary coincidence I knew exactly how to do that very thing, and though it was easily explained, I thought a practical demonstration in her bathroom would be a more helpful, and gentlemanly thing to do. So off we went to her room where I showed her the technique of pulling up the what's-it at the top of the tap that diverted water to the shower.

She smiled, and thanked me, and so I smiled, and said it was a pleasure. Sorting out the shower was such a simple matter of common sense I was reasonably hopeful there might be something more on her mind, but the fear of misreading the situation, and my subsequent humiliation, kept me silent, and unable to make a move. What I needed, I thought, was a more obvious sign, her playfully toying with her hair perhaps (I'd read that was a sign of attraction in a recent Desmond Morris book) or maybe her towel 'accidentally' slipping to the floor. Personally I hoped she would be so kind as to throw herself on the bed, and tell me to get on with it.

None of these things happened. Instead I shuffled about embarrassingly, said goodnight, and went back to my room. I told this story to Lara who congratulated me on being a gentleman.

MY ARM UP A COW

★ ★ ★

This was what was called block filming, scenes from multiple episodes shot over several weeks and it meant you had to keep a close idea of where you were in any story. Chris Timothy had come up to Yorkshire early to spend a week with Jack Watkinson who was the local vet and also our adviser on the show. I met Chris in the bar the night before filming started. He was looking grey-faced. With the exception of Robert Hardy none of us had any idea of what being a vet involved, and I gathered Chris's week had been in turn both exhausting and upsetting. For anyone brought up away from the sometimes harsh reality of rural life, it was an unpleasant experience. Chris bore the brunt of the 'on camera' veterinary work, while I mostly got drunk in the Drover's Arms, impersonated farmers and pretended to be ghostly monks.

The first scene I filmed was also my first appearance in the series, which you might think would be obvious but, in fact is rarely the case.

The director of my first episode was Peter Moffatt, whom I'd never met but had certainly encountered. While still working under the name of Peter Moffett, I'd received letters intended for him, asking to be considered for something he was directing. Eventually I'd sent them on to him with a note saying, 'How about considering me for a job?' I'd never heard back from him. I might have taken a dislike to him but that was impossible, and we would go on to work together several times over the coming years. Though he often gave the impression of gentle bemusement, he had an eye for comedy both on screen, and in his professional life.

Early on he asked, with a twinkle in his eye, which profile I preferred. He once told me a story of working with Margaret Lockwood and an actor whose name I forget, in a fifties film romance. No one had bothered to check which side the actor preferred to be shot from, and unfortunately it turned out to be the same side as Miss Lockwood. The result was that although the story was one of falling desperately in love, all their scenes had to be shot with them walking side by side looking into the distance, and professing undying affection.

My first scene was Tristan arriving at the railway station and being met by James. The BBC couldn't afford a train so the scene was shot at the disused Redmire station with a smoke machine giving the impression of the departing train. Unfortunately, the smoke machine was faulty and the wind instantly blew away the dribble of smoke that was released. In fact, there seemed to be more smoke coming from my Woodbine cigarette than from the machine, so we made do with the train whistle that was added in the edit.

I had few words in that first scene, but it set the tone and I began to think I'd enjoy playing the part. I suggested to Peter that I should sit in the back of the tiny car as if James was my chauffeur, while he struggled with my luggage. Later Chris told me he knew I was going to be all right as Tristan because of the way I said my first line.

'Yes.'

I wish it was always that easy.

Both Chris Timothy and Robert Hardy were big influences on me. Chris was even-tempered, and quick to compliment and support everyone around him. This was his moment, and yet he wanted it to be an ensemble piece, and would sometimes almost obsessively try to take a back seat. Quite early on he decided that Tristan was the funny one, and would often suggest I take his lines. Even though I was young and eager to take any extra lines on offer, it became so regular an occurrence, I found myself insisting we should do it as written. I think he was uncomfortable with idea of being the star, and so, on top of a natural inclination towards altruism, he was determined to be undemanding, generous and easy to work with.

He taught me a lot about how to behave on set, and how to keep success in perspective.

A week into the filming, I was starting to find my feet. The few scenes I'd completed had gone smoothly, at least no one had complained and the director hadn't inundated me with notes. Bill Sellars was on set most of the time, but he rarely intervened. One morning, I found myself in front of him as we queued for coffee. I indicated for him to go ahead of me but he waved it away. I had a sense that he was about to speak.

'They've been watching the rushes in London,' he said. 'Bill's very happy.'

(Bill Cotton was the incoming controller of BBC1, formerly the head of light entertainment, and arguably the most important man at the BBC. I remember watching his dad on a Saturday night in the Billy Cotton Band Show.)

'Really?' I couldn't think of anything else to say.

'Well, he asked to take a look at you, and if he hadn't been happy . . .'

He let the statement hang but the implication was obvious, I hadn't realised my future was quite that perilous.

Unit facilities on television productions were fairly primitive in those days. There were no drivers employed to bring us to and from the unit base, no trailers or caravans for us to sit in. Instead we would pile into the AFM's (assistant floor manager) Land Rover and off we'd go. We'd change in the costume van, and then hang around in the make-up truck until someone took us away to start filming. Hanging around in the make-up truck was the most pleasant part of the day and I discovered that if you made the assistants cups of tea or offered to bring them breakfast from the catering wagon, they would never want you to leave.

About two weeks into the block I was filming a scene where

early one morning James finds Tristan in his car, having thrown up there and fallen asleep. After the first rehearsal Bill Sellars appeared and introduced me to a man with him. Brian Sinclair was the real Tristan, and had recently retired from the ministry of agriculture. He'd obviously been short and dark, just as the books described him – now he was short and a distinguished shade of grey, but he still had the look of the debauched choirboy – an innocent face combined with a mischievous grin. Meeting him was useful because I'd worried about how to make my Tristan endearing even though he behaved appallingly, and now, shaking his hand, I could see how Brian could have managed it. I was even managing to master the Woodbines.

We'd tried filter cigarettes but they weren't around in 1937 when the series was set. So although I hadn't smoked except for one cigarette given to me by my father when I was thirteen, and which nearly left my lungs lying on the ground in our back garden, I was stuck with Woodbines. Endlessly spitting out tiny shards of tobacco that got stuck on the end of my tongue was a problem, but other than that I affected a smoking style that I imagined looked pretty cool.

I had not, of course, consulted the experts and in those days being a 'spark', or member of the lighting department, came with a compulsory smoking requirement. As I walked back to the make-up department one morning, past the generator truck, one of the sparks called out to me, 'Hey, Pete mate, why do you smoke like a prat?'

I was deeply hurt, I had no idea I looked like a prat. Over lunch I took lessons from the professionals, and completely overhauled my technique, trying the 'thumb, and forefinger' method but discarding it in favour of the 'between the forefinger, and middle finger' style but making sure the cigarette is held towards the bottom of the fingers. In the afternoon, full of confidence, I used my new version in the next scene. The next day was a day off and we went for tea at Askrigg Falls. On Sunday we were filming again and Bill Sellars was there bright and early. He took me by the arm and pulled me aside. For a moment I wondered if Bill Cotton had changed his mind.

'You've changed the way you smoke,' he said.

I explained about the sparks and their expert critique and said I felt the smoking should look authentic. He looked at me wondering how to break the news.

'We like you looking like a prat,' he said finally.

The filming block lasted about five weeks, and was a social whirlwind. I drank too much or at least more than I ever had before, and stayed up too late, but somehow developed the ability to learn lines in the make-up chair the following morning. John Nathan-Turner who was the production unit manager was a kind of social secretary, organising dinners, and parties, and general activities for the film unit. Sometimes we would drive over the tops into Swaledale, and have an evening in Reeth which was close to where Robert Hardy stayed. The route was affectionately known as the yellow brick road, because it weaved its way up from Wensleydale around escarpments, and troughs, and never seemed to end. In the darkness driving back you could easily find yourself off the road, with the car leaning at a precarious angle, and hysterical laughter from all of us who should have known better. It wasn't too healthy for the rabbits either.

Robert, or Tim as we called him if invited, sensibly stayed in a separate hotel from us. A classier hotel with a fine restaurant, to which he would sometimes invite us. Usually just Chris, Carol and myself, and occasionally the director. He would order bottles of fine red wine, which I obligingly sipped at, while he talked matter-of-factly about his friendship with Richard Burton, and the years working with Olivier at the RSC. It seemed a world away from my more frivolous acting ambitions, but his approval of me did wonders for my confidence.

IS THERE LIFE OUTSIDE THE BOX?

After the filming in the Yorkshire Dales, we returned to London, and into the steadier regime of rehearsals and studio days. The BBC had a building opposite North Acton tube station that consisted of six floors of rehearsal rooms with three rooms to each floor. On the seventh floor there was a canteen that also served food for the scenery, special effects, and costume departments situated next door. Every imaginable show would rehearse in this building, and lunchtime in the canteen was an autograph hunters' paradise. The rehearsal room for *All Creatures* would have the main sets, the living room, the surgery etc., marked out on the floor with different coloured tape, and metal poles would mark the doors. This was where we worked through, and fine-tuned the scenes before recording them in the studio. The rehearsal period was about ten days per two days' recording at the Pebble Mill studios in Birmingham. Looking back, that seems generous considering there were no rehearsals at all for location filming, but interior scenes were always longer, and wordier, and it gave us the chance to learn the lines, which often meant changing them, and on occasion rewriting entire scenes.

Robert Hardy was very particular about the standard of the scripts, and had a problem with the way Johnny Byrne wrote for Siegfried. We would struggle through a couple of days' rehearsal, and over time I learned what this meant. The following morning he would arrive, and announce he had taken the liberty of reworking the scene, and although he always gave us the option of going back to the original, I for one did not argue. Nor did the director. These were my first substantial scenes with Robert Hardy, and no two rehearsals were ever the same. Sometimes he would bark the lines at me, sometimes spit them at me, nose to nose, sometimes gesticulate wildly, sometimes coil himself in controlled fury. Somehow I had to keep up, and give him as good as I got. He was extraordinarily supportive, and as the weeks went by, I began to enjoy myself. Our first scene together was about Tristan's failure to pass his exams, something I felt fairly well qualified to play, but I never knew what he thought about me until I was informed through my agent that I would now be in all the remaining episodes after Robert had requested more scenes with the two brothers. Tristan's planned return to veterinary college was dropped, and then for the most part forgotten. After recording one bruising Siegfried/Tristan encounter, he took me aside, and told me he would one day like to direct me in *Hamlet*. It was an opportunity that I never took advantage of, which may have been for the best.

The interiors were recorded at Pebble Mill. While Chris, Carol and Robert stayed at a nice hotel in Birmingham, I found I could make money on my expenses by staying at the Bristol Court hotel just around the corner from the studios. It was cheap and falling apart, and according to folklore had been condemned a few years earlier, but reprieved because of lack of hotel beds in the city. If you drew the short straw, something I did with remarkable consistency, you would get the single room with no window, or more often the bedroom that was designated part of the fire escape. This was fun. Even though you were given a key, the door had a fist-sized hole cut into it just above the lock to enable escaping guests to reach in, open your door, and make their way through your room, out of the window and onto the fire escape, hopefully waking you on the way. It also meant anybody passing down the corridor could look directly into your room through the conveniently placed viewing hole.

Unlike Television Centre, Pebble Mill had an intimate family atmosphere. Everyone was on first-name terms, and even though I had a dressing room, I would still spend most of my time loitering in the make-up department. The building used to have a grand reception area but by this time it had been requisitioned by *Pebble Mill at One*, a daily live magazine programme that went out, not surprisingly, at 1 o'clock. Getting to our studios meant making your way across the back of their set often as the show was being broadcast. You could stop and catch some interesting lunchtime entertainment if the guests were good enough.

★ ★ ★

In the early days of *All Creatures* we would camera-rehearse the scenes during the day, and then from 7.30 record them in quick succession. You could go back, and retake, but that would push us ever closer to the deadline of ten o'clock when VT (the videotape department) would turn off the machines. Looking back at those early episodes it's interesting to see what was accepted, or rather what isn't now. Every living-room scene involved glass after glass of whisky being poured and knocked back, and I was barely ever without a cigarette. Of course the whisky was only water with drops of burnt sugar, and I never inhaled the Woodbines for fear of leaving a lung lying around the studio floor, but no one was concerned about my health. The beer, for some reason, was real, which in the drunken pub scenes caused problems. Perhaps too many beer commercials had made me immune from the effects of downing a few pints but I remember Chris Timothy throwing up in a bucket halfway through a scene, and then coming back on set for more.

Skeldale House was at the heart of the series. The exterior was an imposing house in the middle of Askrigg in Wensleydale, actually called Cringley House, and owned by Olive Turner and her husband Charles, who welcomed us with open arms from the first day of filming. Although we never shot any interior scenes there, it was often used for make-up, and costume, and, while relaxing between takes, they would make us tea and coffee, and show us pictures of their children. The couple even appeared as extras in a couple of scenes. In the first series, filming the scenes in Askrigg was an easy affair. No one was that interested, except the odd irate motorist whose trip through the dales was held up by the BBC filming 'some nonsense', but by the second, and third series it would come almost impossible. Every scene outside 'Skeldale House' would be filmed with an audience of up to hundred or so people. Some were there by chance, some came seeking us out, and often a coachload of American tourists would arrive on organised tours of 'Herriot' country. Each take would begin with a request to onlookers not to use flash photography, not to talk loudly, nor to laugh. It was rather like television meets theatre; we would perform the scene for them, they would patiently wait for the shout of 'cut', and then give us a round of applause.

The studio interiors of 'Skeldale House' were also entertaining to do. The staircase went nowhere, and if you had to run downstairs to answer the phone, it meant perching yourself on a small platform just out of shot, and launching yourself into the scene. The surgery was full of a wonderful selection of genuine veterinary implements from the thirties as well as shelves of very dodgy-looking medicines. For my own character of Tristan I decided it would be fun if all I ever did in the surgery was clutch a mortar, and pestle in case Siegfried appeared, aside from the usual smoking, and reading 1937 copies of *Health and Efficiency*.

Then, of course, there were the dogs. There were four main dogs that roamed about the set. Robert Hardy's whippet called Christie, a lovely dog whose only failing was the inability to remain in the same room as Robert once he'd started acting. There were Bill Sellars' two dogs who were large, and fluffy, and extremely loud, and finally John Nathan-Turner's mutt, who would cause the most trouble, and then look at you with wide eyed innocence. If there is a scene that sums up how much we enjoyed making the series, it would be the episode in which I return from college. We rehearsed the scene without the dogs, me walking in the front door, and explaining my concerns about my exam results. Then we rolled tape, and put the dogs in. No one gave a thought to the fact that John's dog was on heat, and the chaos that followed put an end to my plan to play the scene with quiet truthfulness. I made my entrance at least, but the dogs were already barking wildly, and chasing each other around the set. Carol, Mary Hignett and I carried on for a few more lines, but we were all laughing now, and so I gave up. I stopped acting. I carried on with the lines in a distracted way, because no one had actually said cut, but there was no real point because I was sure we would never be heard above the doggie hysteria. Afterwards, we stood there grinning and waiting for the second take. The floor manager listened on his cans and looked at us: 'Message from the gallery – absolutely brilliant, we're moving on.'

* * *

Tuesday, 8 September 2015. Stanley our dog is limping. Once again I'm considered the oracle on all doggy- or pet- related issues and this is my family, who should know better. It's a confusion that even relatively bright and rational people are subject to: I once played a vet on television, so I must know about animals. When people ask for advice I usually offer it, foolishly hoping it'll not be misread as me knowing anything about matters veterinary. I diligently top off the advice with words to that effect, but it's often taken as delightful modesty and a couple of weeks later they will ask about some other animally thing. When we filmed *The Last Detective*, a regular feature was a large St Bernard dog and the same thing happened. I was even given personal responsibility (and a hand towel) for mopping up the drool – which is a fact of life with that breed – because no one else on the crew could bring themselves to do it without gagging. And because 'Peter knows all about dogs and that'.

MY ARM UP A COW

★ ★ ★

Love for Lydia started going out on Friday, 9 September 1977, and although it received good reviews, I didn't get the sense it was going to launch me into the stratosphere, although one Saturday morning a few weeks later, in Guildford High Street, I was recognised from being on television for the first time in my life, and was so excited I had to cut short my shopping trip, and go home to tell everyone.

We had one more short filming block before Christmas to capture the look of the Dales in winter, and the weather was turning colder. Up on the tops it could be cold in the summer, but in the late autumn, your face would go numb, making it difficult to speak. A sympathetic assistant would offer a cup of tea in which I would stick my frozen fingers, rather than drink it. I also ran out of luck avoiding the 'arm up the cow' scenario. Chris, as the diligent vet, seemed to spend most of the filming with his arm up some farm animal or other but up until now Tristan's lassitude had meant I had not been called upon. Now here it was in black and white: *Interior Barn: Tristan is stripped to the waist with his arm up a cow.* I spent so many days worrying about it, I didn't even give much thought to the cold weather. The series was set in 1937 when vets didn't have the luxury of modern 1977 rubber gloves, so therefore neither did the actors portraying them. All we had was a bar of soap, and a bucket of warm water, and Jack Watkinson, our veterinary adviser, to show us what to do. It's very simple he said, a quick up and down the arm with the bar of soap, and in you go.

So on a cold November day with the wind whistling through the cracks in the walls of the wooden barn, in I went. Of course, when I got on with it, it wasn't so bad, and even the cow seemed to quite enjoy it. All I remember is thinking the only warm part of my body is my arm. Afterwards, with a real sense of achievement, I made my way back to get cleaned up, and even the sparks seemed to look at me with new respect, although I felt sorrier for them, having to clean the cow shit off the cables after the filming.

Having completed seven of the thirteen episodes we had a two-week break for Christmas, and were due to start early in the new year.

Things could not have been going better; my life had been turned around, and my career was on track. I had survived having my arm up a cow, and now we heard the series would be broadcast starting in January.

★ ★ ★

Thursday, 12 November 2015. Didn't sleep last night. I had to be up at 6.45 for the car taking me to Elstree Studios where I'm doing a Harry Hill sketch for Children in Need. My contribution is sticking my head out of a cow's bottom, and saying, 'I've been stuck in there for forty years.' (Although I'd like to point out it's only been thirty eight.) There were other relics there, including Tony Blackburn (what's going on with the hair, Tone?), Peter Purves and Jenny Agutter dressed as a nun. There was also a Dalek knocking about as usual. Harry is quiet and unassuming, and I felt bad that lack of sleep made him a little grumpier than usual. The head-out-of-the-cow bit went down well with the studio audience, and I'm sure many will think it my finest work.

★ ★ ★

Sandra and I flew off to New York to meet her parents at the Waldorf Astoria. We flew Laker Airways, the first of the no-frills airlines which had only recently started flying to the USA, and this was my first ever visit to a country I had been writing songs about for ten years. It was like a party excursion, everyone cheered as we took off, and again

144

when we landed, and I realised the other passengers were probably like me – never before being able to afford international travel.

Manhattan: I couldn't believe that steam really came out the drain covers, that car tyres squealed as they went round corners, and the city never slept, but it was all true. On every street corner there were Father Christmases, differing in age and ethnicity, ringing hand-bells and calling, 'Ho, ho, ho, Merry Christmas, everybody!' with varying measures of conviction. In the hotel room of the Waldorf Astoria hotel, I switched on the TV and of all the channels available in New York, the first person I saw was Robert Hardy in an episode of *Elizabeth R*. This must be a good omen, I thought.

All the thrill and excitement living the high life was tempered by the news from London that Chris Timothy, while running around the countryside, had tried to stop a motor vehicle with his legs, failing miserably and managing to shatter the more important bones in his leg instead. To add to his troubles, Chris wasn't quite in the geographical location he should have been when the accident occurred. The whole thing was a bit of a mess, and for a few days nobody knew what would happen next. I was told he was alive, if not exactly well, and was about to be bolted back together with various bits of metal, bolts and screws, and no one knew how long his recovery time would be. The situation was being continually assessed and no one could say how well he would be able to walk in the foreseeable future. The worst-case scenario was recasting James, and delaying the show until we had reshot the scenes. This had shades of *Love for Lydia* about it. I began to wonder why this was happening to me, and whether it was it karma, payback for my general lack of application. At least it wasn't me lying on the operating table while the surgeons fired up their Black & Deckers.

My agent called and said one option being considered was replacing Chris and re-shooting from the beginning, and how would I feel if the replacement was me? I'm not sure how serious an option that was, but it made me feel uncomfortable. I was quite happy playing Tristan, and felt great loyalty to Chris and our oddball little team. When I returned from Washington, DC, I went to visit Chris in hospital, and he seemed in remarkably good spirits for a man whose personal life was now as battered as his body. He was sitting in a chair, and looking more like his old self. It occurred to me that, as we'd already filmed the location scenes for the whole series, all we needed to do was prop him up against a wall, or tie him to a lighting stand in the studio, and we'd be laughing – everyone except for Chris.

The first episode was broadcast on 15 January 1978, a Sunday night, and incredibly, a few weeks later, we were back in Birmingham to continue making the rest of the series. The show received an appalling review on BBC Radio 4's arts programme *Kaleidoscope*, which dampened our spirits slightly. The review, by a working vet, criticised virtually every aspect of the programme, and concluded by saying that no one would want to tune in to watch the exploits of James, Siegfried and Tristan. I'm sure the reviewer wasn't watching us, but within a few weeks, eighteen million other people were, and some church services were moved earlier to accommodate the congregations' new viewing habits.

Chris made remarkable progress and we resumed filming six weeks later. He was immobile without crutches, and recording the scenes to give the impression of movement became an art-form. We'd prop him against the desk in the surgery from where he would announce he was going out on a call. Cut to me saying goodbye, my eyes following him to the door as two aptly named prop guys would carry him over to the door, and lean him against it. Cut back to Chris managing a turn as if he's about to leave. Sometimes it was Siegfried talking to both of us as, out of view, I put Chris's arm around my shoulder, and lugged him over to our next position.

As a result of his predicament, Tristan's involvement was upgraded again; there were scenes that James couldn't manage to pull off while standing or sitting motionless. Chris endured all this with admirable patience, although I suspect he was in more physical pain than he ever let on, and between takes I would catch him sitting, and rubbing his leg with a painful look on his face. In the end it turned out to be a bonding experience for all of us. Very quickly the BBC realised they had an immensely popular show on their hands and Chris's injury notwithstanding, they commissioned a second series and this time they wanted the show to go out in the autumn slot, which meant we would barely finish the first series before starting the next. Chris's leg was improving all the time, but we had lost six or seven weeks, and so had a three-week break in transmission in March to allow post-production to catch up.

I celebrated our success by getting myself a new car – a Renault 5TS, not quite in the Aston Martin league as all my friends expected, but a step up from the Renault 4 van I'd been driving. It had a radio you could actually hear while driving along the motorway, and it was on one of these journeys to Pebble Mill that I first heard *The Hitchhiker's Guide to the Galaxy*, Douglas Adams's brilliant take on science fiction, and a comedy with no studio audience, a rarity at that time.

Apparently 1978 was the year that we really 'never had it so good', when we all had the perfect balance of work, wealth and happiness, when everything peaked, most notably our optimism, before the graph started its slow but relentless downward journey. Personally I couldn't refute it, a young man in his twenties, his blond highlights sparkling in the sunshine, leaning casually on his Renault 5TS, his blonde American girlfriend in heart-shaped sunglasses by his side. I have the photos to prove it. Even his new bank manager wants to take him out to lunch and offer him a mortgage, and his dad manages to bring up his name in the local newsagent's or to the visiting plumber. Only his mother refuses to be swayed by his success, constantly reminding him how lucky he is to be working with Robert Hardy.

As the new series started filming, Chris had managed to find a way of walking that concealed his limp as long as he affected a kind of John Wayne swagger, something that he grew more attached to over the next couple of years. I was now everyone's idea of a lovable wastrel, and in June I was invited to open a local fair. Hawes was a sizeable market town only a few miles from Askrigg where we were regularly filmed. I had been cajoled into doing it by a man in the Drover's Arms, and now I was worried they would expect the outgoing Tristan, and not an introverted actor. Robert Hardy waved my concerns away: 'Do it as Tristan.' So that's what I did.

I can't remember my whole speech but it went something like: 'Hello everyone. Cheers [holding up a pint of beer]. Before I declare this fair open, I'd like to run through what's going on today [pull out a dog-eared piece of paper]. At 2.30 we have an appearance by the Wensleydale Morris dancers in the main area, and at roughly the same time I will be appearing in the beer tent. At 3 o'clock we have a fancy dress competition in the main area, and meanwhile I'll be appearing in the beer tent. At 4 o'clock we have the dog show, and I will be— no, hang on – I think I'm judging that one. So let's say at 4.15 I will be back in the beer tent [and so on] ...'

It all went down quite well, although my mother, who was visiting Yorkshire to admire her son's first personal appearance, was rather confused as to why I would want to spend so long in a beer tent when I didn't drink beer.

Although I was more involved in the filming than I'd been before, I still had a lot of free time and it gave me the chance to explore the Dales, and I would drive around, taking in the extraordinary beauty (apart from the odd cluster of modern bungalows and the television aerials on every rooftop) of the countryside and maybe have lunch in one of the small villages dotted about.

But occasionally the lure of a town, with more than one shop and a post office, proved too much. That's how I ended up in Richmond one Friday afternoon, wandering around the market. I was soon aware of a giggle of girls a short distance away from me, but thought nothing of it and walked on. When I turned around they were still there, so I hurried a little, and they hurried slightly more. It had suddenly turned into a pursuit. I have no idea what I was running away from any more than I knew why they were running after me. There were no more than ten of them, but I felt like I was in a scene from *A Hard Day's Night*, although, I admit, there wasn't that much screaming. I escaped to the safety of my car, and drove back to the hotel.

Later that night I told Chris who was so annoyed he hadn't been there that he decided we should go back the next day. It sounds ridiculous when I mention all these years later but despite the success of the series none of us had experienced this before. The odd autograph was one thing but being chased down the street, now that was something special. On the Saturday morning we parked my car in Richmond, and walked nonchalantly around the market square looking as conspicuous as possible. It was Saturday and the town was crowded, but nobody seemed to have a clue who we were. An hour passed, and with Chris's leg aching, we decided to give up and go back the hotel. We turned and realised we had a group of people in tow. We waved pleasantly, signed a few autographs and, deciding that being recognised wasn't all it was cracked up to be, made our escape through a handy chemist shop, obligingly being let out of the rear of the building.

We never went back to Richmond without sunglasses and hats.

The unexpected success of the series had given Bill Sellars and

Ted Rhodes a headache. We were getting through the stories at an alarming rate and in the first series a single episode might feature four or five stories from the books. James and Helen had been married halfway through the first season. The problem was exacerbated by Alf Wight's insistence that not only should the series only feature stories from his books, but also he wanted the veterinary practice, and the animal treatment, to be at the heart of the show; he especially ruled out any hint of discord in James and Helen's relationship. Keeping Alf Wight 'onside' was a courtesy issue, I don't think he had any legal recourse except to take his name off the titles, but Bill obviously wanted his endorsement and tried to keep him involved in the process where possible. In any event it was probably these restrictions that kept the series popular and on track, and prevented its soapification, a trend that was creeping into the TV drama schedules at that time. Only Tristan seemed to escape these restrictions, and I wasn't about to complain about the succession of girlfriends – even if every relationship ended in disaster.

One Sunday we were invited to tea at Donald (Siegfried) Sinclair's house, a large, and splendid, if slightly disorganised property at the edge of the North York Moors. Both Alf Wight, and Donald's infamous younger brother Brian, my alter ego, were there. Robert Hardy had already told me the story of the two brothers individually giving him their view of the TV series. Donald had said to him, 'Good stuff, but, of course, I was nowhere near as awful as you made me out to be.' This was followed a couple of days later by Brian also congratulating him, but adding, 'You did let Donald of the hook, he was so much worse than you portrayed him.'

That afternoon it was as though the Sinclairs were acting out their lives for our amusement. Along with our tea Donald's wife offered us jam or honey with our crumpets. Brian asked for honey, at which Donald leapt up from his seat exclaiming, 'Honey? No one has honey with tea. Honey is for breakfast time. Never heard anything so ridiculous in my life.' That pretty much ended the jam or honey conversation, and we moved on to other topics. Brian was about to go on a cruise with his wife where he was being paid for giving talks about the real world of 'James Herriot'. Alf Wight was very happy about this, and thought it suited Brian perfectly, while he far preferred staying at home and writing. Donald, I noticed, seemed oddly discomforted, and as though something else was on his mind. I was glancing in his direction when he rose from his chair and quickly left the room, returning a few minutes later with a freshly toasted crumpet on his plate, spread liberally with what looked suspiciously liked honey. I looked at Brian who raised his eyes to the ceiling with a long-suffering expression as if to indicate this had been the story of his life.

That Christmas, Sandra and I flew out to Washington to see her parents. Her brother David and his family had chosen that year to drive across country from California, and her younger brother had come down from Rochester in upstate New York with his girlfriend. This confluence of their family was a rare occurrence, and I suppose to mark it in some indelible way, Sandra and I went down to the town Hall in Rockville, Maryland, and surrounded by her brothers and her parents, and without any of my family knowing anything about it, we got married. We returned to the UK rather shocked by our own impetuousness, and made it up to my disappointed parents by buying a house only two doors away from them. It had been Sandra's idea, but one I was happy to go along with.

By March I was back in the dales, freezing to death and chasing sheep across the snowy hilltops. The show was still incredibly popular, but by now we were all getting itchy feet. We made three series of *All Creatures* before we collectively called it a day. We had taken the books up until the outbreak of war and the departure of James and

Siegfried, and the last episode of the third series, while maybe less amusing than others, contained some of my favourite scenes. The final shot was James driving away from Darrowby, the first two people he waves to are Olive and Charles Turner, the owners of Cringley (Skeldale) House which they had recently sold to be turned into an old people's home . . . It was the end of an era for the characters, and also for us. We were all going off in different directions: Chris was doing a musical, Robert was about to play Winston Churchill, and Carol wanted to write. I had agreed to have a go at a sitcom, eventually two of them as it turned out. What we all knew for certain was that it was absolutely the end of playing TV vets in *All Creatures Great and Small*.

Until we did it again . . . three years later.

8

DAVE PROWSE TRIED TO KILL ME

Tuesday, 14th July 2015. Back at Big Finish for a Weeping Angels story without Janet and Sarah. Janet is mad as hell of course, which makes me happy only because it indicates she's not feeling too bad after her cancer battle. Matthew Kelly is guesting as Leonardo da Vinci, and although we've bumped into each other many times over the years, this is the first time we have worked together since 1981, and *Holding the Fort*. Once again I try to correct the story he often tells that I advised him not to do *Game for a Laugh*. What I said was that he would find it difficult to get good acting work if he went down that route, and I still maintain that was true. It was over twenty years before he escaped the image of the presenter, a job he did brilliantly, by the way. When I told him my recollection of the conversation he patted me gently on the knee, and said, 'It's lovely to see you', meaning, I suppose, that he'll go on telling his version of the story for the rest of his life.

It was lovely to see him too.

$$\ast \quad \ast \quad \ast$$

IS THERE LIFE OUTSIDE THE BOX?

We were due to record the pilot of *Holding the Fort* on 10 August 1979. It's a day that's hard to forget because at 5.30 that afternoon, as we finished a camera rehearsal of the show, the lights went out. They stayed out for ten weeks. Television screens, assuming that you only watched ITV, went black. It was beginning of the great ITV strike and the result of a bitter dispute that had lasted through the spring and summer months. In simple terms, ITV was making loads of money, and the unions wanted more of it for their members. It's true; ITV technicians were the best paid in television, but then so was the management. More problematic was the number of unions involved in any negotiation. The tabloids made absurdly exaggerated claims about union members income. Some so absurd, they almost matched the amounts the management were being paid.

While my promising TV career was on hold I briefly went back to song writing. I wired up my new Teac four track tape recorder and even splashed out on a decent microphone. I was struggling with the lyrics for a song I'd temporarily called 'Dancing in the Dark', when I had a call from Stan Woodward who'd directed our ill-fated episodes of *The Tomorrow People*, a few years before. He asked me if I'd like to write the theme song to a children's series he was planning called *Button Moon*. I'm not even sure how he knew I wrote songs, but I said yes I'd love to. I sat down at the piano unsure where to start on a theme tune, played around a bit and eventually gave up and went back to struggling with lyrics. It was only a minute or two before 'We're dancing in the dark' became 'We're off to Button Moon'. It was a terrible cheat, but I sent Stan the recording a couple of days later, and he was so impressed with the speed and rendition of the finished song, that he invited me to sing on the recording a month later. The show was an unlikely success, and is remembered fondly by those who grew up watching it. Thus, for many years after I've been able to impress people much younger than me and who've never so much as set eyes on me on the TV.

When ITV started broadcasting again on 24 October, no-one was much in the mood for making comedy shows. They'd managed to record the camera rehearsal of our show and eventually, when good humour was restored, they took a good look at it, and we were given the series go-ahead. It was almost a year before we started the series proper, and in the meantime the BBC called with a very good sitcom offer of their own.

Sink or Swim was written by Alex Shearer and I loved it the moment I opened the script. Shortly after, I met with producer/director Gareth Gwenlyn at the Television Centre. He was an unlikely looking director, smartly dressed in a pale suit and tie. He had a rather quiet, inscrutable manner, that didn't exactly make me feel at ease. He'd made some very successful shows such as, *The Fall and Rise of Reginald Perrin, Butterflies* and his current show, *To the Manor Born*.

The meeting took place only a week before I was due to start recording *Holding the Fort* and I was dizzy with the sudden interest in me after a year of not much going on and was also worried that my imminent employment on an ITV show might put him off, especially as the dates clashed by a couple of weeks. Everything I thought might put him off, seemed to make him keener to have me do it, and in end he delayed his start date so I could slip seamlessly from one to the other.

Despite the stress of making the studio audience laugh while you're recording, TV sit-coms take less time out of your life than any other job. They are almost always rehearsed in Church Halls, and, almost always, only in the mornings. This four-hour day includes a generous tea break (now re-designated a tea/fag break) and a gossip about the merits (or not) of last night's television.

Holding the Fort was a six-episode, almost completely studio-bound sit-com, which meant it took only six weeks to complete, and the day we recorded episode five, episode one was being broadcast, fortunately to good reviews. It was written by Laurence Marks and Maurice Gran and Patricia Hodge and I were the leads, with Matthew Kelly as my best friend and soon to be employee. I'd expected Patricia to be hard work but nothing was further from the truth. I felt she was always searching for something that wasn't quite there in the writing and would often present a challenge to the newcomers, Lawrence and Maurice. Matthew Kelly had started out in stage management and had only resorted to acting at the encouragement of all who had worked with him and felt his natural talent and warm eccentricity was wasted, left hidden behind the scenes.

* * *

We finished *Holding the Fort* on Friday night and a week later I was due to start filming *Sink or Swim*. The intervening days gave us just enough time to move house yet again - three doors away, to an identical house, now right next door to my mother and father, and a couple of days after that, as I was lugging tea chests of stuff up the garden path, I heard our fancy new Trimfone warbling somewhere inside the house...

In the space of one week I had finished playing Russell Milburn, was about to morph into Brian Webber, and in my few days off had been offered the chance to play Doctor Who. Not that I could tell anyone of course, I had been sworn to secrecy on pain of...well... I've no idea... on pain of something that John Nathan-Turner never specified. I kept my secret throughout the filming block for *Sink or Swim*, as we created traffic chaos on the roads of Bristol, as I stood atop a narrow boat on the back of a lorry on the M4, and as we disrupted the Acton car auctions in London. I think John's idea was not so much to keep the secret, as to keep the speculation about possible casting on the front pages, speculation that swung between the possibility of a female Doctor to the usual suspects: Richard Griffiths, Geoffrey Bayldon, to the wild card Brian Blessed, who was usually the man behind the Brian Blessed rumour in the first place.

In spite of this, or maybe because of it, I threw myself into the character of Brian with great fervour. It gave me the chance to tap hidden depths of nerdiness, a rich seam that ran deep inside me. Gareth Gwenlan was a revelation, with an ability to make a minor tweak that brought new life to a scene. He knew exactly what would make a scene funnier and what would tip it into farce. Gareth was keen to use an untried actress, Sara Corper, as my girlfriend, and Robert Glenister as my younger brother. Together we made an oddball but effective team, with the only drawback being mine and Robert's inability to look each other in the eye, in some scenes, without a twinkle and then helpless laughter. In the Christmas episode there was a scene where we disagree about a need for a baby Jesus in our nativity decorations. It wasn't a particularly stand-out scene but we never got through it without laughing and when we finally got through it, the occasional smirk could still be seen.

I feel a bit sad telling this story, because of the memories and knowing the show is still there, lying in the BBC vault, but that it's unlikely anyone will get to see it again. Although we made three series, and got excellent ratings, it was cancelled because the BBC didn't think it could have two shows about two brothers, running at the same time, and preferred *Only Fools and Horses* to ours. Still, its early obscurity is a regret.

Meanwhile *Holding the Fort* had been running for a couple of weeks. It was the breakthrough show for Laurence Marks and Maurice Gran. When we started they were still working for the civil service, young and ambitious but not quite assured enough to take the gamble. While perhaps not the best, they were the savviest writers I worked with. Their long-term plan, which they later carried out with some success, was to come up with good ideas for projects, write the first episode, and then commission other writers to do the rest. Then they would keep control of the show and still be free to come up with new ideas, and before long they would take over the comedy world. It was based, more or less, on the American TV sitcom handbook which enabled the making of twenty-six episodes a year rather than the paltry six, that single writer British comedy shows could manage.

All that was to come later. For now it all depended on *Holding the Fort*. After three weeks of good ratings, a few days after we finished recording the series, I heard they had given up the day jobs, and were heading for the big time.

Meanwhile the BBC had begun to run trailers for *Sink or Swim*, and I seemed to be everywhere. Struggling to keep my *Doctor Who* secret, I may have been less tight-lipped than I thought. I'd certainly told my family, and Robert Glenister and Sara Corper, with the same stipulation: *Don't tell anyone else this, it's a big secret . . .*

Which is a bit like inviting them to pass it on in the same way.

So it's possible I was the cause of the phone call on 5 November 1980, from the *Doctor Who* Office to my agent saying the news was out, and they were issuing a statement immediately announcing my casting, and would I be all right talking to the press? I was driven from my rehearsals to the BBC in London, and spent the next four hours talking to journalists on the phone and the odd one in person. For the first hour I rambled a bit, aware I hadn't given much thought to what I might say. In the second hour, I hit my stride and was about as coherent as I got all afternoon. I had never done publicity like this and wasn't sure if I should say the same thing to every reporter or try to make it different each time. Besides, my views were being refined and adjusted as I went along, which should have meant I was getting better at it, except in the third hour a terrible fatigue hit me. I was no longer sure what I'd said in any particular interview and therefore no idea if I was repeating myself, no clue who I was talking to, or where abouts in the country they lived, even if I was going out 'live' or being recorded, and the way things were going, less sure I would still have the job in the morning.

I got home just before nine o'clock in the evening, exhausted, and just in time to see my face at the top of the nine o'clock news. I thought I'd either died or I was now definitely the Fifth Doctor. The news item was followed by one confirming the former actor Ronald Reagan had been elected the 40th President of the United States.

He got second billing.

* * *

By now Sandra was the darling of *Blankety Blank*, a BBC quiz show hosted by Terry Wogan, and since August had been filming *The Hitch-Hikers Guide to the Galaxy* by Douglas Adams. I was a big fan after listening to the radio broadcasts on the long journeys to Pebble Mill, and earlier in the year I'd been teased by an availability check for one of the main parts in the TV version. Sandra, who was everything they weren't looking for in the audition, had nevertheless won over Douglas Adams, and with it the part of Trillian. In the middle of rehearsals one day, Sandra overheard a conversation between the director, Alan Bell, and Douglas that went something like:

'Alan, who can we get to play the Dish of the Day?'

'I'm not worried, it isn't a big part, he doesn't move and he's inside a rubber suit.'

'I think we should get someone interesting though. Great if it they were high-profile.'

'A guest part for someone who doesn't mind not being seen? Which idiot is going to go for that?'

At this point, according to legend, Sandra piped up enthusiastically with, '*Peter will do it*', and the great wheels of the BBC artist-booking system began grinding into action. I was very happy to do it, wanted to do it, would in fact have done it for nothing, but this was the BBC and things were not that simple.

Having spent three years playing Tristan for a 'special low' episode fee (determined as an actor with a regular part but no previous BBC employment), my recently negotiated *Doctor Who* fee had instantly moved me into the 'special high' category (recognising the size and importance of the part), and in consequence, my new 'special low' fee, in relation to my new 'special high' status, was now too high for the special 'low' fee set aside for Dish of the Day.

Feel free to read that paragraph again, but it boils down to the BBC insisting that they had to pay me more money to do the job, while at the same time saying I couldn't do the job because they had to pay me too much money. Seriously, this is the conversation we had.

I insisted I didn't want a fee, but apparently that was out of the question. Alan J.W. Bell, who was now quite taken with the idea of the next Doctor Who being in his series, begged them that I was worth the extra fifty quid, and suggested we could all have a whip-round, but the bookers earnestly shook their heads, and a gloom descended. It was an even more ludicrous impasse that had them licking their lips. The original choice for the master of ceremonies at the Hotel at the End of the Universe had been Jonathan Pryce, an actor now making his mark in films as well as on stage and television. The BBC made his agent an offer that wasn't acceptable, and they, in turn, asked for more money, probably quite a bit more than Jonathan's designated fee, which was on the low side. Once again Alan found himself doing battle with the bookers. 'It's Jonathan Pryce,' he told them, 'he'd be great.' Neither the agent or the BBC would budge, and after a day of deadlock, Pryce pulled out and the director was told to come up with another suggestion. The part was offered to Colin Jeavons, a fine actor who, because of his long history working for the BBC, was immediately offered a higher fee than Jonathan Pryce. However, to cheer up the embattled director, the booking department conjured up a *special* '" low" low' that allowed me to play the part.

I met Dave Prowse while filming the 'Restaurant at the End of the Universe' episode, at the same time as I was struggling to come up with a convincing character for an Amiglean-Major cow. Neither of us had that much to do, so while we hung around we chatted about stuff. I liked him, even if he did try and kill me. He was honest and unaffected in the way he spoke about his life; I thought he was like Britain's answer to Arnold Schwarzenegger, where the answer had been slightly wrong. Both started as body-builders and moved into acting. Here Dave was slightly ahead of the game, becoming the TV superhero known as The Green Cross Code Man, which must have made Arnold steam (if he'd known what the hell it was). Both had arresting vocal styles: the mouthy Austrian accent of Arnold, alongside Dave's cosy West Country burr, and both had their big break in sci-fi films. After that the comparison falls apart a bit, but I thought it was worth mentioning because it struck me that Dave's career had combined luck and misfortune in equal measure, like being cast as Darth Vader, one of most successful villains in movie history, but then no one telling him they weren't using his voice until he sat in the movie theatre at the premiere.

He described ringing his agent about getting an audition when he heard they were making *Superman*. He heard nothing for weeks and then received a call from his agent,

'Dave? Get down to Pinewood, Ilya Salkind the producer has got some great news!'

Jumping in his big American car, driving out to Pinewood studios, his heart pounding, striding into the Salkind's office and hearing him say, 'Dave, this is Christopher Reeve, and he's playing Superman. We'd like *you* to train him.' So instead of playing *Superman* he created the superhero's muscles, something he was very proud of, which led on to a discussion about my muscles, or relative lack of them. He could do wonders, he said. I had broad shoulders and after a few weeks I too could look like Christopher Reeve, and why don't I come down to his gym?

As I sat and listened to him, to the friendly rounded vowels, and trying to ignore this particular strand of the conversation, I suddenly thought, he is *The Dish of the Day*, and so shamelessly, without asking, or thanking him, I stole his voice.

However, I did agree to visit his gym.

Dave's gym was not far from Borough tube station just south of the Thames, and was called The Dave Prowse Star Gym, which pretty much tells you everything you need to know about it. This was where you went if you wanted a body like Christopher Reeve's, although sadly I must point out this was 1981. I wasn't aiming for the full-on *Superman* look, but I'd been seduced by Dave's comments and foolishly thought a little toning up would be easy. On his home territory he was a different animal, dominant and brusque as he took me through a thirty minute work-out on various machines designed to search and destroy every part of your body. All the while he stressed that I could stop anytime I'd had enough, but whenever I said I'd had enough he would tell me I was mistaken and that, in fact, I'd barely started. I understand his disappointment in me; the broad shoulders gave the illusion of fitness and good health, but there was a very good reason why I'd chosen cricket as my favoured sport. It's possible he didn't notice the first flush of my face, the grimacing and the subsequent draining away of blood until I was left a ghostly white and trembling hulk. I was three short of the ten required squat thrusts, and hadn't contemplated the bench presses coming up next, when I was overtaken by an urgent and unstoppable need to throw up.

There were several oiled-up and well-built gentlemen in the gym at that moment, none of whom, I reckoned, would have relished a bout of unrestrained projectile vomiting so I dodged them and made it outside into Marshalsea Street before heaving with as much dignity as I could muster. I never went back to Dave's gym, and afterwards felt there was a slight chill between us.

Sadly it brought to a precipitous end my fitness campaign. Although I did join a health club in Belsize Park in 1994. It cost me three hundred and fifty pounds for the year and I went twice – that's a hundred and seventy-five quid a visit.

9

TAKE THE MONEY OR OPEN THE BOX

Wednesday, 1 July 2015. The temperature in London has hit 37 degrees. This morning I have a read-through for the brilliant *Toast of London*, and once again I'm playing me. This is not an entirely accurate version of me as in this episode I've run away with a foul-mouthed dancer. The read-through was in the old County Hall building by the Thames at Waterloo. While I'm waiting in reception I meet Sophie Colquhoun who is also playing a guest part. She told me she loves read-throughs. 'Really?' I said. 'Why?'

'It's so wonderful to hear it all.'

Now, I admit they're useful, even amusing at times, but I've never got past the idea that everyone else is thinking, Shit, he's terrible, I hope they recast. I think a lot of actors share this paranoia, and so I was surprised Sophie was so confident, and how, in the heat, she managed to look super cool. While we were waiting to start, I asked Sophie where she went to school, although she looks barely old enough to have left.

'Cheltenham Ladies' College,' she tells me.

I nodded wisely as if this information signified something. I've met girls who went to Cheltenham before, and like Sophie they were all well-spoken, confident, and to the point. She fanned herself with the episode script, and gave me a polite smile.

'I apologise if I smell,' she said.

* * *

John Nathan-Turner loved a good memo. Very often they would arrive moments before he left the office for a long break. Partly because he'd procrastinated until he could no longer afford to do so, but generally because it gave no one the chance to reply, giving his memo the whiff of a command rather than a dialogue. Now that he had his Doctor in place the memos began flying in all directions. As I was not there to receive them, he would ring me up and tell me he'd sent them, usually just before he left the office for a long holiday. They covered his thoughts on my opening story, on new title sequences, the number and nature of companions in the TARDIS, and of course my costume. The costume was his preoccupation of the moment, and from day one I'd made my thoughts clear and never deviated from them.

Of course, I had no say in the matter except the actor's inalienable right to sulk if he isn't happy, which is a powerful tool in the hands of the right man. Luckily there was a general agreement about most things, a certain British eccentricity, and a sporty tone to emphasise youth. John had thoughts about a polo outfit, complete with riding boots and jodhpurs. I said, 'How about a cricket outfit?' Then one evening he had an epiphany about a morning suit. I politely suggested a cricket outfit might be better. In the end it was handed to the designer, Colin Lavers, to come up with something, courtesy of a memo sent just before JNT went on holiday. We had a meeting in early March at Television Centre at which Colin showed us designs he'd made, which I regarded as a partial victory for the how-about-a-cricket-outfit lobby. I still argued why the Doctor couldn't simply walk into his wardrobe room and pick an outfit, off-the-peg, but I was alone in this viewpoint and frankly fed up with all the costume chat and the lack of how-the-hell-do-I-play-the-part chat, so I said yes it looked great, by which I meant comfy, and that was it.

I couldn't even be bothered to sulk, which is a terrible abrogation of an actor's duty. Now John had mentioned an additional but unformed idea of me wearing something unusual on my lapel. I was probably too busy admiring myself in the costume department's multi-angled mirror to take him seriously, until a week later at a photo call outside TV centre, he took me aside and said,

'Celery.'

I don't like celery, but I had no objection to wearing it on my lapel (I might have changed that view if I'd known I would be asked to take a mouthful of the stuff when we recorded my opening story). My only stipulation was that he explained the reason for the decorative vegetable (obviously I used a less decorative description) before I left the series. Then I went away and forgot about it for the three years.

At the end of January I had recorded the regeneration sequence, at the tail-end of Tom Baker's final studio. At the tail-end was meant to be immediately after the supper break, between seven and ten o'clock, but as usual something had gone wrong. Tom was unhappy and the tension was obvious. The companions, very nearly *my* companions, looked apprehensive, as they tried not to get in the way. This was not the friendly, almost family atmosphere of Pebble Mill. By the time the afternoon session ended the studio was over an hour-and-a-half behind, and somehow I ended up in the BBC club bar, standing at one of the pillar-cum-drinks-tables with Tom himself. It was slightly uncomfortable for both of us. He was still grumpy about 'all the fucking about', that had delayed recording *again,* and yet I sensed he felt he should pass something on to me. He leaned across, as if to say something profound, informative and loosely encouraging. Unfortunately, the noise in the bar was too much and I didn't catch what he said. I know I could have asked him to repeat it, but in the moment, with missing it a second time a real possibility, I just didn't. Instead I smiled slowly and nodded, and he winked, showed his teeth in something akin to a grin, and nodded back. I felt we had an understanding, even if I had no idea what that understanding was.

Later, sitting in the small room off the studio floor, my face bandaged and plastered with white make-up, I watched a monitor on which nothing much was happening, and the studio clock, which ticked past nine o'clock. It was the final gantry scene, the one in which the Doctor falls and sparks his regeneration, and there seemed to be some problem with shooting off the set. All this heightened the level of irritation and was only solved when Tom swore at several people not directly the cause of the problem. Then, at nine-forty-five, we started the scene we should have been doing at seven o'clock, which I would find out later, was only marginally worse than usual. At nine-fifty I was dressed in Tom's coat and scarf, and lined myself up, lying in the place where he had fallen, I could see a ghost image of him on the monitor, I moved my head half an inch to the left and turned it a few degrees to the right. I knew that at exactly ten o'clock either the lights or the videotape machines would be switched off – it all depended on who was vying for that week's Most Militant Department award. As nothing could be recorded without both being switched on, it didn't matter, but I knew one of them was poised. At ten o'clock, something, or everything would stop.

Nine-fifty-six.

We got the shot, and out I came. Tom's scarf dragged along the floor.

Into make-up.

Nine-fifty-seven.

While one make-up girl washed and dried my hair, two more dabbed ivory base all over my face. It was . . . brilliant.

Nine-fifty-nine.

I was back in position, lining myself up again. VT machines rolled tape. 'Now sit up,' someone called. I sat up, looked around. Genuine amazement on my face.

The King is dead. Long live the King.

Ten o'clock.

The lights went out. This week's award goes to: the lighting department.

I started work on *Doctor Who* Season 19 on 30 March 1981. A large table was set up in the rehearsal room at North Acton, and a great number of people turned up to join in the fun. This was the read-through, which are no fun at all. Although I'd met a few of those present, at that moment I couldn't remember anybody's name. The tradition is for the director to go around the table introducing everyone, a monumental challenge, and a pointless one as nobody really listens. I wedged myself between Janet Fielding and Sarah Sutton, two of my companions and a kind of buffer zone between me and the great unknown. Opposite me was our guest star, Stratford Johns; I grew up watching him on *Z Cars* and *Softly, Softly*, where he was tough and uncompromising, but here he looked rather friendly.

In 1963, as part of a school science trip, we had visited BBC Television Centre and had a guided tour of the *Z Cars* set. The actors must have been there, but we didn't see them, only the police station set, and the cut-away cars with the screen behind that gave the impression of driving the mean streets of Newtown. So real on our murky black and white TV and yet so small and insubstantial in real life. It wasn't a let-down, it was magical, a moment when I thought, I want to be a part of this. Now I was a part of it. In less than two weeks' time I could possibly be in the same studio I'd visited eighteen years before, and acting opposite the man who played Detective Inspector Barlow, only this time he would be dressed as a very large green frog.

I started out with three companions, Adric, Nyssa and Tegan. That's too many. Someone had to go, and I knew it was meant to be Nyssa. The initial drafts of *Four to Doomsday* didn't include her character, which meant she was supposed to bite the dust sometime in the first three stories. I'd asked JNT to keep her on for a while, and was relieved she was there – at least it gave the illusion of influence.

Our first day in the studio was also my thirtieth birthday, and on a technical level it went well; I found myself picking up where I'd left off on *The Tomorrow People*, and understood what helped or hindered the camera, and effects team, which in turn saved time, making me popular on the set.

Beyond that, I was a mess.

The idea of starting with the fourth story in the season was JNT's. I didn't request it. All the same it suited me very well. I had no clue what I was doing and thought if I managed to figure it out by the time we recorded the first story the following September, the viewers might not notice the onset of extreme vagueness during story four.

The real reason we didn't start with *Castrovalva* was the minor inconvenience that there was no script, and in the end the fourth story wasn't as bad as I'd feared. The set incorporated the real studio walls, which were wobble free, and Paul Shelley made us laugh.

I was rather proud of the spacewalk sequence in which I was towed around the studio balancing horizontally on an office chair with the back removed, and I relaxed enough to try to persuade Bert Kwouk to slip in a bit of crazy karate. The production manager was Henry Foster, a man who went on to train other production managers. At one point I slipped into the studio gallery where John Black, the director, was watching the studio monitors on which Stratford Johns was declaiming gloriously in his green frog costume. At the end of the scene they reset for another take and John asked Henry to gently suggest to Stratford that he take the performance level down the tiniest bit, which should have been Henry's cue to translate the message into something more reassuring and whisper in the actor's ear, but Henry, who seemed to have learned the BBC handbook backwards, called loudly across the studio floor, 'Hey Stratford, note from upstairs. They think you're way over the top.'

I often wonder how the training thing worked out.

After my costume, John's next obsession was casting. Celebrity always trumped acting ability in John's book, but thankfully they often co-existed. In *Kinda* we had Richard Todd, not only the hero of so many post-war British films (he won the Battle of Britain in his Spitfire and destroyed German dams in his Avro Lancaster bomber), but a fine actor too. He was older now but had lost none of his star quality. Fortunately, Matthew Waterhouse was there to take care of him, to proffer a little advice – after all, the poor man had mainly done feature films, nearly fifty of them, and had only limited experience of television, and there was stuff he needed to know, and Matthew was ready to tell him in a sober and patient manner. Stuff like warning Richard Todd not to look at the camera because it breaks the fourth wall; heaven knows how he'd managed for the previous forty years. In my book Matthew is here today because Richard Todd was a gentleman and didn't drop a bouncing bomb on his head. (Peter Grimwade, the director, thought the story might have worked better if we'd filmed it on a South Sea island. I don't want to state the obvious, but doesn't everything work better on a South Sea island?)

Despite me being on set, making notes for a future edition of *How to Act* by Matthew Waterhouse, *Kinda* was Janet Fielding's story. She even managed to get Sarah Sutton out of the way for two whole episodes, allowing us an unimpeded view of the evil and possessed creature she was. Mind you, she's from Brisbane so it wasn't much of a surprise.

But if you'd met Janet back in 1981, away from the *Doctor Who* set, you might never have guessed her origins. Sometime before she started on *Doctor Who*, she'd hooked up with a guy called Nick who would turn up to every studio. Nick didn't like the name Janet, so he called her by her second name, Claire. Nick didn't like the Australian accent, so outside of the show she spoke in a rather husky British manner. In rehearsals she once told me that she'd forgotten how to do an Australian accent, a statement she now vehemently denies, but come on, now that we all know she's from Brisbane, who do you believe?

If you meet her now, you'll find she's recovered her full Australian-ness, and is damn proud of it. She has battled cancer and is doing great work for charity in the seaside town of Ramsgate. I was always fond of her but now doubly so, and I sincerely hope one day they let her back into Brisbane . . . if Ramsgate ever lets her go.

★   ★   ★

Sunday, 19 April 2015. Spent Sunday at a convention in Portsmouth, sitting alongside Sarah Sutton. I tried to ply her for memories of our time on *Doctor Who*, but she insists she remembers nothing, only shadows. It's when I persuaded her to share those shadows that I realised that, while I saw myself as a kindly avuncular figure, I failed to notice her predicament.

★   ★   ★

The reason I wanted Sarah to stay on was self-interest. Despite being one of the youngest and therefore lumped together with Matthew as an uncomfortable duo, she was actually an experienced child actress. I thought she was very good and under-used and would have blossomed with better scripts and intelligent direction, which is what she'd been used to and exactly what there was no time for on *Doctor Who*.

It's a difficult transition for any actor new to television after working in the theatre or arriving direct from drama school. You move from a world where your performance is watched closely, where you're praised if a scene is good, and given the freedom to try something else if it isn't, and are plunged into the often cold and technical approach of the TV studio. The general rule in series television is that if you're doing good work, no one says anything to you, and once you get used to that way of working, it's fine. It was only much later I discovered Sarah was despondent during this period, a combination of too many scenes with Matthew, and a lack of encouragement and guidance, and when she finally got the attention of a director, it made matters worse.

One lunchtime, during the filming of *Kinda*, our director Peter Grimwade found Matthew and Sarah in the make-up room and in front of several people lambasted them for reasons that were more to do with his own inadequacies than theirs. They didn't know their lines properly, he said, they weren't doing the moves they'd rehearsed and they weren't focused on set, they were being – he barked at them – unprofessional.

This word is kryptonite to an actor, it's a dagger to the heart, and I've never been sure why. A French first assistant director once accused me of being unprofessional and I turned on him in a cold fury and he hurriedly backed away with a fearful and surprised look in his eye. I think it surprised both of us. Interestingly, while my anger was real and heartfelt, in the same moment I was thinking, Hang on, I'm pretty good at this cold fury thing, I wish someone should offer me a job playing a psycho.

Sarah, being a nicer and more sensitive person than me, was upset by

Grimwade's rant, even after it turned out it was the result of a similar clobbering by JNT on him. She had thought her professionalism was second to none, and she was right. Once she had returned from temporary exile, one thing was obvious: she wasn't going anywhere. Contractually she had to miss two episodes, and if she'd already missed them I realised they intended keeping her for the rest of the season. Janet had already been told she was staying, so unless it was me leaving, there was only one other possibility. . .

Before we started filming *The Visitation* JNT told me of his plan to kill off Adric. The actual killing thing was a bit of a surprise, but after a while it grew on me. After all, I thought, no one dies in *Doctor Who* (I'm talking regulars here, I know about the other poor buggers), and yet every week lives of the Doctor and companions are threatened. Sometimes we die, and then it turns out we haven't, quite. If for once, one of us did, we'd raise the jeopardy factor sky high. Yes I thought . . . killing Adric is a good idea.

It wasn't.

It was a deeply flawed notion.

The truth is many fans watched, comfortable with the knowledge that the regulars would survive, and the threat of us dying at the end-of-episode cliffhanger wasn't diminished one bit. So we traumatised millions of children, and I'd like to take this opportunity to apologise to them all, even though I would like to point out . . .

. . . IT WAS ABSOLUTELY NOT MY IDEA TO KILL ADRIC.

* * *

In 2006 my two sons were five and seven years old. They loved *Doctor Who*, a passion that had started when I'd dug out some old VHS tapes a couple of years before. Louis had started school with an iron curtain of shyness that was only breached when he talked to his school friends about Doctor Daddy. Of course his school friends had no idea what he was going on about for at least another year and half, when the series returned to television in its younger, brighter, all bells and whistles format. After that Doctor Daddy was never spoken of again, the old tapes and DVDs gathered dust, and cobwebs formed across the fronts of the DVD shelves and probably across me as well. Then at the end of the first season, which was only twelve weeks long, children started having withdrawal symptoms. Across the land they stared blankly into space, or would sit on the sofa rather than crouch behind it, so much so that parents, in an attempt to save their offspring from distress, searched the cable channels, or in some cases, their VHS and DVD collections, and discovered an almost infinite supply, an alternative universe, of other Doctors. These were the now re-designated *classic* series. Yes, the picture was a funny shape, and the effects a bit lame and fizzy, the music a bit weird and the action didn't exactly race along, but it filled a space.

There was only one problem.

I remember picking Louis up from school one day, chatting to another parent until the children came out. When they did, the mum turned her son towards me and said,

'Look, this is the Doctor Who you were watching last night.'

The child looked at me, looked past me, looked up at his mother, and for the life of him could not see a young blond-haired demigod anywhere in the playground.

Then along came David Tennant, saving the universe in his pyjamas, and once again the old codgers faded gently into the mists of time. Meanwhile, in an attempt to impress my children, I had taken advantage of contacts and arranged a visit to the set when they filmed in London.

David Tennant and Billie Piper were there and had their picture taken with the boys. My youngest, Joel, was so besotted with Billie he couldn't bring himself to show his face and so hid behind tightly clasped hands, and couldn't bring himself to speak. At the end of that season, there was a rumour that Rose was going to die. The boys were distraught, and rather than let them be traumatised, I sent an email to Russell T. Davies, briefly explaining, and asking him if Rose's death was a fact or not. I received a brief reply;

Dear Peter
You killed Adric. What do you care?
Russell

* * *

Matthew didn't like the idea at all, although his main focus was that dying meant he couldn't return to the series, even if the public demanded it, which he was sure they would. I tried to argue that no one would forget his departure, that it would forever be etched in the hearts of eighteen-year-old Welsh boys living in Swansea (they may not have been my exact words) and that he would die a hero. None of this washed with Matthew and he was dead grumpy about it, which, because we are cruel and heartless people, tended to make Janet, Sarah and myself giggle a bit. By the time we finished *The Visitation*, Matthew was like a dead man walking.

Not only would his departure not be forgotten, I reiterated, he had a great story to go out on too. *Earthshock* was written by Eric Sayward, the new script editor, and was a gripping Cyberman adventure, and with a good design team and an excellent cast, it would remain my favourite up until the last story of my final season, despite JNT, having a celebrity moment, casting Beryl Reid as the freighter captain.

Everyone loved Beryl. She was fun and eccentric, and lived in a house filled with of cats, but casting her as a hardened and ruthless space-freighter captain, whose ship is invaded by Cybermen, perhaps wasn't the best idea. When she put her mind to it she was fine, but she revelled in not understanding it so much, and the comedy mileage of the director's attempts to explain was such that we spent too many happy hours laughing when we might have been rehearsing.

Then we blew up Adric.

But before that there was the strange incident of the woman with the script.

My father worked for Sony, who made very good televisions, some with tiny scratches on them which made the sets 'graded stock' and so available to employees at a very cheap rate, and that's how I came to have a Sony Profeel monitor, and how I came to see the woman with the script. The evening episode two of *Earthshock* went out, I sat at home watching the Cybermen break out of their packing cases and march menacingly up the stairs: there, as plain as day, was a woman following the Cyber army across the screen. I rang up JNT who obviously thought I was mad, because no one, not when the scene was recorded, not in editing, not in the final broadcast check, had seen her. The next day they all went back and looked again and there she was.

Then we blew up Adric.

And it was a great end to the episode, Adric saves mankind inadvertently by failing to deactivate the bomb and wiping out the dinosaurs, and the final scene in which my two remaining companions and I realise what's happened, and the credits roll in silence, is a classic. In rehearsal it had been impossible to keep a straight face, not least because Matthew was watching keenly to make sure we took it seriously, which we did, which is precisely what made it so difficult not to laugh.

It reminded me of a scene from *All Creatures* where I took a call from the local milkman and had to come into the living room and tell the others simply, 'That was old Tom on the phone, his horse just died.'

The director wanted the scene to end with a collective and sombre moment of reflection, which was asking for trouble, and though in rehearsal we never managed to get through it without laughter, I imagined that filming it would bring us to our senses.

It didn't.

Take one: Tristan enters and sits at the dining room table.

Tristan: That was Tom on the phone, his horse has just died.

At the end of the sentence Tristan catches Siegfried's eye, they both start laughing.

Take two: Tristan enters and sits at the dining room table.

Tristan: That was old Tom on the phone, his horse has just di—

James snorts with laughter before Tristan can finish. Helen joins in.

Take three: Tristan enters and sits at the dining room table

Tristan: That was old Tom . . .

He turns around and walks straight back out, his voice already wavering.

Take four: Tristan enters and everyone laughs.

There is only one thing to be done at a time like this: a serious telling-off from a floor manager that will cure most corpsing. But what happens now is the furious and slightly hysterical director appears on the studio floor appalled at our behaviour, and lectures us about how the death of Tom's horse will cause great hardship to the old man, and that people in the village won't have their milk delivered, which as we are sitting in a studio in the middle of Birmingham in 1978, strikes us as the silliest thing we have ever heard and makes us laugh even more. Eventually, after a tea break we managed to get to the end of the scene, but the director never got his moment of reflection, they cut a millisecond before we laughed.

Now here I was again, and it's important you understand we weren't laughing at Adric's demise, because I admit I have often joked about it since, and I know they are jokes Matthew may not have always appreciated. No, the desire to laugh, or corpsing as actors call it, is never a solitary offence, it takes two (or more) to tango. It is nerves, with a pinch of embarrassment about the nature of acting, but most importantly the seed of suspicion that the other actor knows you want to laugh, and he knows you know he knows, and in a moment you are guffawing like an idiot. This time it wasn't so bad, and the scene was moving, and worked well. All the same we didn't look at each other, and I was ready with the scene from *Tomb of the Cybermen*, which for once was entirely appropriate.

My first season ended with *Time-Flight*, written by Peter Grimwade, who turned out to be a better writer than he was director. Unfortunately for him and the rest of us, the budget was all but gone, and no amount of decent writing can make up for polystyrene monsters and a foot-long model of Concorde at the back of a perspective set in Studio 8 of Television Centre. The few days of filming started off well enough, where we actually shot scenes on board the real plane, parked outside a hangar at Heathrow. Even the rehearsals were a joy, with a cast that was hell-bent on enjoying the experience. Nigel Stock, an actor I had grown up watching and who I imagined would be a serious and intense actor, proved to be as silly as everyone else and his death scene was one of the most spectacular I have ever witnessed. It was after the filming and the rehearsals that it all went downhill.

The moment I walked into Studio 8 and saw the set, my heart sank. I asked how Concorde had managed to touch down on a landscape of rocks? I pointed out that a perspective set has to slope upwards to the horizon; otherwise it looks like Studio 8 in Television Centre. Of course there was nothing to be done, but that was the moment I started to question how long I should stay with the series. John Nathan-Turner was already talking to me about the twentieth anniversary special which he wanted to be a part of my third season.

There was a problem because I was committed to another series of *Sink or Swim*, which had proved very popular, and to *Holding the Fort*, which I had also promised to do. John wanted me to say no to *Sink or Swim*, enabling him to complete and transmit my second season in the autumn of 1982, and make *The Five Doctors* special as part of the 1983 season and coincide exactly with the anniversary date in November.

There followed a spat between the comedy and drama departments that dragged on for weeks. I bravely hid in a corner somewhere and waited for things to die down. The corner turned out to be London Weekend Television, where I slipped in a third series of *Holding the Fort* while no one was looking. We also found time to move again, this time to a house by the River Thames in Weybridge, just down the road from where my father and my friend Dave had worked for many years, and where I had also temped in the summer holidays while at drama school. I regularly passed the factory (now closed down) and it seemed a world away from the life I was leading now.

In the end, the combination of John Howard Davies and Gareth Gwenlan proved too much for Nathan-Turner and I was sent over to light entertainment for two vital months. John was disappointed but undaunted, especially as, in compensation, he was promised a week of foreign filming to open the second season. He commissioned a story set in Amsterdam and in May 1982 we all embarked for a week of fun. We stayed in a hotel not far from the red-light district and on our very first night we all went for a walk around the area. Janet dressed up for the occasion and while she looked very pretty as she walked the streets of Amsterdam, it did leave her open to certain misunderstandings. I looked around at one point and saw her with two men and smiling in some confusion as she tried and failed to understand what was happening.

My proudest moment was shooting a scene in Dam Square: I am actually Omega who has made himself in the Doctor's image and is now decaying horribly. They covered my face in green slime and Rice Krispies (an effective combination often used by the BBC make-up department), and told me to stagger across the crowded square, while they filmed from the top of a nearby building. This meant that no one in the square that afternoon was aware we were filming, and because the show was not broadcast in the Netherlands, no one had any idea who I was either. Just some decaying alien who happened to be passing through the city as bits dripped off him, I suppose. I did a pretty good job of scaring the wits out of the people of the city, and even threw in a 'nearly getting run over by a tram' bit for good measure, although, as usual, most of the credit must go to the breakfast cereal and green slime.

I know I was good because John told me how effective it was. Just before he told me it was cut because the episode was over-running.

* * *

Wednesday, 4 November 2015. Martin Clunes turned up at the stage door saying it was nice to see me 'strut my stuff'. *Doctor Who* was his first TV part, and since he became well known he has been haunted by the clip of him in a toga, although I remember his legs were much admired by my companions.

* * *

Having been rescued from a life in the red-light streets of Amsterdam, Janet was back with a vengeance and *Snakedance* was her story, a continuation of the Mara fable started in *Kinda*. She was happy about the script but not so wild about her new costume.

IS THERE LIFE OUTSIDE THE BOX?

Since the beginning of season two, both Janet and Sarah had suffered a costume rethink, apparently brought about by the father of a fan who wrote to the BBC complaining that the companions were wearing too many clothes. The letter was sent to the *Doctor Who* office and landed on Nathan-Turner's desk. As a result, Janet went from a high-necked stewardess outfit to a boob tube and shorts. Apparently, she reminded me every ten minutes, the top was very uncomfortable and either dug into her flesh or started slipping down, depending on the mood she was in. I'm sure she was distracted by the desire to be good in the episode as well, but I refuse to accept her assertion that this had any connection with the events at lunchtime on our first studio day. We were walking back from lunch around the circular corridor that connects the studios in TV centre. I was striding ahead trying to escape from Janet's complaints about her costume slipping down all the time. As I recall the conversation went something like this:

'This bloody thing.'

'Yes we know, it keeps slipping down.'

'It's all right for you, you don't have to wear the thing and hoick it up every ten minutes.'

I stopped, turned back and looked at her seriously.

'Janet, do me a favour and reach up as high as you can above your head.'

Here's the thing. It's my contention that if a bloke asks a girl who's wearing a boob tube, to reach as far as she can above her head, most sensible girls of a modest nature would decline the request and that is what I expected Janet to do. But Janet, being Janet, reached as far above her head as she could, without giving the slightest consideration as to the consequences of doing so. The inevitable happened. Worse than that, the inevitable happened at the precise moment the camera crew appeared from the other direction around the circular corridor.

After allowing the events to set clearly in my mind, I adopted the modus operandi of my Doctor and ran away.

There was strike trouble brewing. There was always some union unrest going on around this time. The lights would go off bang-on ten o'clock, or the VT operators would switch off the machines halfway through a line, but on this occasion I think it was the scene shifters. The union agreement specified the number of scene shifters required to do the job, the management said they needed half that number. Impossible said the union, even though they knew the management estimates to be about right and that at any given moment, half the crew were off doing other jobs to bring in a little extra money.

These things are never as black-and-white as we would like them to be. It meant our season was disrupted and the number of episodes reduced. *Enlightenment* had to be rescheduled and we lost the original casting of Peter Sallis as one of the captains. Sarah Sutton had left at the end of *Terminus*, and we'd picked up Mark Strickson to play Turlough in *Mawdryn Undead*. I was against Sarah leaving and thought she was never given the chance to shine. Her departure was the result of JNT's desire to have companions with attitude; the result had thus far given me Tegan, who never wanted to be there, Adric – desperate to get back to E-space – and Turlough, who wanted to kill me.

I believed Sarah had a raw deal and was never given a chance to shine, but no amount of leading actor cajoling and wheedling would make him change his mind. He wanted to replace Nyssa with an American companion, an idea I thought was so ill-conceived that our usually friendly discussions became a little more edgy. I had nothing against Americans – for God's sake, at that time I was married to one – but I was sure what the American fans loved was our uniquely British take on sci-fi, right down to the wobbly sets and dodgy effects. John thought an American companion would make the show more popular across the Atlantic and possibly lead to co-production money to film a story over there. He'd tried a similar approach with Tegan, even making her an air-stewardess in the hope of doing a deal with Qantas to fly the film crew out to Australia. That had come to nothing and eventually he abandoned the American companion plan too, only for it to resurface a year later.

So there was Turlough, which was a problem from the start. No one could figure out how long he should carry on trying to kill me. John Nathan-Turner was equivocal, Eric Saward couldn't get a straight answer, and Mark became increasingly frustrated at being locked up in episode one and only getting out three episodes later, in order to sidestep the whole issue.

Then John hit us with his idea for a *Doctor Who* Pantomime. That's to say a production of *Cinderella* featuring myself and Anthony Ainley, and making it a family affair by getting Sandra to play the fairy godmother. John loved pantomimes, and had always dreamed of putting on his own, and we were effectively both a willing and captive cast. He booked Tunbridge Wells Assembly Halls and brought in Gary Downie, his boyfriend, as choreographer. We were still in the final stages of the second season when we started rehearsals and would often split our time between the two, and I often wondered if the BBC head of series turned a blind eye to its passive involvement in John's production.

* * *

Sunday, 8 March 2015. After a week of rehearsals we had the read-through today. This is because a couple of the cast are doing *Singin' in the Rain* in Paris, and today is the only day they can get back to London. They all threw themselves into the reading and I'm beginning to wonder if I can catch up. Our choreographer, Stephen Mear, who has also been in Paris, introduced himself and announced we'd worked together on the famous *Doctor Who* Pantomime in Tunbridge Wells in 1982, it was his first job as a dancer he said. We did the Betty, Keppel and Wilson routine together (I was Betty of course). He's going to send a photo in case I need it for the book.

★ ★ ★

The pantomime went down very well, helped by a considerable influx of fans from the States, who made the journey eager to be utterly confused by men dressed as women, women dressed as men, and the Doctor and Master throwing custard pies at each other.

I was giving my 'Buttons', which went down rather well except for one performance when I nearly knocked out a small child with a miniature Mars bar, accidently hurled, with deadly speed and accuracy, into the balcony.

We filmed *The Five Doctors* at the end of March. Patrick Troughton and Jon Pertwee were aboard and Richard Hurndall was drafted in to play the first incarnation. Tom Baker, perhaps feeling the chill of life after *Doctor Who*, declined to take part. As for the rest of us, we were left feeling the chill of filming on the bleak and wintery hillsides of North Wales.

I made the decision to leave the series while sitting on my bed in a hotel room in Richmond, North Yorkshire. JNT had been pushing me to do a fourth year (I was yet to start my third), and my agent had called me for the second time that day. It would have meant better money (within reason – this was the BBC after all), and a chance to have more say in story development, but it also broke my unwritten 'three series and out' rule, and the similar advice Patrick Troughton had given me.

We were in the middle of filming the first *All Creatures Great and Small Christmas Special*, and the previous night, over a thick gammon steak and eggs, in a pub in Middleham, I'd discussed my future choices with Chris Timothy. I'd already had a similar talk with Robert Hardy, and both agreed it was time for me to move on. That's what I told my agent. There was a hesitation before he asked me if I was sure, and even though I wasn't sure at all, something told me it was the braver option. Apart from the stand-alone *Five Doctors*, I hadn't been happy with the strike-hit second season, on top of which the idea of an American companion had reared its ugly head again, and despite his assurances to the contrary, JNT's megalomaniac tendencies were becoming more apparent. So I burned my bridges and tried to imagine a life after *Doctor Who*, never imagining that there wouldn't really be one.

* * *

Monday, 23 November 2015. The last week of *Gypsy*. At lunchtime I attended a gathering, and made a short speech outside Broadcasting House in support of the BBC who are struggling with government attempts to dismantle the corporation. This particular rally was for *Doctor Who* fans (it's the fifty-second anniversary of the first broadcast), and so I gave my speech, via a loudhailer, to various Cybermen, Masters, and other versions of me. Quite surreal.

* * *

During my final season, I got to do a Dalek story, which had looked doubtful after Terry Nation had withheld permission for the previous two years. At the end of *Resurrection of the Daleks*, I left Tegan behind, and less than a week later we flew to Lanzarote to film *Planet of Fire*.

The part of Timanov had been offered to Peter Wyngard, whose agent (a little surprisingly as Wyngard hadn't worked much in recent years) came back insisting his client would only accept the role if he was allowed to play it 'old'. A demand that baffled director and producer alike as both agreed he was old. That hiccup soothed away, we began rehearsing a couple of days before we left. Peter Wyngard was indeed playing it 'old'. He wanted a walking stick, he hunched his shoulders, and assumed a quivery voice, all of which worked splendidly. Costume fittings were done in Lanzarote and I was not present when Peter tried his costume on, but I gathered later he was very pleased with it. It looked a little like something out of *Lawrence of Arabia,* and I can only suppose he looked in the mirror and thought, Yes, I can still do it!

Because somewhere between rehearsals and the first scene we filmed, the stick, the hunched shoulders and quivery voice disappeared, and were replaced by a heavily shaded moustache and eyebrows, a puffed-out chest, and a large booming voice. Beneath his robes he had also plumped for clogs to give him an extra inch in height, and this caused great problems for the sound department, who couldn't figure out where the loud clump, clump, clump, was coming from. The story also marked the first appearance of Peri played by Nicola Bryant, whose entrance, jumping into the sea and being rescued by Turlough, caused much consternation when we filmed it.

We'd arrived at the location, a deserted beach away from the popular areas of the island, very early in the morning, long before it became obvious it was a beach intended for nudists. I think JNT had a pretty good idea but he was saying nothing. The TARDIS had been set up in the middle of the beach, and by ten o'clock was attracting great interest, mostly from naked German men. It made the materialisation scene difficult to film without the odd passing nudist appearing and disappearing along the police box. There were female nudists too, although in the presence of the leery British crew they chose modesty over the boldness of their male counterparts.

So Nicola jumped off the boat and started shouting for help. The camera was set up on the beach, and Mark Strickson was ready to act, but that didn't stop four or five naked German men from rushing into the water to save her. We aborted the take, explained to the nudists that this was pretend, and pointed out the camera and the eager actor, and then we tried again. This time Nicola got to cry and splash about for a few more seconds, before several other naked German men, who'd been relaxing on the rocks a little way off the beach, did exactly the same thing. JNT was keen to take personal charge of explaining the situation, and what should have been a simple shoot, took most of the day.

The Caves of Androzani was my last, and probably best, story (notwithstanding the last thirty seconds during which I turned into Colin Baker).

At the beginning of the final rehearsal week in Acton, I remembered the promised explanation of the celery had not been forthcoming. Perhaps I had an inkling of how many times, over the next thirty years, I would be asked why the hell I was wearing it, so I demanded (requested) a reason. The script editor, Eric Saward locked himself in the green room for a few minutes and emerged with a pretty good explanation. So we had a great cast, an excellent script, and no unresolved issues. Except that our director seemed as mad as a hatter. Graeme Harper reminded me of an animated garden gnome, and wouldn't stand still for long enough for me to question his directing skills. If I did manage to point out that this shot crossed the line, or that move wouldn't work, he waved me away muttering, 'It will. It will, don't worry. Trust me.'

Of course I didn't trust him because I was sure I knew better. I'd been doing this *Doctor Who* thing for three years and had observed all the techniques the average television director employed to make average and serviceable programming. Alec Wheal and his steady team of studio cameramen didn't know what to make of it, especially when Graeme left the gallery upstairs and set up camp on the studio floor. It was a master stroke, because slowly his energy enthused us and I quite forgot about whether it would cut together, and instead threw myself into the story with a vigour I had never had before. Graeme Harper was something different. We were all infected, the actors and the technicians, and when Colin squeezed into my costume on my last day, I was beginning to have second thoughts.

So it goes. I'd made the decision to leave eight months before and had been content it was the right choice. But on that last day, it was different. Somehow, against all the odds, they'd found someone to replace me, and now he was lying on the floor of my TARDIS with my companion all over him. I stuffed as much of my costume as I could into my bag, and quietly left by the side door.

It was January 1984, the end of three exciting but frustrating years. I felt, along with many others, that *Doctor Who* was underfunded, unappreciated and would only get more problematic as time went on. In the last two years we'd been hit by strikes and work-to-rule disputes, and John's grip on the series was threatening to choke it to death. A few months later as I was driving on the North Circular road, I heard an interview with Colin Baker talking excitedly about his plans for the show. Every idea was an inherent criticism of what came before, but it was hard to be angered by what he said. He'd find out soon enough, his wriggle-room was non-existent, and his great notions would come to nothing.

10

PLAYING
THE DOTS

Wednesday, 1 July 2015. At the end of the first show Michelle our dresser was called to the stage door; someone had come round to see Imelda. Michelle came back and told me it was an old American bloke, and she made him wait while she went to ask Imelda. I asked her what his name was, 'It was . . . Somebody . . . Prince,' she said, 'could have been Harold.' I looked at her seriously, 'Michelle, are you saying it's Harold "Hal" Prince, the most famous Broadway director and producer of the last half-century who you left waiting at stage door?' Later Imelda confirmed this, casually telling Lara and me that Hal Prince had come by and said that he'd seen every production of *Gypsy* over the last fifty years, and this one blew all of them out of the water.

★   ★   ★

In May of 1984 Sandra and I headed off on a tour of *Barefoot in the Park*. It was a remount or more accurately a remodelling of the production we had done in Bromley three years before. Everyone in the cast except the two of us were different; the man upstairs was now played by Gerald Flood who'd been in *Doctor Who* with me, playing King John, and his alter ego Kamelion in *The King's Demons*. Flood's wife was the costume mistress, employed I suspect to look after Gerald who was ailing slightly in his later years. By the end of ten weeks we were pushing it a bit with Sandra's waistline. As an old lady was overheard saying in a matinee in Leeds, 'That one's got a bun in the oven.'

In July we appeared on TV-am ostensibly to publicise the remainder of the tour, but their presenter Anne Diamond, who knew about it, was determined to have the pregnancy announced on the show. She hinted and cajoled and in the end we had no option but to go along with it, and indeed our concern was not for privacy, but for fear of tempting fate that still something might go wrong. The announcement cemented us as a TV couple who, without chasing publicity, were happy to live their lives in the public eye. As so often happens, that easy acquiescence would come back to torment us a few years later. After the tour I went off to film an episode of the BBC's *Miss Marple* in which I was cast as the murderer. It's rather prestigious to be offered the murderer's part, and I was keen to do it. It tends to take the *who* out of whodunit, and here was a chance to get away from being the nice guy. At the read-through and in rehearsals, I trawled through my repertoire of murderous tics and psychotic glances, forgetting the first rule of whodunits: everyone can behave suspiciously except the killer. The director, took me aside, and gently suggested I should play it like Tristan until the reveal scene, when I was welcome to go as nuts as I liked.

I met Joan Hickson only briefly. She was frail by this time, and protected from the parade of guest actors passing through, which in our episode included Tom Wilkinson, Selina Cadell, Timothy

West, and Clive Merrison. We also had Fabia Drake, who was old enough to have met Agatha Christie and was not an admirer of her work. She was sure Christie had written the books without any firm idea who the murderer was, then simply re-read the manuscript and picked the least likely character, inserting a load of old plot nonsense, as she put it, to explain their guilt. In *A Pocketful of Rye*, for example, my character, Lance, wasn't even in the country when one of the murders is committed. Only in Miss Marple's denouement speech do you discover he flew from Paris in the morning, committed the murder, and then flew back to Paris in the afternoon.

The director was primarily known as a TV producer, having worked in that capacity on *Nanny* and *The Cleopatras* as well as the previous series of *Miss Marple*. Now, as unofficial payback, he had the chance to direct one of the episodes. It turned out not to be as easy as he hoped. For a start, he approached the task with a solemnity that we and the crew, for various reasons, were unable to match. I suppose we weren't the most serious bunch of actors anyway, and the mix of the two approaches only made us sillier. Tom Wilkinson thought it would be fun to have alternative names so called me Dave Peterson, and in return I called him Will Tomkinson. My favourite was Merry Cliveson. Tom would quite happily refer to us by these names when discussing a scene with the director, which confused the poor man further. It all came to a head one day in a big scene in the hallway of the main house. A scream is heard (added in the edit), and we all emerge from different rooms to see what's happened. We assumed that would be the end of the shot, but our director felt we had fallen short on initiative, and shouted that as we had just heard a scream, we wouldn't just stand there. We looked at each other blankly for a moment, after which he angrily suggested we would call the police. Another moment of bafflement

– then Tom Wilkinson raised his hand apologetically: 'Excuse me, but I think you'll find I am the police.'

In the late autumn of 1984, I took part in a celebrity initiative show for the Christmas schedules, called *Take Off*. After landing the Concorde flight simulator with a display of 'spectacular recklessness' (noted by the Chief Concorde training officer) – though at least I put it on the runway (which is more than my celebrity colleagues managed) – and driving the Challenger tank simulator with similar disregard, I was handed two free tickets on the supersonic airliner. It was a great feeling but couldn't quite eclipse the birth of my daughter Georgia, four minutes into Christmas Day, 1984. It should have made her the first Christmas baby had the nurse not forgotten to make the phone call. The pregnancy had gone well, except for the closing stages which involved Sandra in twenty-three hours of labour that ended with the bump turning out not to be the baby boy we were expecting. It was odd because the result of every test predicted it would be: Sandra's head in the toilet bowl, the ring on a piece of thread moving from side to side, the shape of the bulge, its width and elevation, all declared this was a boy. There was even a chance meeting with Lynsey de Paul at the *Sun* TV Awards, who laid her hands on the lump and announced confidently, 'It's a boy, I'm never wrong.' Later, it turned out she was never right, she just never remembered to go back and ask the follow-up question – What did you actually have? A day after she was born we took Georgia back to our newly extended house on the Hamm Court Estate in Weybridge.

Everything in my life was damn near perfect, maybe too perfect. We had four cars in the driveway of our house by the river Thames, and a beautiful baby daughter in a traditional crib at the end of our bed. I didn't have a job, of course, but who needs one when you have two complimentary tickets for Concorde waiting to take you on the trip of a lifetime. Actually by the time we went on the trip of a lifetime I did have a job, a *Magnum PI* special. On the down side, 'Déjà Vu' (1985) was one of the only episodes not shot on location in Hawaii, but in the south of England. Universal Pictures, as one of the executives put it, had come over with suitcases full of money to spend in the UK. I didn't take this as literally suitcases of dosh, but the pound had slumped to an all-time low against the US currency, only just falling short of one dollar to a pound. Universal hired Leeds Castle in Kent, a beautiful building dating back to the twelfth century but restored in the nineteenth, that was often used for international summits, and came fully staffed, including two butlers. It was the main location in the episode, and meant to be the ancestral home of Magnum's patron, Robin Masters, always unseen but voiced by Orson Welles, no less. Everyone in the cast, and the directors and producers, stayed on site in the castle. Tom Selleck, who was as charming in real life as he was on the telly, had what might be called the royal suite, but I wasn't complaining. I was put in a well-appointed room with a four-poster bed and the thickest feather mattress I had ever slept on (I had never slept on a feather mattress before).

My early scenes were with Tom Selleck and John Hillerman, and they were not what I expected. We'd block the scene, and then be released while stand-ins walked through the moves for the camera operator and sound department. We were free to relax in our trailers, or if it was a nice day sit outside on the chairs provided. Tom and John would run the words with their respective personal assistants, regardless of whether or not they happened to be sitting next to each other. Being much lower down the pay scale, I didn't have a personal assistant and couldn't run the scene with anyone, and so twiddled my thumbs anxiously until we were called back to set and the director called for a take. The lack of rehearsal was unnerving, especially as

IS THERE LIFE OUTSIDE THE BOX?

Tom Selleck in his downtime would often adjust his lines to better fit his disarming style of acting, which often left you guessing as to when he'd finished speaking. Hillerman was much more fastidious but they had a chemistry and a shorthand between them, born of years working on the series.

The director, Russ Mayberry, a veteran of American television, would never run a shot from beginning to end, instead he would film the odd line in close-up, a couple of speeches in a two-shot, and so. Later he told me that because the editing was done by the producers and executives back in Hollywood, this was the only way he could control the final cut.

Tom's stand-in and personal assistant (whose name was Tom), had been with him for several years. He was similar in build and height, had styled his hair the same way, and had grown the Selleck moustache, but there the similarities ended. It didn't stop the public mistaking him for the real thing, and if asked he would, without hesitation, sign autographs as Selleck. He was quick to explain that if he didn't, people would go away thinking it was that the star had refused to sign, which would damage Selleck's image more than the odd bogus signature.

A few days later the remaining two regulars turned up. Roger E. Mosley and Larry Manetti were fresh from a few days' holiday in Italy, where things had not gone according to plan. Larry had wanted to go to Italy to try the pizza, which he assumed would be the finest in the world – it was a huge disappointment, and left him depressed and disillusioned. With every pizza he tried, his spirits and his opinion of Italy sank a little lower. The more miserable Larry became the more Roger was amused. On the final day Larry cheered up after meeting a guy selling flick knives outside the Colosseum just before they left for the airport, and decided they were perfect to present to his colleagues as gifts from the land of his forefathers. Hillerman was appalled – he was sick to death of gifts he didn't want, and even had a new Porsche sitting in his garage in Los Angeles, an end-of-series surprise from Tom Selleck the previous year. He didn't drive, he told me, but didn't feel able to get rid of it.

In the evenings, we dined in the castle and were waited upon by our pair of butlers. How the Americans loved them. John Hillerman was so taken with the experience, he wanted to take one back to LA. Strangely, the Americans had no problem hailing the butlers by their surnames; the British contingent were hopeless, finding ourselves apologetically asking, 'Sorry, would it be all right? Don't want to trouble you . . . could I possibly have a top-up . . . please?'

A day filming *Magnum* would go like this. I was woken by the butler or deputy butler at the appointed hour, and made my way down to breakfast. Afterwards I would stroll along to the make-up and costume rooms, and, sipping freshly brewed coffee, would be handed the schedule for the day. Unlike Tom Selleck and the others, I did not have a Mercedes at my disposal twenty-four hours a day, but there was usually a spare one waiting to drive me the three hundred yards to the set. This was encouraged to protect us from the general public but took a lot longer than walking, because of the traffic jam caused by as many as six Mercedes cars and prop vans and lighting trucks manoeuvring their way around the Leeds Castle grounds.

A couple of days after I finished, at the age of three months, Georgia was ready to fly supersonic. We'd booked the tickets, planned the holiday, and bought a carrycot that became known as the Green Bag. Now all we had to do was turn up at the Concorde check-in lounge, and we were away. Word had already been slipped to the pilots via the Chief Concorde training officer, and I was hopeful I might get another glimpse of the flight deck.

We arrived at Heathrow bright and early, with three suitcases, a baby and a buggy, and that's when we heard about the TWA strike. There was no reason to think it was a problem for us, but it soon became clear it was. We were asked to stand to one side, as check-in personnel whispered and looked in our direction. It turned out our seats were complimentary and only existed when there were no paying customers who wanted them. They were sorry, they told us, but we were bumped off the flight. Georgia was asleep around my neck in a harness, while we complained and pleaded in vain. The airline staff said there was nothing they could do and perhaps we could try again tomorrow. We picked up our bags, and headed off, a telephone ringing at the desk as we walked away. We had reached the door of the Concorde lounge when we were stopped, called back by a suddenly friendly attendant, who said that if we followed her she would put us on the plane. We followed her, not understanding, while she advised me that I would be sitting in the cockpit for take-off, along with the manager of the Bank of England. Events had taken such a bizarre turn that I was half expecting the Queen of Hearts to turn up. Sandra and Georgia were shown to a seat, I squeezed in the cockpit with the pilots, the flight engineer, and the manager of the bank of England, and off we went. Somewhere over the Atlantic, at the speed of sound, we started chatting.

Apparently the flight crew had been going through the list of pre-flight checks, when the purser entered, and told them the flight was boarding, to which the pilot answered, 'Oh there's some chap off the telly on board, tell him he can come up to the cockpit once we're flying.'

'They've been bumped off the flight,' said the purser.

'I was told he was on the flight, Mike sent me a note.'

'TWA strike,' said the purser.

The pilot and the co-pilot exchanged a look. These were Concorde pilots they were messing with.

'Tell them we're not taking off till he's on board.'

The message was sent back to the gate, and much as the ground staff remonstrated with the pilots, they were as stubborn as the ground staff had been with us, which was why the purser went to the manager of the Bank of England, and politely asked if he might give up his seat and instead join the crew and some bloke off the telly, on the flight deck for the journey to Miami. He didn't mind at all.

They switched the afterburners on after Bristol, and you could feel the plane accelerate away, until the sky above our heads turned the darker blue of space. I wanted to know every detail of flying this incredible plane, whilst they wondered if I'd really put my arm up a cow.

In Florida we stayed with Aunt Olga and Uncle Ben, before going on to California to see Sandra's brother, and returning via Washington, DC. This was definitely the 'Show the Baby' tour. The in-laws lived in Bethesda, a quiet and affluent suburb of Washington, DC, in a large white clapboard house that backed onto woodland. We were visiting at the right time of year, after the raw cold of the Washington winter and before the wet blanket of stifling humidity settled over the city.

* * *

Tuesday, 20 October 2015. Bumped into Haydn Gwynne in the corridor outside my dressing room. I first met her when she had the smallest part imaginable in one scene in the first episode of *A Very Peculiar Practice*. Even then she had a presence about her. She reminded me that we also did a courtroom drama together for Granada TV, in which I was accused of her rape. Happy days.

IS THERE LIFE OUTSIDE THE BOX?

★ ★ ★

I arrived to find a message to call my agent about a meeting at the BBC. It was important enough to send the scripts. They didn't arrive until the day before we left, and so I read them through the night on the flight home. The series, called *A Very Peculiar Practice*, was written by Andrew Davies. I knew the moment I started reading that this was something special and a step up from the TV work I'd done before. It wasn't an offer, however, and I would have to meet the director and producer in a couple of days' time. Because it was such an intelligent script I sat down to figure out something intelligent to say when asked the question every actor trembles at, 'What did you think of the script?' I thought I came up with a couple of acute observations, and went off happily to meet David Tucker, the director, and the producer Ken Riddington. Tucker, who was soft-spoken and whose face, in repose, was less than friendly, asked me if I'd read the script. Riddington fidgeted, jangling keys in his pocket, something I was to become used to over the years. I replied, 'Yes I have, I've read them all.' Tucker nodded, and looked at me. He'd mastered the technique of the psychoanalyst and said nothing, allowing me stumble on, desperate to fill the awkward silence.

After I'd laid out my various minor observations about the script, Tucker nodded sagely and said nothing. Was he impressed or bored to death? It was hard to tell which, but I was heartened enough to add that I thought that one particular line in one particular episode wasn't particularly necessary. I knew the moment I said it I had stepped out over the edge. Tucker looked at me long and hard and gently cleared his throat: 'Well, I think you're entirely wrong about that.' It was a bad end to the interview, and by the time Ken walked me out with an uncomfortable, almost apologetic air, I had written off my chances. It was the beginning of rush hour and Shepherd's Bush was crazy with traffic. I found a phone box and called my agent mostly because I wanted to explain my failure. He answered the phone by saying they had just called to offer me the part.

★ ★ ★

David Tucker, who is now a friend enough to have given the best man's speech at my wedding, even though he wasn't actually the best man, categorically denies his reticence, but there is an actor out there who claims to have been offered the part before me until someone at the BBC stepped in, and demanded a better-known actor. I have not heard of this actor since he told me the story nearly twenty years ago, and I wondered at the time why he wanted me to know. Tucker insists I was always his first choice, though this might be because he was looking forward to years of clobbering me over the head with his Cambridge degree.

In late spring of that year my mother broke her leg. She had been walking our dogs, Spot and Alice, on the towpath by the River Wey when she was hit from behind by a large dog trying to get past her. In the following weeks, my mother, the matriarch, the woman whom I had always seen as indomitable, was reduced to a shadow of her former self. Yes, it was a bad break, considering the fluffiness of the dog, and she was hospitalised for five weeks, but, to me, that didn't explain the change in her character. It was as though the spirit had been sucked out of her, and even when she was eventually discharged, and came back to stay with us in Weybridge, she was discomforted, and liable to moments of panic when confronted with simple everyday tasks.

I found this change in her difficult to cope with. I had hardly ever seen a vulnerable side to her, and I didn't like it. I didn't like it when she got distressed about the bleak future she saw for herself. In the end for all the wrong reasons I probably did the best thing. I told her to stop feeling sorry for herself, that she was exactly the same woman she had been before the accident, and that I needed her to be that woman again. It was the kind of speech she might have given me twenty years before, and maybe this was payback time. However ill-judged it might have seemed, she responded almost immediately, as if the reassurance she was still depended on, was all she needed. She never fully recovered her nerve with dogs on the towpath but who could blame her?

★ ★ ★

We started filming in the early summer, once again with the uncomfortable mix of filmed exteriors and video interiors. The cast, for the most part, was excellent, with Graham Crowden as Jock, the head of the practice, and David Troughton as Bob, and Amanda Hillwood as my eventual girlfriend. We were all impressed with Amanda because she was married to Matt Frewer whose alter ego was Max Headroom, an incredibly popular icon in *The Max Headroom Show*. The only problem was the actress playing Rose-Marie. She looked perfect, and even sounded perfect, but she couldn't help but come across like a head girl rather than the sensuous, Machiavellian woman she was supposed to be. Andrew's idea was that Rose-Marie should look like she was wearing nothing underneath her white coat, and so during the studio someone came up with the idea of sowing buttons on the inside to give the impression of nipples. There followed much discussion, and debate about the exact positioning of the buttons for maximum nipple effect. After recording the first episode, the actress was recast, and replaced by Barbara Flynn who captured the part perfectly without ever resorting to buttons.

David Tucker is a heck of a director, getting out of Graham Crowden the performance of his career, but the first few days

Above left: The seventeen-year-old Peter Moffett on stage in the Byfleet Players production of *Tom Jones*. I am giving my 'Master Blifil'. My mother couldn't stop laughing. My father fell asleep.

© The Byfleet Players

Above right: Cast and crew of *Love for Lydia*, watching playback. Those admiring themselves include Sherrie Hewson, me, Mel Martin, Chris Blake and Jeremy Irons.

Below: The cast of *Grime Goes Green*. I'm afraid I can't remember who the bloke on my right was.

© Video Arts

ACTOR

You know you've made it when you're on a knitting pattern, complete with your duplicated autograph and a job description. This was a response to the considerable demand for 'Tristan'-styled Fair Isle sweaters – mostly from the girl on my right.

© Sirdar

Above: On location with *Campion*. My Auntie Olga was visiting from Florida – she was tremendously impressed with my suit and my manservant.

Below: In the garden of the eight-bedroom house in Wargrave. Considering the size of the mortgage, I look surprisingly calm.

Above: Filming *At Home with the Braithwaites*, and hanging with Smarty and Churmy. The best surrogate daughters you could wish for.

Below: The modern(ish) family, at my parents' fortieth wedding anniversary. My sisters, Pamela and Barbara. are in the red and green.

Above left: Another typical *Doctor Who* convention fan, who turned up dressed as me.

© *Catherine Ashmore*

Above right: *The Complete Guide to Parenting*: this is what happens if you don't read the contract.

Below: *Distant Shores*: Samantha Bond can't understand what the fuss is about.

Above: With my wife Elizabeth, after I won the Golden Nymph award in Monte Carlo. Five minutes later, I dropped it as I walked in to the dinner. It didn't survive.

Below: A filming day for the *Doctor Who* episode *Time Crash* in 2007. Louis, Louis, Joel, and Josh – the Moffetts and the Moffats, lend their support.

Spamalot. The closest I will ever get to being in *Monty Python's Flying Circus*.

Above: January 2011 – A relaxing Sunday afternoon at home. Except that Joel appears to be strangling Stanley the dog.

Below: Opening night of *Gypsy*. April 2015.

of rehearsal were interesting for all of us. After the read-through Tucker took David Troughton aside, and told him he was no longer giving the performance for which he'd been cast, which was unfortunate as David could not remember how he'd played it at the audition. Lindy Whiteford played the Irish nurse Maureen Gahagan and Gillian Raine, the former Mrs Leonard Rossiter, was the scary receptionist.

The exterior filming was done at Keele and Birmingham universities. Andrew had written it as the University of East Anglia, but they had previously been stung by not reading the script of Malcolm Bradbury's *The History Man* properly and were later horrified to discover that the series featured the sexual exploits of a professor and his students. The institution subsequently vowed never to let the BBC darken its doors again. Even so, both Keele and Birmingham only allowed us to film on the understanding it was a combination of both, and therefore possibly neither.

The first day I spent shooting driving sequences around the Birmingham campus, a camera rigged on the bonnet facing me. Lights were also bolted on, and pointed at my face, making it almost impossible for me to see where I was going. Having survived the first day without killing any luckless students, I nearly didn't make it past the first week myself. Filming a sequence in the university swimming pool that involved me nearly drowning, I very nearly drowned. I had warned everyone I was not a strong swimmer, there was nothing you could have done to persuade my father into swimming so I didn't exactly have a good role model, and I thought that if I stopped swimming, and pretended to drown, I would in fact be drowning. Tucker, a strong swimmer himself, found it hard to contemplate anyone who was otherwise. He seemed to think drowning wouldn't be a problem because the action entailed Amanda Hillwood jumping in and saving me, and, as long as she jumped in on cue, she would almost certainly reach me before my lungs filled with water and I died. This was of course a great comfort, although I did point out Amanda was only *playing* a lifeguard rather than actually being one, and while she certainly looked the part that was hardly a substitute for having a certificate hanging on her wall.

Ignoring my concerns, the camera crew started to film, and I started to drown, which unsurprisingly involved flapping my arms about, and swallowing water. After what seemed an eternity, and very nearly was, I was aware of Amanda jumping in, which reassured me somewhat until suddenly my head was pushed under water, and held there by her powerful grip. I was pretty sure this wasn't how you saved someone's life, but I was rather too busy drowning to ask questions.

In the end, as Tucker has pointed out to me on a number of occasions, I didn't die, and filming continued apace. We shot a scene in the Keele Students' Union building that had to be bleak, depressing and desolate. To achieve this effect, the prop guys turned up with bags of rubbish to scatter around the place. They took one look inside the building, and put the bags back in the van deciding it was more desolate, depressing and bleak than they could ever have made it.

Peculiar Practice featured two nuns who appeared in every episode, sometimes scavenging around the rubbish bins, or driving recklessly around the campus in a mini. It was Andrew's theory that, wherever you went in life, there were always two nuns knocking around, and although Sonia and Elaine were only classed as supporting artistes they became part of the family. The real students had no idea what was going on, though they loved the idea of a few extra quid for being extras. They were good at it too. In one dream sequence an entire lecture theatre full of them had to advance on the faculty sitting on stage shouting abuse, something they obviously relished.

The studio followed the usual pattern of ten-day rehearsals followed by two or three days' recording. Once again we used the Pebble Mill studios in Birmingham so I was surrounded by familiar faces.

In the London rehearsals we all treated Andrew's script with reverence, and there was no cutting or rewriting of scenes. We wanted to do it exactly as it was on the page. All of us were reverent but some were more reverent than others. Tucker was way ahead of us. After rehearsing a scene in which I had an unfinished line, as in 'unfinished . . .', he looked at me thoughtfully, and said, 'There are three dots at the end of that sentence, I think you're only playing two.' On another occasion after a long discussion about the meaning of a particular line, we agreed to disagree for a whole day until Andrew Davies turned up, and put us right. Tucker told him what he thought it meant and I put forward my own interpretation. 'I don't know what it means,' said Andrew, shrugging, 'I just thought it was funny.'

The show had an interesting history. Andrew had been writing something else for the BBC about three female mature students, but after struggling to write three of the episodes, he gave up. Unfortunately he'd already been paid seventeen thousand pounds, which they wanted back unless he could come up with something else. A few weeks later he presented them with *A Very Peculiar Practice*. In episode five of the series Stephen Daker meets a character called Ron Rust, who's at the university researching a TV series he has to write because he owes the BBC seventeen thousand quid. As, Andrew later said, 'Necessity was the mother of invention.'

Along with the regular cast we had steady roll call of actors playing students who went on to greater things, including Hugh Grant, Oliver Parker, Paul Jesson, Simon Russell Beale, Kathy Burke, and Mark Addy. We also had John Bird as the Vice-Chancellor, and Timothy West as a homicidal lecturer. In early October we returned to Keele to film the last block of the series. The last two scenes of episode seven were set in the car park where first, Chen my Chinese flatmate leaves, followed by my girlfriend Lynn in the very last scene. The two scenes were originally supposed to have been one. Overnight, with us only halfway through the set-ups, there was the first snowfall of the year, covering the campus with three or four inches, a continuity problem that would be hard to miss. We sat around most of the following morning with Ken Riddington jangling his keys in overdrive, and all of us hoping the sun would break through, and melt away the winter wonderland but it was never going to happen. Then I had an idea. Perhaps I could apply my bodging technique to film making. Why not mix through from where we left off in the summer, and make it look like time had passed, and it was the end of the Christmas term? Ken Riddington thought I was a genius, for the most part because it would save his budget from disappearing in a costly remount. Even Tucker had to admit it wasn't a bad solution in the circumstances.

We finished the series knowing we had made something special but also knowing that as it was for BBC2 it was unlikely to set the ratings on fire. It was a one-off as far as Andrew was concerned. He had paid back his seventeen thousand pounds, and wasn't interested in doing more. It was never intended to be a 'first of many' series anyway, and none of us speculated about doing more. Only days after I finished *A Very Peculiar Practice*, I was back in Yorkshire to film a second *All Creatures* Christmas Special.

I can't remember when the idea of making another series of the show came up, but it was probably long before anyone mentioned it to the actors. Not that we raised too many objections, I felt I had done enough other work to prove to myself that Tristan hadn't hindered my prospects. Quite the reverse, as *Doctor Who* had proved, Tristan was a stepping stone to other parts. The Christmas special would be Carol

Drinkwater's last appearance as Helen; she had moved to the south of France and was determined to pursue a career as a novelist.

That Christmas, Sandra and I did Panto in Wimbledon. *Aladdin* was a much grander affair than the Assembly Hall in Tunbridge Wells although as is often the case with the bigger productions, it was a panto clone. Our *Aladdin* had been in done in Manchester the previous year, even down to us being told the moves our counterparts had done. The sweet and ultimately tragic Lena Zavaroni was in the cast, as well as such contemporary favourites as Spit the Dog. Lena had suffered from anorexia ever since stage school, and while she talked positively about the future, there was an overwhelming sadness about her. She died in 1999, after years fighting depression. I also can't remember the panto in Wimbledon without recalling turning on the car radio outside the theatre, and hearing about the *Challenger* Shuttle disaster.

At home, Sandra's parents were coming over for Christmas, and Georgia had taken her first steps at only ten months old, and spoken her first word confirming her parent's conviction that she was the brightest child that had ever lived. Ominously her first word was chequebook, the poor child brainwashed by the most common enquiry heard around our house that year, 'Honey, where's the chequebook?', and I was going a bit mad with the chequebook myself, buying a new Sony video camera with the exciting new video 8 format.

That Christmas I filmed Georgia's first birthday, and over the next few years would record hours of her growing up. No holiday, no family celebration, no Sunday afternoon at home, went by without my video camera being there – It was bloody annoying for everyone but I was relentless, and in some ways, given the rise of mobile phone video, ahead of my time.

Nineteen-eighty-six was the year of touring theatre. After the success of *Barefoot in the Park* I was high on the commercial theatre wish-list. Someone came up with the idea of *The Owl and the*

Pussycat, a play by Bill Manhof that had been made into a successful film with Barbra Streisand and George Segal. It was a two-hander and the producer's idea was for Sandra and me to play the leads, but by the time they caught up with us, Sandra had committed to a tour of *The Seven Year Itch*. I was happy to wait until later in the year but theatres had been booked and so they wanted a replacement. Stephanie Lawrence was a star of musical theatre, playing the lead in *Evita* and *Starlight Express*, but now she wanted to conquer straight theatre, and the part of Doris in Manhof's play was an ideal way to start.

Lou Stein, who was about to become the artistic director of the Palace Theatre in Watford, was brought in to direct. There were problems almost immediately. I had never done a musical, and so had no way of knowing if Stephanie's particular approach to rehearsing was her own or was, as she insisted, 'the way we do it in musical theatre'.

This being a touring production, rehearsals were short: less than four weeks before we were due to tech the show, and Stephanie's inability to grasp that time was short was only the beginning. Lou, who was becoming aware there was a long road to travel, encouraged us both to lose the scripts as quickly as possible, and my usual obsession with learning the words only added to the problems. Stephanie complained I was putting her off by knowing the words and not having the script in my hand. I explained it was just my way of doing it and I was not trying to embarrass her and it was fine by me if she held on to the script for as long as she wanted. This was probably not the wisest thing to say as Stephanie seemed happy to hold on to the script well into the final week of rehearsal at which point Lou explained he needed to see a semblance of a performance in order to judge 'where we are'. Stephanie replied that she had never been asked to give a performance before the opening night.

PLAYING THE DOTS

That night came all too soon at the Theatre Royal, in Bath. The dress rehearsal had been lacklustre but at least we had got through it, and I knew the audience would lift us. Nothing prepared me for what followed. Stephanie burst onstage with a furious energy that would have been magnificent if only it had been directed at me, but strangely she appeared to be delivering all her speeches directly to the audience. When I had a line she gave the briefest look in my direction and then resumed her full frontal performance. When Lou came to my dressing room afterwards, we looked at each other in silence before I raised my hand and said, 'Hello, I'm over here?'

By the time we came to play the Yvonne Arnaud Theatre in Guildford we had a workable show and, as I sat in the green room chatting to Val May, who'd run the theatre for almost twenty years, I was almost looking forward to the week. I still had a few niggles: every night we would go up at least ten minutes late, apparently because 'Beginners please' to Stephanie, meant begin to get into your costume rather than begin your journey to the stage, and as getting into costume took fifteen minutes or so . . .

Then they called the half-hour, and someone came in to tell me Stephanie had not yet arrived. This is the point when you normally put the understudy on stand-by, except we didn't have an understudy, we had an assistant stage manager who was understudy in name only and had not rehearsed or had time to learn the lines. By the quarter, the understudy is going on – this is reversible if the actor turns up, but only at the understudy's discretion. At 7.30, when the show should have started there was still no sign of Stephanie and all we knew was she had left her home in London at 6.30 p.m., leaving herself only twenty-five minutes to get to Guildford.

Val May stepped in and insisted we hold the curtain, which we held for forty-five minutes until Stephanie turned up explaining the traffic had been bad. The shit hit the fan. Stephanie was given a verbal warning and her agent was sent a stern letter, the understudy was told to learn the lines, but no one really believed it would happen again. The next week it did. We were in Southampton, I think, and this time there was no last-minute reprieve. There was no one answering her phone at home and her agent had no idea where she was other than that she was commuting. The manager didn't want to hold the curtain on account of the paucity of late-night transport in the area, and so the company manager went in front of the curtain and made the announcement that Miss Lawrence was indisposed and that the understudy would play the part. The audience were disappointed of course and sighed accordingly and then the understudy and I went on stage having never rehearsed together and with her having only a passing knowledge of the script. At least it was a two-hander, I thought, so if she stopped speaking I knew it was down to me to pick up the slack, but I didn't quite foresee the randomness of her memory. She would say a line from the first scene, and follow up with a line from the third and then go back to the second, while I tried to respond with an appropriate bit of dialogue that may, or may not have been from the same act – or even the same play. And so it went on. I'm pretty sure none of it made any sense but it must have made a heck of an interesting evening, and at the end of each scene or whenever the DSM decided we'd confused people enough and cued a blackout, we would dive into the quick-change area on opposite sides of the stage and regroup for our next adventure.

About twenty-five minutes into the second half I dashed off for yet another change, having no idea which bits we'd missed out or had done twice or how long the play might last before we were sure we'd covered everything. At least, I was thinking, there had been no embarrassing pauses, and now we were in the final straight. I went back on and the lights came up – and there was Stephanie Lawrence standing there, almost inviting applause. And how they applauded. The poor girl had overcome her indisposition, they thought, she'd risen from her sickbed, cast aside her melancholy and grief or whatever had kept her from performing, and here she is – let's give her a cheer!

What had actually happened was that Stephanie had taken the wrong road and rather than find her way to the theatre from where she ended up, had retraced her route back to London before trying again. I don't even blame her, she was only obeying orders. When she finally arrived at the theatre with only half an hour to go, it was the theatre manager who insisted she go on. Despite everything it was hard not to like Stephanie. She hardly seemed aware that she causing disruption and she seemed disconnected from the world around her. On this tour there was no sign of drinking that would eventually end her life fourteen years later.

* * *

By the end of 1986 it was agreed that the original cast, minus Carol Drinkwater, would re-assemble to film another series of *All Creatures Great and Small*. Lynda Bellingham took over the role of Helen, a more mother-like figure than her predecessor. The date was set for the spring of the following year, dangerously close to the date set for a second series of *A Very Peculiar Practice*. Fortunately for me, Andrew Davies was having a little difficulty coming up with good storyline, which meant that as long as he eventually got it right, say three months later, I could do both. Eventually Andrew delivered a script which the director, David Tucker described with typical circumspection, as 'really awful'.

Now I was worried. Much as I loved the idea of playing Tristan again, I knew *Peculiar Practice* was a step in the right direction.

There was a meeting with the director and writer, at which by Davies's own admission, Tucker sat him down and told him what to write. An exaggeration perhaps but within a week of the meeting there was a new first episode that was fresh and exciting, and others soon followed. Meanwhile I had decamped to Yorkshire where we slipped back into making *All Creatures* with unnerving ease, and now the studios were back in Birmingham where it had all begun. It turned out to be the last full series I would appear in, as other projects overlapped or prevented me from turning up at all. At first the storylines sent me away tuberculin testing cows in Ireland, from where I would send letters home recounting some mishap or other that would then be mentioned in the episode. Over the years, people have told me how much they enjoyed these scenes that were never actually filmed.

In the new series of *Peculiar Practice* Andrew had written in a new female lead character of Grete Grotowska, a Polish art lecturer at the University of Lowlands and I got a call to come in and read with the actresses auditioning for the part. This was difficult, I was not officially a part of the casting process and I knew it would look like I was. There were several well-known faces, some with excellent Polish accents, but there was one genuine Polish actress who had won the hearts of David and Andrew. Ken Riddington, the producer, wasn't convinced.

'She wasn't bad . . .' he told them, leaving the sentence hanging.

'But . . . ?' Tucker prompted.

'. . . I'm worried her breasts aren't big enough.'

Tucker looked at him stony-faced.

There was a kind of logic to poor Ken's concerns. In the script Grete demands I proceed with a breast examination even though there isn't a nurse present, which leaves me open to charges of misconduct, and Ken thought that larger breasts were important in highlighting my doctor's dilemma. The rest of us (I had somehow been drawn into the discussion), took the view that breasts were breasts whatever the size and that smaller ones wouldn't lessen the misconduct. In the end common sense, smaller breasts and Joanna Kanska all won the day, and we started filming at Keele University in August.

It turned out that Joanna, who'd made perfect sense of the script at the audition. spoke almost no English at all and had learned all her lines phonetically. I discovered this while trying to have a simple conversation with her in the coffee bar at Keele University. She was unabashed and even with her broken English, she made it clear that my primary job for the rest of the series would be to coach her through the lines. I did this at every available opportunity, while she chain-smoked cigarettes, and looked distant and beautiful in the way women from Eastern Europe do so effortlessly.

In the evening Ken, who had quite forgotten his mammarian concerns, insisted we all went out to dinner. I sensed it was the most fun he'd had in years. If you'd run a poll at the BBC asking who is the least likely producer to be found dancing on a table in a Greek restaurant at eleven o'clock at night in Stoke-on-Trent – Ken Riddington's name would be close to the top of the list. And yet there he was – slightly pissed and enchanted, as we all were, by the seductress from Eastern Europe.

On the morning of 16 October the alarm went off at 6.30 a.m. and I switched on the TV, and was immediately confused because breakfast television seemed to be broadcasting in the dark. We were filming at Birmingham University in a thin strip of the country that was completely unaffected by the great storm of 1987. I was frustrated I'd missed it, and spent much of the day catching up with news, as it came in. Our home in Wargrave had been battered and several formerly upright trees, along with our front porch, were scattered haphazardly around the garden, and the house cut off from the rest of the village. It was much the same all over the south of England. In Birmingham, life carried on as usual.

The following year, after the trees had been cut up and the porch rebuilt, I constructed a tree house with a log staircase rising eight feet to the front door, where Georgia would serve me imaginary tea and biscuits. I never told her the tree house was for me.

When studio rehearsals started, one of the first scenes to be tackled was Ken Riddington's favourite: the breast examination. David Tucker, wanting to get it right, arranged for a real doctor to come along to demonstrate how it should be done. I thought it would ease the embarrassment for Joanna, and me, if a no-nonsense GP showed us the technique. The special rehearsal took place one lunch break, and was confined to Joanna, David Tucker and myself. The no-nonsense doctor turned out to be a young and attractive woman, who showed none of the embarrassment I was feeling, as she guided my hand through the squeezing, prodding and massaging Joanna's more than adequate chest.

The second series was a perfectly aimed attack on Margaret Thatcher's plan to bring a corporate business model into the university system. It was shown on BBC 2 and never repeated, and was finally released on DVD in 2008.

Earlier in the year I'd done an episode of *Tales of the Unexpected* with Liza Goddard. In the hotel bar after the last day of filming, Paul Annett, the director, asked me if I'd heard of the Campion detective novels by Margery Allingham. I told him I hadn't and he suggested I read a couple of them. 'Just a thought,' he said, and sidled off see Liza. I didn't take it that seriously, but seriously enough to seek and find a Campion novel in a second-hand bookshop. Seven months later we were almost at the end of *Peculiar Practice*, and in a scene off, I grabbed a coffee and went up to the gallery to watch the recording. Tucker was in the thick of a difficult scene and so I sat next to Ken Riddington who was reading a book, and trying not to notice we were slightly behind schedule. After ten minutes of being ignored, I got up and leant over to see what book he was reading – it was *Look to the Lady* by Marjorie Allingham. Before I left, I touched him on the shoulder and whispered, 'I'd be good in that.'

A month later the BBC came through with an offer for a series of *Campion*.

In January of 1988 we drove Sandra's parents' old Chevy Malibu across America, from Washington DC to Los Angeles. We made a short detour in Oklahoma, leaving Interstate 40 and visiting the small town of Moffett (population 239). We didn't stop.

In Arizona we visited London Bridge, which wasn't worth visiting when it was in London, let alone in the middle of Arizona. We had a choice of detouring there or going north to Las Vegas, and by popular vote we chose London Bridge. It's never a good idea to give a three-year-old child a choice between blackjack tables and a big red bus. They just don't get it. We got to West Hollywood on day five and settled into an apartment next to Norm's breakfast restaurant, a couple of blocks up from Trashy Lingerie, and within sight of the Beverly Centre, which in 1988, was a really cool place to hang out.

Sandra was there for pilot season, a pilgrimage she would make for the next four years. Occasionally I would be called in for a meeting, and it always followed the same pattern. Once they discovered I wasn't available they were desperate to have me stay. I flew home a few weeks later, leaving Sandra and Georgia in the safe hands of our nanny, Louise.

I was back to do the first series of *Campion*.

We were shooting on film, which at the time, with the trend towards the cheaper video format, was an indication of the prestige of the project. It was the first thing my agent had mentioned when he called to give me details of the offer. To save money the BBC purchased Albert Campion's red Lagonda for £25,000, which sounded crazy, but to hire it for the series would have cost much more, and by the time it was sold for a profit at the end of the second series, it had in effect cost them nothing.

The first script was written by Alan Plater and directed by Martin Friend whom I had worked with on *Anna of the Five Towns*. That first day of filming in Suffolk, I had a free afternoon and was sent off to master the art of Lagonda driving. Those in the know will realise that's no easy task. The car was a jewel of individuality, not least because the accelerator and brake pedals were reversed, the brakes worked on an occasional basis, and there was no synchromesh on the gearbox. This meant learning what I'd only ever heard about: the ancient skill of double declutching. Now I can double declutch like a master, but on that first afternoon, as they attempted to film in the usually peaceful countryside, all that could be heard was the continuous grinding of the gearbox when I got it wrong.

* * *

Tuesday, 17 February 2015. Big Finish. The last time I was here David Richardson asked me if I had any ideas for future projects. Since then I had the thought that audio adventures of Campion might be something to think about. We've lost Brian Glover with his brilliant take on Yorkshire cockney, so I suggested Alun Armstrong might produce the same magic. David was interested.

* * *

Campion was one of the last shows made before the move to the cost-effective, but punishing, two-week turn-around. We were given three weeks for each episode, luxurious by today's standards, and our budget, while not excessive, never seemed to hold us back. Even the usually vexed Ken Riddington was hard pressed to find a reason to rattle his keys.

Magersfontein Lugg, Campion's ex-convict manservant, was played by Brian Glover and I can't find enough good things to say about him. He was wise, easy-going, hugely talented in everything from wrestling to writing, with acting slotting in somewhere in between. For many years he'd been the proud Yorkshire voice of Tetley's tea bags, in fact Brian was so synonymous with all things Yorkshire, it was disconcerting to hear him use a cockney accent. Above all he lived life to the full and partied with the best of us. I'm assured by those he sashayed with around the dance floor, he could move pretty well too.

He arrived on set one morning with a spent but contented look on his face. There had been a lively party the night before and Brian had been at the heart of it until I lost sight of him around midnight. He sidled up and stood beside me, waited a moment, then turned his head and whispered, 'If anyone asks, I was with you last night,' and walked away.

Nothing more was said, nor did it need to be.

★ ★ ★

Monday, 30 March 2015. Had an email (via Georgia) from Jane Perry who worked as a runner on *Campion.* She was diagnosed with MS in 1995 but still manages to be president of BECCTU and is asking me to sponsor her to run the London Marathon, raising money for the MS charity. I asked her about a half-remembered incident from 1989 that had made me laugh – 'Yes' she said, 'all true.'

★ ★ ★

IS THERE LIFE OUTSIDE THE BOX?

It's not easy being a runner on a film set. The same job on television is even more demanding, and in 1989 your job description covered being a unit driver as well. All Jane Perry had to do was pick up the actress Hilary Mason at 7 a.m. and drive her to set. The rest of the unit had arrived on time and were waiting to start, but at 7.45, there was still no sign of Jane or Hilary. The first assistant director, an efficient and uncompromising woman called Viv, was getting twitchy, but five minutes late, while annoying, was something the schedule could cope with. By eight o'clock she was angry, there was nothing we could do that morning without Hilary and so the third assistant was sent off to call the hotel. At 8.15, camera and sound were set up and waiting and we knew the car had left the hotel on time. By 8.25 Viv was pacing up and down, telling anyone that would listen that she knew it was a mistake to give a job to someone as inexperienced as Jane. By 8.45, Jane had lost her job. She was incompetent and she would be fired the moment she turned up on set. Around ten to nine the mood changed very slightly. And five minutes later Viv, along with the rest of us, started to worry and hope that the two of them were all right. At 9.00 the third assistant was sent off to phone the police and see if anyone had reported an accident. By ten past, we were all convinced they were lying dead in a ditch somewhere, and Viv was wringing her hands in distress.

Jane and Hilary turned up at 9.20, having been lost in the country lanes of Suffolk for an hour and a half. Hilary was very apologetic, and Jane was crying like someone who was about to be fired. Fortunately, Viv hadn't a clue about anything prior to the moment she'd started to worry about her runner. She flung her arms around her, told her not to worry and sent her off to have a nice cup of tea and a rest.

If things are worth doing, they're worth doing well.

We did two series of *Campion* and I wished we'd done more. I loved the books and the stories but there was a problem dramatising them. The plotting was intricate and didn't lend itself to simplification the way Agatha Christie books did, and because the two episodes of each story were a week apart, it wasn't easy to remember what had happened in the previous episode. Nevertheless, they were successful and if the BBC had not wanted more contemporary and cheaply made detective series, might have carried on much longer.

11

MY TEN YEARS IN THE WILDERNESS

Saturday, 27 February 2016. Had dinner at Nigel Planer's house in London. Interesting time finding his house as neither of us could figure out how to get to Borough Underground station. Nigel and I are trying to corner the market in 'older blokes in musicals', and he had his eye on taking over from me in *Legally Blonde* but I ended up staying for the whole run. So I reckon I owe him one. He has developed his grumpiness into an art form, has eight projects on the go but is unable to move forward with any of them; he is brutal but very funny about it; I understand his frustration. We were both recently asked to read for a remake of an eighties BBC comedy show. We both agreed about the script, but whereas he went along, I declined to with the same result – neither of us are doing it. Over coffee a man called Ben Harrison explained he'd been a producer, then turned to me and said I'd once worked for him.

'Video Arts,' he said.

'That'll be *Grime Goes Green*,' I replied.

IS THERE LIFE OUTSIDE THE BOX?

* * *

I had no idea I'd been in the wilderness until, in 2001, the *Daily Mail* announced it was nice to see me back after the ten years of being in it. There was at least a small amount of truth in their assessment, which for the *Daily Mail* is surprising. By 1991 the succession of TV series which I had seamlessly moved between were drying up. My marriage to Sandra was disintegrating, and a stupidly high mortgage along with threatening letters from the collector of taxes only added to the stress of our lives. This is no plea for sympathy, I had been very fortunate, but we had been needlessly living at the edge of our means for several years, and now the dip in lucrative job offers had tipped us well beyond it. I was feeling the dull weight of anxiety a little more with each day that went by. Even so there was the occasional pleasant surprise.

Video Arts was a production company with an enviable reputation for making training programmes and had been set up by John Cleese and Anthony Jay who, only the year before, had sold it on for 43 million pounds. The script they sent me, which would also feature John Cleese and so enough to make me accept, was intended to teach companies to be environmentally friendly. The teacher in this case was a character described as a 'Prince Charles lookalike'.

Five minutes after I accepted the job the phone rang again.

I was on the floor in the attic room of our house playing with Georgia, and I rolled over towards the phone and picked it up, only expecting the usual job confirmation from my agent. The call was from John Cleese.

'So pleased you're doing it.'

'Yes, so am I.'

'I should tell you. Obviously keep this to yourself. The Prince is not going to be a lookalike.'

I assumed he meant he couldn't find one.

'Oh that's a shame.'

'No, it's not a shame. Not a shame at all. It's him. Prince Charles.'

There is a moment while I take this in.

'Wow.'

'Yes. Absolutely. Wow.'

After I had for years of listened to him on the radio and followed his every TV appearance, Cleese was something of a godlike figure to me. I knew enough about him not to expect him to be funny off screen, and he wasn't, but even his studied seriousness made me smile. At the time he was still rankled by divorce number two, and over breakfast on the first morning asked me how long I had been married.

'Nearly twelve years,' I told him.

'Twelve years?' He beat his chest in a pantomime of choking on his coffee. 'Oh God, that's far too long.'

He wasn't far off. Within a couple of years, I would find myself in the same predicament.

We filmed *Grime Goes Green* over four days at Fountain Television in New Malden, where my sister Pamela had worked until a few months before. The first three days we shot everything except the scene with the prince 'lookalike', and I nearly gave the game away several times by not quite understanding who exactly knew exactly who was turning up on Thursday. In fact, of the cast, John Cleese had only told me. I'm not sure why I was entrusted with the information but it was clearly misplaced. 'It's going to be interesting on Thursday; will we have to walk backwards off the set?' I murmured to Josette Simon in make-up. Over lunch, I remarked casually, 'We'd better remember our lines on Thursday or it's off to the Tower.'

They all looked at me thinking I was an idiot making bad jokes about a Prince Charles lookalike. I was an idiot but at least I was making bad jokes talking about the real thing. On Wednesday morning the cleaners moved into Fountain Television. Everything that could be polished was buffed to within an inch of its life. Light bulbs that had sat dead in their sockets were replaced with bright new ones, and flowers and plants started arriving by the bucket load. At tea break everyone was told the truth, and I wondered what they thought I had been droning on about. The next morning, we were told, the car park would be closed as well as the roads immediately around the studios. We had to arrive early for security checks, including the once-over to prevent unofficial photos.

The Prince glided in at about ten o'clock in a convoy of spectacularly unimpressive black cars. He was surrounded by an entourage of well-groomed young men, dressed in black, of course, with broad friendly smiles. You might almost call them inconspicuous were it not for the seriously official shoes, and a slight shortness of length in the trouser department. He was of course perfectly charming and as a consequence for a good number of years dropped off my list of the first against the wall when the revolution comes. He seemed bemused by the world around him, but how could he not be? Here was a man who had never been in a traffic jam or travelled by bus or tried to make his way down a busy shopping street. Real life moved to one side as he travelled through it, and if it didn't there were men in serious shoes to shove it out of the way. A few years later, an actress told me a story of Prince Andrew calling to ask her out to the opera (she had met him at a function earlier in the evening but had no idea how he got her number). He asked her where she lived so he could send a car. 'Ealing,' she replied.

'Where's that?' he said.

Back in New Malden, we were all getting on famously. Although the film was being directed by Peter Robinson, Prince Charles was more personally directed by Cleese. I think they were good friends or at least knew each other socially, and I'd go so far as to say Charles was a bit of a fanboy. The rest of the cast, including myself, grinned, and gawped at him in that way you can't stop yourself doing, even though you're thinking he's no different from us. In my case we were both crap at school so we should have had a lot in common. Only Bryan Pringle maintained a lugubrious air to the end. After we wrapped, we all posed for a group photo which still hangs on my wall today, together with others of me with Tony Blair, with George W. Bush and with Nelson Mandela . . . all these Photoshopped for a television series I did years later. I never saw the finished *Grime Goes Green*, but I don't think Charles' acting would have won many awards but then, come to think of it, neither did mine.

* * *

If I had to pinpoint a job that sent me spiralling into my dark decade, it might be *Fiddlers Three*, a sitcom for Yorkshire Television written by Eric Chappell. It was funny enough, but somewhat similar, I discovered later, to his series *The Squirrels*, made ten years before. This was an offer, and after a couple of days' deliberation we started negotiations. At the same time, I had an availability check for a new BBC comedy called *The Brittas Empire*. The script was great but I was being pressed for an answer by Yorkshire TV, and felt I had to accept the offer on the table. I'm not suggesting I would have got the part because Chris Barrie created a wonderfully eccentric character for the part of Gordon Brittas and very different from the way I would have played it, but as a general note to myself, maybe I was a little timid in not taking the chance on it.

The lure of *Fiddlers Three* was the money which I desperately needed at that moment. We were living unhappily in an eight-bedroom riverside house with mortgage debt and interest on unpaid tax rising by the day. The bank managers who had been so keen to lend us money a few years earlier were now polite asking if they could please have it back. It was our own fault of course. We'd spent too much on kitchens and cars, on clothes and gadgets, on redecorating every room in the house. Why did we need an eight-bedroom house anyway? And on the river? When we first bought it I had stood on the riverbank every day amazed at my good fortune – now it struck me it was weeks since I'd so much as given the river a second glance.

I'm probably being slightly unfair to *Fiddlers Three*. We had a very good cast, Paula Wilcox played my wife, Charles Kay was my boss, and Tyler Butterworth and Peter Blake my office rivals, and if you judge a job by how much fun you have making it, *Fiddlers* would be right up there. We rehearsed in a church hall in Kensington from Mondays to Wednesdays, but only in the mornings, and then only in between chatting, and various coffee breaks. Every day Peter Blake would arrive, and proudly place his new mobile phone on the desk in front of him as if at any moment he might get that all-important call. To be fair he couldn't have kept it in his pocket as it was the size of a house brick. Tyler Butterworth would give Peter a troubled look, and then glance at me, which meant we had to stop for another coffee break until I recovered my composure. We all loved Charles Kay because he was Charles Kay, and Cindy Marshall-Day was Cindy Marshall-Day. Peter Blake's phone didn't ring until the last day of rehearsal of the series, three months later. It was his girlfriend asking where he kept the cat food.

Every Thursday, we would catch the train to Leeds, and record the show the following night in front of a live audience. There is nothing quite like this experience. It's the worst of both worlds; do you try to make the studio audience laugh or keep it subtle for the viewers at home? I'm baffled how anyone thought the studio audience was a good idea. It trickled down from the early days of American radio, and we should have plugged the leak years ago. It makes me nervous just writing about it. The viewers will laugh at the clever, well-written jokes, a studio audience will howl if someone says knickers. First the warm-up man welcomes the audience, and tells a few jokes that you hope are not funnier than the ones in the show. This can happen. When I made *Sink or Swim* in the early eighties we often had Felix Bowness as our warm-up man, who would get the studio audience into such a state of frenzied laughter I thought they would laugh at anything. In fact, by the time we came to record they were exhausted. At Yorkshire TV the warm-up man was pretty good, and after a few gentle jokes, would introduce the cast. I would try and make a wry comment, something like: 'I hope you find the show funny, because if you don't we're going to lock the doors, and keep doing it until you do.'

After which we got down to business, started the big videotape machines, and ran the opening titles. I would take my place on set, trying to remember the last-minute line change as the make-up girl dabs the shiny patch on the end of my nose that won't seem to go away, and the floor manager counts down from five on his fingers, and cues me in, all of which brings me to the other studio-audience dilemma. If you screw it up you have to retake a scene, but by then the audience has heard all the jokes, so while they reset, the warm-up man will step in, and ask them to pretend they haven't so the audience, eager to please, laughs too loudly, and often before the end of the funny line. On the other hand, every audience loves a cock-up – it means they're seeing something they shouldn't, and it also relaxes them. So early on there is often either a deliberate mistake, or at least a casual approach to getting it right.

Afterwards we would all go for dinner. Paula usually brought along her boyfriend Skip, a charming and amiable American who happened to be the son of the legendary arranger and band leader Nelson Riddle, but more importantly had introduced the UK to the VideoPlus+ system of VCR programming. That may sound antiquated now but I was fascinated. Peter Blake really came into his own at these dinners, rather fancying himself as an epicurean. It was Paula who first noticed that in a French restaurant he would talk to the waiters in a French accent, in an Italian, like an Italian, etc. – even adopting stereotypical gestures.

He would order his own expensive bottle of red rather than drink the house red the rest of the table were enjoying, and keep it firmly within his grasp. He was apoplectic if you cut the cheese incorrectly, which needless to say we started doing deliberately. All this might sound as though I had a problem with him, but I didn't at all. I was probably being over-sensitive. However, I sensed an antagonism between us, as if he really couldn't understand why I was starring in the series. I couldn't blame him for that. I had gone from job to job throughout the eighties, never finishing one without knowing what I was doing next, and appearing in at least two, sometimes three, series a year. It would have made me sick had I not been the one doing it. There was one week, I was reliably informed, when I was on television, in one programme or another, every day. I'm surprised there wasn't a contract out on me.

Maybe there was. Maybe that's how I ended up in the wilderness.

* * *

In 1972, a few weeks before we left drama school, each student was given an assessment by the teaching faculty of our future prospects. It was a daft idea, because it either left you suicidal or with dangerously inflated expectations. I was going to need extraordinary patience, I thought, as they had confidently predicted I wouldn't work until I was forty. Their assessment was so utterly wrong I had almost forgotten about it, but this year I was forty and I began to worry that they had simply got it upside-down: I would work until I was forty and that would be it. It very nearly was.

On my fortieth birthday Sandra was in California trying to get a break in another pilot season. Louise, Georgia's nanny, decided to help me celebrate. She and a friend, Sheila, from down the road whose husband's birthday was a few days later, arranged a surprise.

I was woken at six o'clock in the morning, and told to get dressed. We drove down the M4 watching the rush-hour traffic building up in the other direction, and ended up in a field outside Newbury. Even before I saw the balloon I had a fair idea what was in store for me. Sheila's husband Paul looked as uncertain as I did, but this was a birthday surprise, and the two women were smiling broadly. For one thing it wasn't the tranquil morning I associated with ballooning. It was I thought, as I climbed into the surprisingly large wicker basket, what you might call windy. There were ten of us, all intrepid first-time balloonists, together with our experienced pilot. Despite never having been up in one, the sight of hot air balloons was not uncommon where we lived. A couple of years before one had brushed the side of our house before drifting lazily off into the distance. It looked so elegant and relaxing. I still didn't fancy it.

The deceptive thing about ballooning, I discovered, is that you're moving with the wind, so that no matter how fast you are going, no matter how much ground you are covering, the air around you is always perfectly still. You may look down at the stunning views of the English countryside, and notice the world is moving quite quickly beneath you, but that's not a problem while you're high up, and enjoying the spectacle. It's when you start descending that you, literally, and figuratively, come down to earth.

The general plan when ballooning, in case you haven't been as lucky as me, is that the ground crew jumps in a motor vehicle, and follows the course of the balloon as best they can, so that when you drift gently down to earth, they can be there to meet you. This assumes a modest rate of travel and it soon became obvious that this was an assumption we had chosen to ignore. While we headed south towards the English Channel at an alarming rate, the Land Rover was trundling down the A34 towards Portsmouth. A quiet panic had broken out in the basket although it may only have been me. After all I was standing closest to the pilot, and it was me who heard him speak quietly into his walkie-talkie, one hand covering his mouth, and say, 'We're going over Gibbet's Ridge, and we're going like the clappers.'

We were.

As we descended this became apparent to everyone. As in an aircraft, when you come into land you appear to get faster, so it was with our balloon. In fact, we were coming in exactly like an aircraft, not the gentle wafting down I had seen before. Our pilot suggested as calmly as he could, which wasn't calmly at all, that we should crouch down below the edge of the basket on account of the balloon occasionally tipping over, and being dragged a short distance before stopping. I was quite happy to do this immediately. After all, this wasn't the right time to ask him why we had chosen to go ballooning in the middle of a gale. The last thing I saw before I ducked down was us narrowly missing the top of a hedge as we headed into an open field.

There was a bump, and then nothing. Not even the threatened tipping up. I looked over the top of the basket, and saw the reason. We had landed all right. Bounced, to be more accurate, and now we were airborne again, and heading towards a rather tall, and substantial tree. I decided to crouch down again, and bravely close my eyes. We hit it with a jarring thud, bits of tree flying all around us, and the stub of a tree branch piercing the basket about a foot away from me.

We were miraculously upright, but stranded about thirty-five feet above the ground, with the wind catching the tattered remains of the balloon, and threatening to drag us out of the tree again. Fortunately, the remains of the branch held the basket firmly in place . . . at least for the moment. I had always been pretty good at climbing trees, and I was bloody brilliant at climbing down this one. I was the first on the ground without giving a moment's thought for anyone else's safety. But I was forty, for God's sake.

Eventually we all made it down the tree safely, which meant we could concentrate on our next problem. We were in a field in the middle of nowhere, and with no way of explaining to the ground crew in the Land Rover where we were.

They found us two hours later. Louise and Paul's wife laughing hysterically at our misadventure. They took us back to Newbury, and even had the nerve to hand us a certificate confirming we had completed a trip in a hot air balloon.

I was forty, but I was alive.

As I sat in the car on the way back, I felt amazing. People have come a lot closer to disaster and survived but I felt like every day from now on would be a bonus. The next few years turned out to be difficult and challenging, but in some way the best years of my life. This was the wilderness. Bring it on.

* * *

It started at the Festival Theatre in a south-coast town called Chichester. I had a meeting with Michael Rudman, who at the time was putting together the 1991 season, and he told me he'd got Annie Castledine directing *Arsenic and Old Lace*, and asked if I would like to play Mortimer Brewster. I said yes immediately. The film, which starred Cary Grant, was one of my favourites, and it was also a chance to do something other than touring productions. When he mentioned her name I had no idea who Annie Castledine was, but he said her name with such reverence it was clear I ought to have done. I discovered she had a reputation as a radical spirit while running Derby Playhouse, and the idea of her and Rudman taking on the Chichester elite appealed to me.

We rehearsed the first few weeks in London, although I use the term loosely. What we did was watch old films, tried some improvisations based on what might be happening to us offstage, and threw balls and other objects to each other while in character. I wasn't quite used to this approach and found it hard to understand how it would help us get a show ready in five weeks' time. There was also a contradiction in Annie. At the start of each day she encouraged us to sit quietly for a few minutes, and then walk around the rehearsal set feeling the props and furniture, while she sat on her chair drinking coffee and chain-smoking fags.

After about two weeks' rehearsal, I stopped humming to myself, and fondling the furniture, and made myself coffee too. We would talk while we sipped, Annie taking deep drags of her cigarette, and me crunching my chocolate Hobnob as we slowly got to know each other. When we finally blocked through the play, she insisted she wouldn't tell us where to move, but allow us to find our own actions and movement, within the space. This kind of personal responsibility didn't sit well with many of us (and I'm not convinced it did with Annie), and during one ponderous rehearsal in which none of us could decide where we wanted to stand, our frustrated director threw her principles out of the window and barked at us, 'Why don't *you* walk across to the sideboard. Now *you* can sit on the window seat. And the rest of you, stop fucking wandering about!'

When we moved down to Chichester it became apparent it was round one to the traditionalists. Michael Rudman had been replaced by old Chichester favourite Patrick Garland. A meeting was called for everyone involved in the season, and would be addressed by Patrick himself. Wearing a pastel-coloured sweater, he told us he believed in being perfectly straight with people, and therefore wanted to tell us exactly what had happened, and he assured us the best way of doing this was by quoting from a lesser-known Shakespearian sonnet. Which he then went on and quothed.

That was all we got. I had no bloody idea what he was talking about, but he certainly wasn't telling us what happened. Annie Castledine was fuming, but the whole episode had the effect of coalescing us into a tightly knit company. We saw ourselves as the last vestige of Rudman's season, and were proud of it. The cast had Rosemary Harris, and Elizabeth Spriggs as the kindly murderous aunts, Bernard Bresslaw as my lunatic brother, and Alan Corduner as his accomplice. Bresslaw was a revelation. Having watched him in *Carry On* films all my life I found him the antithesis of what I had expected: intelligent and softly spoken, with a quick-wit. He arrived having done extensive research on the play and the period in which it was written.

The Chichester audiences loved it, and there was even talk of a transfer but the idea suffered from the show not being part of Garland's repertoire: Foolishly, I didn't stay in Chichester itself but rented a cottage about seven miles away. It was infested with mice, and each night I lay in bed throwing shoes at the skirting board to frighten them into silence long enough to let me fall asleep.

After a few weeks Chris Timothy turned up in the next play, a production of *Henry VIII*, starring Keith Michell. It's Shakespeare's dullest play, with no action, no comedy, and precious little intrigue, and the whole cast did its best, including an outstanding performance by Fiona Fullerton's corseted bosom, which rose and fell with such enthusiasm it stole the show whenever it appeared. Poor Keith

Michell as Henry did his best to convince us he was playing the title role, but it was Ms Fullerton's cleavage that got the reviews. What we all missed, as I discovered while examining documents of the time, was the bloke playing the 'blink and you miss him' parts of Gentleman/Surveyor/Porter, and whose name was Colin Farrell.

★ ★ ★

Arsenic and Old Lace finished in July of '91, by which time I'd heard we had been given the go-ahead for *A Very Polish Practice*, a final special of Andrew Davies's *Peculiar Practice*. Most of the credit should go to Joanna Kanska who gave Andrew a story idea set in Poland, and told him to write it. She had that way about her. Anyone who can get Ken Riddington to dance on a table can do just about anything. David Tucker was also at the heart of it as usual, pushing Andrew to finish the script to the satisfaction of the BBC. Ken Riddington was the producer, although he didn't last long – He somehow managed to break his leg while getting off the plane in Warsaw, and flew straight home again.

This was my first visit to an Eastern Bloc country, and it was eye opening. The Russians had gone, at least those governing the country had. For the Russians who remained there was a reversal of fortune. Always despised, at least they had once been privileged, now they found themselves relegated to the bottom of the heap. At the local market held each day in the sports stadium, they had once commanded the central tiers to set up their stalls, now they made do with whatever space the Polish didn't use. We'd been advised to bring US dollars as that was the currency the Poles found most desirable. The zloty was still legal tender but its value had nosedived, and by exchanging a few pounds you could become a zloty millionaire. Shelves in the food shops were mostly empty, but people didn't seem to go hungry. I had the impression there was a brisk and effective black market in most goods, which Andrew had reflected in the plot of our film.

Bob Buzzard was back, crackling with nervous energy, and played with his usual brilliance by David Troughton. At the airport in London he had bought an expensive bottle of whisky because he was convinced you couldn't get the real stuff in Poland, and he was partial, as he said, to a small tipple at the end of a filming day. The first evening in the bar of the hotel he discovered good Polish vodka, and the whisky remained unopened for the entire shoot. We were staying at the one of the finest hotels in Warsaw, which at that time wasn't saying an awful lot. In the evenings the bar was busy with a mix of European businessmen and attractive women, and, of course, us.

We got talking to a woman who was an architect, who was there with her friend. It was only when we noticed them repeatedly leaving with men, and returning half an hour or so later, we realised she was architect by day, prostitute by night. I gathered that earning a little extra money this way was not unusual at that transitional time. She'd given us no clue of her second career, so I assume she was chatting to us in her tea break before going back to her usual clientele – the foreign businessmen. The next night we noticed they were back in the bar. Later in the shoot the bar was closed temporarily while we filmed a scene in there, and because of our experience David Tucker had three extras playing prostitutes. The management caught onto to this, furiously insisting their hotel would never have prostitutes hanging around. We had to gently point out they were sitting in the lobby at that moment, waiting to come in the moment the bar reopened.

Alfred Molina played the black market boss and Joanna's ex-boyfriend. On our day off, the cast ventured out in the city together. In Joanna Kanska we had a perfect guide to Warsaw. In between the beautiful palaces of Lazienki and Wilanow, parts of the city had been infected with the Soviet brutalist style, and the horizon was dominated by depressing utilitarian tenement blocks, all in stark contrast to the charm of the old town, which was the new town, having been reconstructed after the Second World War. Joanna was the celebrity in Warsaw, not from anything she had done there but from her appearances in *Capital City*, an ITV series that had proved incredibly popular in communist Poland. She would be stopped, and asked for her autograph while we stood there like lemons.

In those days, the Polish car of choice – maybe because there was no choice, was the Polski Fiat. I drove one in the film. Tiny and as basic as it gets, and especially interesting on cobbled streets, I grew to love it, and wanted to take it home. Although home, at this time, wasn't as appealing as it used to be. Coming home meant coming home to debt, and long conversations with the tax office about every option short of bankruptcy. We had Christmas inclusive of Georgia's birthday, a more muted affair than usual but still a fair old pile of presents for her to open, and then Sandra was off to try her luck again with the Hollywood pilot season. We still had the apartment in West Hollywood, but it was becoming a liability, and we decided this would be the last hurrah. I still had money coming in as January was always good for a BBC residuals cheque. There were voice-overs, and the odd corporate video, but nothing short of a big fat commercial would get us out of the stew.

I was offered a guest part in *Kinsey*, a variation on the 'maverick lawyer solves crimes' idea, and which starred Leigh Lawson, and was made by BBC Birmingham. It wasn't a hard decision to make. I knew I would be working with people I knew, and besides, it was a job. Most actors start off playing small parts, and graduate to lead roles, I began to wonder if I was doing it in reverse; I had started with such a procession of leading parts, now it was time to pay my dues.

We started off filming in Birmingham, but the bulk of the story was set in Spain where ironically the BBC were about to start work on *Eldorado*, the exciting new, and ultimately doomed, soap opera that was intended to take the ratings by storm, and set new standards for quality early-evening drama. It certainly did that.

Meanwhile we flew out to Malaga. Leigh Lawson had insisted on a trailer for series two of *Kinsey*. These days it would be automatic, but back then it was not a given, and the BBC had found him the smallest, silliest-looking caravan that fulfilled their contractual obligations. It was sad to see it tucked away, almost forgotten in the corner of the unit base, the runt of the litter among the chunky make-up trailers, prop vans and lighting trucks, and then to see the star of the show wriggle his way out, brush himself down, doing his best to maintain his dignity. But when the show departed for Spain, Leigh lost his dinky caravan which proved too costly to send.

In the episode I was a sports agent in love with a beautiful young Spanish tennis star played by an actress called Esperanza Campuzano, who in every respect was perfect for the part except for the minor detail that she'd never played tennis before. No one, not the director, not the producer, and certainly not me, minded one jot about this. We gazed at her, enchanted, as the camera rolled, and a club player served slow half-volleys, all of which went past her before she could move her racket at all. Next, someone tried gently lobbing tennis balls over the net which she also tried in vain to make contact with. Finally, she ran around prettily, swinging the racket with gusto, and hitting invisible tennis balls to all corners of the court. In our minds it didn't matter at all, she was there as an actress, a job she did really well, despite the handicap of not actually being able speak English. She was the daughter of a well-known Spanish musician Felipe Campuzano as I found out in the bar that evening as we took it in turns to help her with translation.

IS THERE LIFE OUTSIDE THE BOX?

The following afternoon we had to shoot a scene where we were spotted kissing by Kinsey. Halfway through the lunch break the director took the two of us aside, and said he wanted us to practise. He wanted it to look passionate, he said, and to be obvious the affair had been going on for some time, so he didn't want the first few takes to be tentative. I was afraid she might think I'd put him up to this; I was conscious she was almost twenty years younger than me, but instead she smiled, and nodded, and off we went. Once we had rehearsed it a few times, done the long shot, the mid-shot, the close-up, and the reverse angle, I was exhausted. It's hard to know how to gauge the conversational moments in between having your tongue down the throat of a beautiful young woman who you've only just met, and who doesn't speak much English but I decided to take up the position of apologist. It's something that's become almost instinctive: if in any doubt I keep saying sorry. Apparently it's bloody annoying. She was having none of it.

'Sorry.'

'*Qué pasa?*'

'Sorry what? I was just saying sorry.'

'*Qué?* Err . . . What for?'

'Well, you know. Are you OK?'

She shrugs lightly, and smiles. A voice shouts 'Action!'. She throws her arms around my neck, and off we go again.

I have no idea how long I spent passionately kissing Miss Campuzano that day, but it took me back to a school coach trip to somewhere I've forgotten when I kissed Jocelyn Guersouille for an hour and a half without our lips once separating, beating Roger Lawson and his girlfriend into a miserable second place.

★ ★ ★

Thursday, 25 June 2015. Luke Street tells me his father is watching the show tonight. They lived in Lyme Regis where I filmed *Harnessing Peacocks*, and apparently his dad was employed as my body double for a scene in a bed in which he had to grunt. I have no idea why I couldn't grunt myself.

★ ★ ★

In July, after a couple of months out of work, I got a leading part in an adaptation by Andrew Davies of a Mary Wesley novel, *Harnessing Peacocks*. We filmed for the most part in Lyme Regis in Dorset so once again I was away from home. The director was Jimmy Cellan Jones, a veteran of TV, whose immediately observable quirk was his insistence on wearing open sandals with no socks, no matter what the weather. Serena Scott Thomas (younger sister of Kristen) was Hebe, the heroine of the film, with a list of lovers that included David Harewood, Richard Huw, Nick LePrevost, Sir John Mills and me.

Jimmy told me he knew he was taking a chance with Serena but was convinced he could coax a great performance from her. However, sometimes I felt it was at the cost to other actors' performances. He would always save her close shots until last and often ask her to hold back on the emotion or, to be brutal, the acting, until then. I was caught out by this in a couple of scenes. After filming the scene on me in which I smile with joy as we each reveal the truth of our first meeting, the camera turned round to film Serena who was suddenly playing the same scene tearfully and distressed. The resulting image of me smiling joyfully while she sobbed, was not quite what I intended.

Jimmy decided Serena should use his precious vintage Mini as her character's car, I can only imagine because he wanted it immortalised on film. This was a bad idea. A few days into the filming they attached a side mount to the car to film while Serena drove, and misjudging the extra width, she clipped a wall, destroying the camera, and severely reshaping vital parts of Jimmy's car.

The biggest thrill was working with John Mills. I'd watched so many of his films growing up that I felt I already knew him. A kinder and less affected man you could not hope to meet. He was eighty-four by this time, with failing eyesight, but was uncomplaining and undemanding, and had time for everyone. He was accompanied as ever by his wife Mary, a marriage that had lasted fifty years. He only had peripheral vision after an eye operation that went wrong, and consequently while the camera was filming Sir John, I was asked to move out of the way while the runner held up a white card which was just about the only thing he could see directly in front of him. I suggested a better idea would be to stick the white card to my forehead so I could at least play the scene with him. He thought this was a fine idea, and suggested that everyone he knew should have white cards permanently attached to their heads.

★ ★ ★

Dimensions in Time was the *Doctor Who* contribution to *Children in Need*. Or was it the *EastEnders* contribution? Or was it the *Doctor Who* Thirtieth Anniversary Special? Nobody knows. Some say it was a demonstration of how terrible 3D would someday look when it eventually appeared on our televisions. Whatever the point of it was it has now taken its rightful place in the pantheon of *Doctor Who*. Right at the very bottom.

On the other hand for those who were looking for a celebration of thirty years since the first broadcast of *Doctor Who*, this was all you got.

I suppose you could question whether you can have an anniversary special for a show that had been cancelled six years previously, and no one really knows if the BBC, as in the actual BBC, ever intended to make one. This is the story of how we ended up with the lamentable *Dimensions in Time* as the only celebration of the programme. It's my story, and if you don't like it go and make up your own.

In the latter part of 1992 someone sitting in an office at BBC Enterprises – not to be confused with the BBC, which actually made television programmes – thought it would be a good idea to make a special to celebrate thirty years of *Doctor Who*. So far so good. After that everything went off the rails.

There are those who claim Tom Baker went to the BBC, and said that he wanted to be Doctor Who again. Whether he did or not, it seems unlikely that it would have led to the project being handed to BBC Enterprises (not to be confused with the BBC, which actually made TV programmes). In fact, the 'those' who claim it was Tom's idea, is probably only Adrian Rigelsford, who was commissioned to write, *The Dark Dimension* despite simply being a fan of the series without any known writing credits. And the commission probably only emanated from someone working at BBC Enterprises (not to be confused with the BBC, which actually, etc… etc…)

I heard the rumours of the special in December 1993. No details. Only that Enterprises had told their big brother down the road not to bother with an anniversary special as they were handling it. Although I heard about the pronouncement, it didn't seem to have made an impression on anyone working in the drama department. By January I'd heard rumours that although we were all in it, it was a Fourth Doctor story, at which time I thought it might be a good idea for my agent to make a telephone call. He made several but none of them were returned. He asked for a script, for intended filming dates. Nothing. Then at the beginning of March, without contacting any of the other Doctors, without checking anyone's availability or desire to be involved, and without negotiation of any kind, BBC Enterprises announced we were all on board, and filming would commence shortly. At which point we politely informed them that it wouldn't.

It was a non-starter. Sylvester McCoy was still the incumbent Doctor, and should have been the central Doctor in any celebration. Tom hadn't endeared himself by refusing to associate with us, and even when obliged to, always separating himself by a couple of steps. The idea of asking us to play supporting roles in a Tom Baker script was deluded, naive, and, for Jon Pertwee especially, insulting. The whole idea faded, withered on the vine, another nail in the coffin of BBC Enterprises.

★ ★ ★

In November of 1992 I had a meeting with David Thacker who ran the Young Vic in London. My agent was keen for me do some good theatre and had worked hard to get me seen. I could tell Thacker was suspicious.

'Why have you never done this sort of theatre before?'

We were sitting in David Thacker's tiny office above the theatre. I didn't know what 'this sort of theatre' was, but I guessed he meant cutting-edge and low wages.

'I've never been asked.'

'Really?'

'Never.'

'How's your American accent?'

'Well, I'm married to an American.'

I was still married to an American, but I wasn't sure for how much longer.

Whatever the reason, I was offered the job, and it was just the fix I needed.

The Last Yankee was the latest play by Arthur Miller, at the time arguably the world's greatest living playwright. It was to have simultaneous premieres in New York and London, and there was a rumour, still unconfirmed, that Miller might be joining us at some point during rehearsals.

After the read-through, David Thacker gave us a tour of the Young Vic. He was very proud of his theatre family and we were taken into each department where we waved politely, and they waved back. It reminded me of my early days with Nottingham Playhouse and I felt I was re-inventing myself or at least getting back to basics. At lunchtimes we would go next door to the pub and talk about the play. This was proper acting. Zoë Wanamaker had been in the third year at drama school when I was a newly arrived student, and she was very much the star of her year and someone we first looked at with awe. Now I found myself kissing her passionately at almost every rehearsal, something I had trouble getting used to. Helen Burns and David Healy made up the rest of the cast, and we rehearsed for about four or five weeks, interrupted by a break for Christmas.

In the last week Arthur Miller flew over to spend a day with us and watch a run of the play. Here he was, the great Arthur Miller, unassuming yet charismatic, and talking to us about his life and philosophy. It became even more clear to me that my character, Leroy, espoused everything that Miller believed in, and that I was, in effect, playing the man himself. Then, before we ran the play, we each had the chance to have a photograph taken on the hospital set. Zoë went first, chatting easily with him, as if she and Arthur might have the best of friends, and I wondered what on earth I was going to say to him. By then Helen was taking her turn, looking relaxed and rather smitten, while I was trying to get the obvious question out of my head:

IS THERE LIFE OUTSIDE THE BOX?

So, Arthur, what was it like sleeping with Marilyn?

Suddenly it was happening. I was there on the bed with Arthur Miller and he was smiling and saying hello. This was a privilege very few people would have. This was the greatest living playwright, and a man whose personal philosophy and life I would be representing on stage, whatever I said it had better be good.

'So,' I said thoughtfully, without any idea what I might say next, he raised his eyebrows in expectation. I decided to stick with the facts.

'So, we're both wearing denim shirts then?'

He looked at me quizzically and for what seemed like eternity but might have been no more than the time it takes to look quizzical.

'Yeah,' said Arthur, confirming the acuteness of my observation.

The camera flashed, and we were done.

We opened on 6 January 1993, to excellent reviews. Sandra and I were still sharing same house, but the marriage was effectively over. For a few months we had been seeing a psychoanalyst, which had achieved nothing except confirm our determination to blame each other. We would attend the hour-long sessions at the end of which he would sum-up his thoughts – I only heard the criticisms of her, she only heard those about me. On the journey home there were such intense recriminations as we listed each other's faults, we would often end up with both tears and laughter. Sandra was in the West End appearing in a Ray Cooney farce at the Playhouse Theatre. We were separated only by the Hungerford Bridge over the Thames, but it might as well have been an ocean. We decided to separate. I planned to get a flat near to where we lived in Wargrave. The reason for this was Georgia's well-being, which was uppermost in our minds even though we had made a mess of the marriage. I was given the task of explaining to Georgia about the separation. We sat in the car outside her friend Emily's house as I told her; she looked straight ahead, avoiding eye contact. When I was done, she said rather brightly and reassuringly, 'OK.' There were no tears and no visible emotion at all. She sat there telling me it was fine and then we drove home as if nothing had happened. Later she told me knew it was coming and just wanted me to get on with it.

The Last Yankee was playing to capacity houses at the Young Vic, but it did little to raise my spirits. Ironically I was still having problems kissing Zoë, as we'd never discussed it in rehearsal and had got used to a slightly timid 'lips only' style. Given my circumstance at the time, it didn't seem an easy topic for discussion.

We were two weeks into the run when in the heat of the moment, a properly passionate kiss evolved. I waited for Zoë as she came offstage so I could apologise, afraid she might be offended.

'About fucking time,' she said.

* * *

Thursday, 3 September 2015. Jason Watkins is here tonight with his wife Clara who used to be Clare, and whom I went out with briefly when she was taking a break from sensible relationships. We met when I was doing *The Last Yankee*, back in 1993 when she worked as a dresser. I asked her what she could recall about the director David Thacker, and she said she couldn't think of anything. In fact, all she could recall about that time was a couple having sex in a flat across the road, while everyone watched from the window of the costume department. When the man realised they had been seen, he stood up and took a bow.

* * *

In 2005, only a few months after *Doctor Who* returned to our screens, it was announced that David Tennant would replace Christopher Eccleston and become the Tenth Doctor. The next day Clare called me.

'What about the new Doctor Who then?'

'David Tennant? Yes, I think he'll be good.'

'Yeah sure, but it's him, though.'

'Who?'

'David Tennant. You remember? The bloke in the pub.'

We were sitting in the pub next door to the Young Vic in January 1993, a bunch of us from the theatre killing time between the shows, when a young man came up and enthusiastically engaged me in conversation about *Doctor Who*, which he knew far more about than I had forgotten. I do remember the incident, although in my memory he sat with us at the table, much to the amusement of my colleagues. Clare said she didn't know about that but she was sure of one thing – his name was David Tennant. It was only recently, after he was firmly cemented within our family, that I checked the facts.

'David, did we ever meet in the pub next to the Young Vic in 1993?' I said casually

'Yes', said David, slightly sheepishly. 'I think we did.'

Case closed.

The show transferred to the Duke of York's Theatre and ran for three more months but with Margot Lester replacing Zoë Wanamaker. It was while we were playing there that the news of Sandra and I splitting up hit the newspapers. For the tabloids it was great news. We had been a relatively high-profile TV couple and when that goes wrong it's manna from heaven. Not that we had courted the press or lived our lives deliberately in the public eye, but I had realised over the last year that the pressure of being a showbiz couple had somehow influenced us, delaying the end in a way that wasn't helpful. Now those very same forces were keeping us apart and creating acrimony where it wasn't necessary. Journalists would wait by the stage door and had to be avoided by climbing the stairs to the top the theatre and precariously crossing the roof into the Garrick Theatre. They also turned up at the house in Wargrave, coming up to the front door and trying to take pictures through it. It lasted about a week before they finally got bored and moved elsewhere.

* * *

Monday, 8 February 2016. We're having a wall built along one side of the garden, to replace the sagging fence. Dave the builder was impressed with the plaster pillars in the garden, especially when he was told were from a James Bond film – Timothy Dalton's *The Living Daylights*: interior Afghanistan camp. The top of one has fallen off, but considering they were built for a film set and used for a week, they've lasted amazingly well in our garden.

* * *

Shortly before the end of the run at the Young Vic I bumped into Tyler Butterworth in the Sainsbury's car park in Vauxhall, a chance meeting that led to a short, shared shopping experience and an avalanche of changes in my life. Staying in Wargrave was a bad idea, he advised me, reaching for the low-fat crispbread and sugar-free Swiss-style muesli. I was starting to think it would be a mistake, I told him, grabbing a couple of packets of chocolate digestives and a box of Weetabix, but I didn't know where else to go. He had a thought: a friend of his, a make-up artist called Naomi Donne, had a successful career in the USA and wanted to rent out her flat in Belsize Park. Naomi Donne was not unknown to me, but then Naomi wasn't unknown to anybody who worked at the BBC around the time as she did. As well as being strikingly attractive, free-spirited and funny, she brought her own particular outrageous style to the BBC make-up department, often standing astride her artiste while applying their make-up, insisting it gave her a far better view of what she was doing. Many years before, she'd convinced me it would be a great wheeze if she made me up as my female companion Tegan on the set of *Doctor Who*, I even squeezed into her dress, and appeared on set. Everyone makes mistakes.

The flat was so different from where I imagined I might end up living, and so much the antithesis of blokiness, that I agreed to rent it on the spot. There was a large living room with a Chesterfield sofa, and on either side of the sliding door into the compact garden were two pillars from the set of a Timothy Dalton James Bond film. There were muslin drapes everywhere, and in the bedroom a large antique dressing table and a mahogany bedstead.

★ ★ ★

It's amazing how *The Decorator* tour nearly slipped my mind, if only because of all the reasons it shouldn't have done. It was a play by Donald Churchill. An actor who managed to combine both skills by making one work for the other: the central male character in his plays were almost always written with himself in mind whether or not he managed to convince the managements to allow him to play them. Donald had sadly died the previous year while in Spain filming a TV series called *El Cid*, and his plays were enjoying a resurgence, turning out to be very successful in the newly liberated countries of the Eastern bloc, though unfortunately for us, our tour took us no further east than Norwich. Along with me, *The Decorator* starred Gabrielle Drake and Erika Hoffman. I had never met Gabrielle although she had made an impact on me during my first acting job at Nottingham Playhouse. In those heady days a rep company would hand out slips of paper which allowed the actors free admission to cinemas during the day. If there were decent films showing you had seen them all by Tuesday afternoon so the rest of the week you watched just about anything that was on. That's how I came across *The Au Pair Girls*.

What a film that was.

This was the era of the sex comedy where the remains of the British film industry discovered they could still make a reasonable return and dodge the censor, with a bit of simulated sex and nudity as long as it was all a bit of a laugh. Even Norman Wisdom was inveigled but I remember almost nothing about the film except for Gabrielle Drake being naked for a good deal of it.

Now, I was forty-one, with a malignant growth of a mortgage, and had accepted *The Decorator* as a way of holding the threat of insolvency at bay. Working with Gabrielle and Erika turned out to be a bright spot in the gloom. We all agreed the play needed a bit of work, and the ending, especially, seemed like a work in progress. It had been done originally with Terry Scott, an actor best known for *Terry and June*, a popular sitcom, and I could see it was well suited to his particular style. Terry, I was told, had become proprietorial over the play and was unhappy that anyone else should have a go at it. No one told me this until we played the Yvonne Arnaud in Guildford and he turned up in my dressing room after the performance and, without introducing himself, announced that he had 'made this play' and that I was all right in it (no more than that, he implied), and abruptly disappeared into the night.

The tour was an 'escape from troubles at home tour', a succession of pleasant lunches and sightseeing, as we plotted a circuitous route around the country. Somewhere along the way I admitted to Gabrielle my history with *The Au Pair Girls* and she laughed herself silly; I also told her I was a fan of her brother, Nick Drake, who tragically killed himself before his musical genius was fully appreciated.

★ ★ ★

By the time I finished the run the dust had settled and I was another out-of-work actor in a one-bedroom flat. My first night there was like being transplanted into someone else's life, one that had passed me by the first time round. I should have been twenty-two; instead I was twenty years older than that and hanging out with Clare, a much younger, weird and wonderful girl from Golders Green who was now an aspiring drama student. There was sadness too, a second marriage was history and now there was our eight-year-old daughter to look after. Then there was the small matter of the Inland Revenue asking for ninety thousand pounds I didn't have, not to mention maintenance payments knocking on the door. I lit one of the big candles by the fireplace and sat on the large chesterfield sofa and considered my bleak employment prospects. For the first time in a few years I realised I wasn't worrying about it. There was nothing else that could be taken away from me, and I could only earn what I could earn. I guess I had reached the heart of the wilderness where everything is peaceful and serene, where people can scream at you and you can't hear a word they say.

As for marriage, I was determined never to do it again.

I didn't have much time to sit around my beautiful flat. By early September I had been persuaded to make a video-film directed by Bill Baggs, a radio producer from Nottingham who wanted to branch out with an angle on making low-budget sci-fi films. He was casting actors from *Doctor Who*, although the stories were not connected to the series. *The Airzone Solution* initially had three ex-Doctors in myself, Colin Baker and Sylvester McCoy, and an ex-companion in Nicola Bryant. Throw in a young Alan Cumming and I guess Bill Baggs was onto a winner. As far as I can remember it was shot on a tiny budget in and around Nottingham University a few days before the autumn term started. Then Jon Pertwee heard what we were doing and insisted on being in it too. There was only one day of filming left, so a scene was hastily written involving a long speech for Jon, which he had no time to learn, so the words were written out on an enormous white card which I held up in front of my face while he read them out. After John Mills I was becoming used to all types of card work.

* * *

Wednesday, 12 August 2015. Tonight after my final scene of the show, Jim Carter came into my dressing room to say hello and to tell me he'd finally finished on *Downton Abbey* that day. I asked him if he was sad it was over and he was quite emphatic that though he had enjoyed the job, he wasn't. Too many hours of his life standing around filling wine glasses was how he put it. We worked together on *Black Beauty* twenty-two years ago when Imelda was pregnant with their daughter, who was born a day after he finished filming. Just another example of her perfect timing.

* * *

Black Beauty was my first motion picture. I had done bucketloads of TV but this was what Hollywood film people called a theatrical release. Everything is different on a proper film. Almost none of it for the better. It was a treat, of course, to be picked up in a late-model Mercedes and driven into Pinewood and delivered to the door of my Winnebago, to have my breakfast order taken, and have it smartly delivered to me. But there are too many people working on a film for you ever to feel like a team. On the smaller, leaner TV film unit, you know everyone's name inside the first week. Here every day seemed to bring a new face I was sure I hadn't seen before. (Often this was true, the level of hirings and firings especially of those at the bottom of the food chain, those who got the blame for the day-to-day cock-ups, could reach epic proportions.) It didn't help that I was kept safely away from everyone in my trailer whenever I wasn't on set. If you so much as popped your head out of the door, runners and third assistants would come at you from all angles, ask what you needed and shovel you back inside. I was aware this wasn't a big budget feature – in Hollywood terms it was low end – but remember I had come from filming *The Airzone Solution*, where a half-panini for lunch was pushing the boat out, and firing the runner only saved you slipping your sister-in-law's boyfriend a ten-pound note at the end of the week.

Before we got down to filming we had a read-through of the script. If you don't know the book its peculiarity is that the story is told by the horse. For the purposes of the table read, an actor called Dominic Guard played Black Beauty and he did a fine job and I assumed he would voice the film. However, in the end it was done by Alan Cumming, a fine actor but a confusing choice that gave a horse born in Yorkshire, and never venturing anywhere north of there, a distinctly Scottish accent.

The film crew was mostly British. The director, producer, executive producers, associate producers, Warner Bros. executives and vice-presidents were over from America. You could tell them apart because the Americans were the ones reaching for their cell phones at the end of every take. The first assistant would shout 'Cut' and out they came. They would wander in circles, weaving around each other with a finger in one ear to block out the sound of the other conversations. The mobile network was so bad in those days, heaven knows who they were talking to. Maybe each other.

The star of the film was a beautiful American Quarter Horse called Docs Keepin Time (I never managed to find out why). He had been flown over in his own chartered jet and like every movie star, had brought along his own entourage, including his stand-in. In this case the stand-in was slightly smaller and had no white flash on its nose, requiring the wig department to glue a hair piece in position whenever she was used. All the horses were trained by the extraordinary Rex Peterson, the go-to horse wrangler at that time, who had flown over with the animals and was able to get Docs to do just about anything short of narrating the story.

Around the animal stars, Caroline Thompson, the director, had collected a host of British talent. Sean Bean, who is listed as the star, only appears before opening credits. I, and my sickly wife Rosalind Ayres, come and go fairly quickly, along with the slightly meatier part of my groom, played by the laconic Jim Carter. David Thewlis probably had the most to do, but it was essentially a film full of cameos: Eleanor Bron, Alun Armstrong, John McEnery, and Peter Cook in his last film appearance. My daughter Georgia almost made her first appearance too when she came along to be a supporting artist in a street scene. They dressed her beautifully in period costume, made a work of art of her hair, and then sat her down for eight hours before releasing her, after dropping the shot. I was disappointed for her but she couldn't have cared less – she was £38 richer.

By this time we were several days behind schedule, a problem that was a particular concern to Jim Carter, with fatherhood fast approaching.

Caroline Thompson was a writer who had worked with Tim Burton, and had now been given the chance to direct her own screenplay. She was perfectly able but seemed to be in the thrall of the avalanche of advice that came her way. She only gave me one note that I can remember: when we filmed the storm scene in which Jim and I have to push the cart that's stuck fast in the mud, Caroline took me aside and told me not to grimace too much when pushing myself as it spoiled my features. I was flattered by her concern but as I was wearing a hat pulled down over my head, in torrential rain, covered in mud, and in the middle of the night, there were other things on my mind. Filming a rain scene is possibly the most uncomfortable experience on my long list of Things Actors Would Rather Not Be Doing. I'm not talking about simply filming in the rain, which for the most part cannot be seen on film, but a rain scene where they deploy a great number of tall sprinkler pipes to shower more water down on your head in one minute than would fall in an hour and half of nature's own. Double that amount if you're filming a storm scene at Pinewood in the middle of a cold October night. We rehearsed without water first so we would know precisely what we would be doing before the cameras rolled and the artificial deluge made it impossible. Even before they called 'Action!' (which I didn't hear because of the noise of the water hitting me) everybody in the scene was soaked to the skin, I could barely open my eyes or mouth for the force of the wind machines lashing the rain horizontally into my face. It was the first of many takes and of many angles and by the time dawn broke I was taken back to my trailer a pale and shrivelled shadow of my former self.

When the film was complete, including months of post production, we had two viewings. The first was cast and crew, at which grown men and women sobbed as the story unfolded, fearful of their children's reaction to the family viewing the following week. We should have known better. Children, being the cruel and heartless creatures they sometimes are, simply enjoyed the film, indifferent to the tragedy of the odd dead horse.

Living in Belsize Park was a different world, or rather, living on my own was. I realised it was something I had never done in my life, having gone from living with parents at home, to sharing a flat, to living with a girlfriend or wife. Now here I was only a mile from where I had been to drama school, and only fifteen minutes from the centre of London. Belsize Park was cool. Squeezed between the cosmopolitan buzz of Camden Town and the fashionable elegance of Hampstead, it was the best of both worlds. Here I answered to nobody. I cooked and cleaned for myself, even if I lived on the edge of organised chaos. My Sundays were taken up visiting Georgia and taking her and her friends to a cinema or theme park. Sometimes I would persuade Georgia to let us visit the go-kart track, which I suspect was enjoyed only by me (there's little that's more therapeutic for a recently divorced forty-two-year-old man than scything your way through a field of nine-year-old girls imagining you're Nigel Mansell). I was also fortunate to find myself a few minutes from Joanna Kanska who had been living in the same top-floor flat in Golders Green since the days of *A Very Peculiar Practice*. We had kept in touch over the years but now she helped kick-start my social life. I found myself welcomed into the Polish community, or at least into Joanna's extended family and friends. I knew only one line of the language, which I had learned for *A Very Polish Practice* – '*Przepraszam, ale to jest nieporozumienie*' ('Sorry there's been a misunderstanding') – but it seemed to cover every circumstance, calamitous or otherwise.

The Last Yankee and *Black Beauty* (which was not as well paid as I'd hoped) had taken up most of 1993, and I had fallen behind with my outgoings. I was paying Sandra far more than I was earning, and with the interest on a £90,000 overdraft and various outstanding tax demands, I was desperately playing catch-up. I was fairly indiscriminate about the jobs I accepted and a series of dog-training spots on morning television and a sketch on *The Good Sex Guide*, all helped, but I was hopeful 1994 would be more fruitful. It started well, financially, with an offer of a sitcom initially called *The Other Couple*, but by the time we started was renamed *Ain't Misbehavin'*, and also starred Nicola Pagett and Lesley Manville. We made two series, one at the beginning of the year, the other in November. It was exactly what my accountant wanted to hear. In between I did a twelve-week run in the West End of *An Absolute Turkey*. I was taking over from Griff Rhys Jones, and in theory the show was directed by Peter Hall. In fact he rarely showed up, and when he did, he never sat down or took off his coat. It was always a great thrill when we heard he was watching, but by the time I finished my scenes he had usually left the building. Notes, such as they were, being handed on by the assistant director. I tried not to take it personally, adopting the philosophical attitude of the neglected television actor: no notes means you're doing fine.

★ ★ ★

Wednesday, 23 March 2016. New York City. Five hours to kill before a flight to Salt Lake City and I'm sitting in the Soho House in the meatpacking district of downtown Manhattan. I'd intended to check my bags in at the hotel but the queue was so damn long I jumped in a cab and brought everything down here before realising I wasn't quite sure where it was. I got out at 14th and 9th, which I had a feeling was fairly close, and was dragging my suitcase along the street when a voice called out 'Peter!' It was Podge, who managed the London club in the wild and crazy years of the nineties, and who is now running the New York branch for a second time (having tried to retire but finding he missed it too much). It was like seeing an old wartime buddy, without me having any idea what that might be like.

Later he found me working at my computer and I told him about the book.

'Maybe I should write one too,' he said.

'You'd have some great stories.'

MY TEN YEARS IN THE WILDERNESS

'I might have to change a few names.'

'Mine might be one of them,' I said.

★ ★ ★

For the first time in my life I was partying like an idiot and was rarely home before the birds were chirruping and dawn broke in the eastern sky. We would start off at the Soho House in Greek Street and end up in Gerry's bar, an exclusive basement drinking-hole in the heart of Soho, or cram into one of the shady and unlicensed clubs on the top floor of dilapidated buildings on Old Compton Street. I was forty-three and apart from one puff of a 'funny' roll-up in Amsterdam in 1973, I had never taken drugs. Now someone offered me a little pill and I thought why the hell not, why not be a little wild in the wilderness? So we sat around a large table in The Green Room, a busy theatrical club in St John Street just off the Strand, and I waited for something to happen. It didn't. Maybe I was too old for this, I thought, maybe it only worked if you were eighteen and jumping up and down in a thumping club in Camden. I took a sip of my drink and looked at the others, and wondered if they were feeling anything. It didn't look like it, I didn't even know if any of them had taken anything, although, I noted, I'd never realised before how beautiful they all were. How could I have missed it? Their perfect faces glowed and their smiles radiated outwards filling the room and I thought, at that moment, how much I liked them all, perhaps even loved them deeply and profoundly, and that I had an overwhelming need to hug them.

The following day, still in the throes of love and goodwill, I rang Sandra to offer to pay for a holiday for her and Georgia – she accused me of being manipulative and slammed down the phone.

In March 1995, Naomi called to say she was selling the flat and would I like to buy it? I asked her to give me a few days but I knew it was a non-starter. The pantomime I had done that Christmas had helped me pay the January tax, but I couldn't imagine my understanding bank manager extending me a mortgage. It was a Friday afternoon and I had already put off calling Naomi for several days, when the phone rang. My first thought was that it was her calling from New York, but it was my agent asking if I was free to do a live TV commercial for Pedigree Chum from the Crufts dog show that Sunday night. The request had come via the man who lived in the top flat upstairs and who worked for Bates Dorland, the advertising agency and had suggested me when Eamonn Holmes suddenly dropped out after discovering it would breach his TV-am contract. It was all such a rush; I didn't have time to think about the money. Ten minutes later my agent called back.

'I wanted to make sure you were OK with everything before I give the go-ahead.'

'OK.'

'You have to be up there first thing tomorrow to rehearse in the afternoon'.

'OK.'

'Then on Sunday it's live on TV the moment they announce the winner.'

'OK.'

'Now the money: they have a set budget.'

That's never good news.

'How much?' I was not optimistic.

'Forty-two thousand pounds,' she said.

That evening I called Naomi and told her I was pretty sure I was going to buy the flat.

* * *

Tuesday, 23 February 2015. Second day of rehearsals of *Gypsy* at Three Mills Studios, blocking through the scenes. This is necessary for the whole show, despite this being a remount of the Chichester Festival production. The Savoy theatre space is much smaller both on and off stage, and it will be a major feat to get the multiple sets to fit, and at the moment these sets amount to no more than different coloured tape outlines on the floor. Had lunch with Louise Gold and Julie LeGrand, who make up two thirds of the strippers. Julie's husband Peter, who is a sound recordist and was filming on the lot, also joined us. When I was introduced, he reminded me we'd worked together one crazy weekend back in 1995 at the Crufts dog show.

* * *

Whether it was inspiration provided by a forty-two thousand pound windfall, or natural enthusiasm for selling dog food, it's hard to say, but I enjoyed my new found role. I arrived on Saturday morning and after a production meeting, we rehearsed briefly, without interfering with the ongoing doggie competitions, did the same on Sunday, and in the evening, as the winner was announced, the camera crew and I launched ourselves into the main arena. With an over-excited standard poodle named Montravia Tommy Gun in the background, I announced, live on television to an astonished world, that once again the proud winner was a dog fed on Pedigree Chum. It was very exciting and went so well, that I imagined I might be doing it once a year for the foreseeable future.

Needless to say, I was never asked again.

My agency had a party. They'd never had one before, or since, and try as I might I cannot discover what was the significance of the occasion. The shining light of the party was Anna Friel, a recent signing and very much in the spotlight because of the notorious lesbian kiss in the Saturday afternoon soap, *Brookside*. She was nineteen years old, beautiful, and enjoying every moment of it. All evening she was surrounded by a throng of young and handsome actors, all imagining they were in with a chance. At the end of the evening Anna wanted to go on to a club, and while I tried to decline, she took me by the hands and insisted I go with them. That's how I ended up in Brown's, a small but exclusive club in Covent Garden, sitting in the VIP section, while Anna, still surrounded by the young hopefuls, danced the night away downstairs.

When we'd arrived, she'd whispered to me, 'Don't leave me alone with them,' and, therefore, as her appointed protector I had made numerous visits downstairs to check she was OK. Now at half-past two I'd had enough and went down to tell her I was going home.

'No, wait, I'll leave with you', she said, leaving her would-be suitors looking pretty sick. I looked at them as if to say, *Don't mess with big boys*, by which time Anna had grabbed her coat and was pulling me towards the door, and there might even have been a small delusional part of me that wondered what was going to happen next . . .

What happened next was we left the club, arm in arm – into a hail of flashbulbs.

I was brought back to a sobering reality by Anna's obvious distress that the press might jump to the wrong conclusion.

STOP PRESS: *Actress Anna Friel (19), pictured leaving Brown's in the early hours, arm in arm with actor Peter Davison, who is more than twice her age.*

And while I tried to reassure her that everything would be fine, the wrong conclusion didn't sound so bad to me. She needn't have worried – no pictures ever appeared. I assume gossip columnists across the tabloid world took one look at the photos and collectively cried 'no chance'.

12

LOVE AND DEATH

Saturday, 20 June 2015. Val, my mother-in-law, came to see the show this afternoon with her friends Ian, and Mair. After the show they come round to the dressing room, and Mair, whom I expected to be effusive, has been so moved by the show that she is speechless, and it's Val who is showering me with compliments. Does this mean after nearly twenty years with her daughter I have made an impact?

★ ★ ★

At the age of forty-four I found myself in the precarious world of dating, more at the instigation of others than my own desire for a settled relationship. I was done with marriage, I said to myself, from now on it would be sex, drugs, and rock and roll, and while this was more a statement of glorious intent, rather than something I would actually get around to, it gave me a sense of living in the moment. At the same time I ended up dating, and drifting dangerously close to, women whose biological clock was ticking loudly.

One Sunday I went so far as to introduce one of them to Georgia, and the three of us went for Sunday lunch in my friend Tyler Butterworth's back garden. The day was significant because Georgia largely ignored the girl's overtures, instead choosing to spend her time making daisy chains with another friend of Tyler's, who was destined to become the love of my life. Considering the cathartic affect she would have on me, there is some confusion about when we properly met. I remember when I first heard about her: I was talking to Tyler on the telephone, trying to arrange a day to meet up.

'I can't do tomorrow, I'm meeting up with Lizzie.'

'Lizzie? Who's Lizzie?' I said, a little teasingly.

'No, nothing like that,' he replied. 'She's an actress friend I'm writing with.'

'Really?'

'Yes, really. Legs up to her armpits, but just a friend. Really.'

This was followed at some point by the garden party and the daisy chains and the assertion that I have forgotten that's where I met Georgia's new friend, and future stepmother.

Then there was dinner at a restaurant, Tyler and a few friends. It was just before Christmas 1995 and I arrived late and squeezed in opposite a very beautiful girl who was introduced to me as Lizzie – at that time I had no way of estimating the length of her legs. I ended up in a conversation with a woman next to me who worked for Camelot, the company that ran the National Lottery, who told me (and took two hours to do so) that everyone who'd won millions had needed psychiatric help, which meant I didn't pay enough attention to the girl opposite me and so when I left early to go to the theatre I looked directly at her and asked if anyone would like to come along.

Not surprisingly, she didn't leap at the chance, and I left presuming she wasn't the least bit interested.

About four months later, in April 1996, Tyler invited me for a meal at Black's, a low-key, members-only establishment, across the road from the much trendier Groucho Club. There were meant to be four of us, although one of our party was running late. Lizzie turned up ten minutes later, appearing in the doorway like a vision of cool sophistication, only slightly scuppered by running up three flights of stairs. Over coffee, by which time we were already reduced to three, we chatted pleasantly until Tyler, with an extraordinarily bad performance of just remembering he had to be somewhere else, got up from the table, announced he had to catch a train and dashed out of the door. Elizabeth and I were slightly lost for words, and left together for the rest of our lives.

★   ★   ★

She'd expected me to be a public-school-educated stuffed shirt; I imagined she was probably a prim and obsessively tidy actress. We were both about as wrong as it's possible to be.

This is my favourite Elizabeth story.

After her father died she brings his old bicycle down to London. It has great sentimental value and she treasures it. Every day she rides it to Earl's Court station and chains it to the railings. One day she comes back and the bicycle is not there and she is furious and heartbroken, but she realises there is little she can do, so does not report it stolen. Months go by. Then one day she comes out of the tube station and she's shocked and stunned to see her dad's bike is there, chained to the railings, exactly where she used to leave it. Outraged at the nerve of the thief she goes to the police station to report it.

The policeman took down the details, promising to catch the

culprit, and finished his report by asking her on which side of the station she'd left the bicycle. Which is the moment Elizabeth realised there were two exits to the station and her bicycle had never been stolen, but had been sitting there chained up for several months because she happened to come out of the other exit on the day she found it had been 'stolen'.

In those first moments after Tyler abandoned us, I discovered she was learning to play classical piano and lived in Shepherd's Bush. Apparently I expressed an interest in learning classical piano myself, and even visiting Shepherd's Bush to do it, something which she rightly interpreted as being a bit too keen. I persuaded her to have dinner the following week, and was even invited back to her flat for coffee, which was when any illusions I'd had about her evaporated into the ether. It wasn't the four-inch gap at the bottom of the kitchen door, or the way she had brought the outside in by having the floor around it bare earth, or the fact she had no working oven, and had blown up the microwave by cooking a baked potato for an hour and a half. Or the hallway that was only plastered halfway up because the insurance money covering the damp repairs had run out along with the plasterers. Nor was it the bathroom floor, covered with a bed sheet, tacked down around the edges, with a chipped plaster statue of the Virgin Mary beside the sink, adorned with items of underwear.

I sat in the lumpy armchair, sipping my instant coffee and reflected on my life so far. Right in front of me was the do-it-yourself mosaic tiling around the old gas fire, unfinished and stuck directly over the old tiles and covering the flue. That was what changed my life.

Here was a girl who needed saving every bit as much as me.

Elizabeth didn't want children, at least that was the assumption, and all her friends agreed she would be the most disorganised and hopeless mother in the world, and that even if she had a baby she'd almost certainly leave it somewhere, possibly chained to the railings outside a tube station.

She was in the middle of rehearsing a play in Northampton, when she came home one day and told me she was pregnant. She was worried about my reaction and it's true that until it happened I'd not considered the possibility and I can remember the furrow of her brow as she told me. I also remember my reaction, which was like a door opening that I hadn't realised was there, an unforeseen but not unwelcome change of circumstance. Then at four months we lost the baby. Somewhere along the way it died in the womb. We knew a few days before we went to the hospital to abort the foetus, which was the hardest part of all. It seemed cruelly clinical and neither of us fully expressed the shock and grief we felt. Instead we found ourselves actively trying for another baby as if that had been the plan all along.

I am getting ahead of myself. Before the dinner with Elizabeth, before I was saved, there will always be *Dial M for Murder*.

★   ★   ★

In January of 1996, in a chilly rehearsal room on the top floor of the Old Vic theatre in Waterloo, we gathered for a read-through of *Dial M for Murder*. Commercial tours can be depressing and cut-price affairs, but this one was done in style, and from the beginning I set out to enjoy every minute. It was sponsored by Mobil and was well organised, well paid, and impressively budgeted. It also came with the promise, usually unfulfilled, of a West End run. Catherine (Katie) Rabbett was playing the object of my murderous intent, with John Vine as the detective, and Richard Linton, affectionately known as Lanky, was the trusty friend. Catherine had a television profile, but her reputation, as far as the public was concerned, was for being a former girlfriend of the Duke of York, something that would casually come up in conversation as if one dated a prince and went back to his place (presumably the palace) every day.

I was happy to see the smiling face of Lisa Brindley, who had also been wardrobe mistress on the tour of *The Decorator*, a few years before. Three weeks later we opened the tour in Norwich and spent the next few weeks drunkenly (not far from the truth) zig-zagging from one city to another, up and down the British Isles. In every town there would be a Mobil reception, attended by local VIPs, and another chance to party. I think something told me this would be my last hurrah, but I was determined to give it my all. Then, to our surprise, we went into the Apollo Theatre for a six-month run in the West End, courtesy of Bill Kenwright who had seen the show in Guildford, and whose finest quality was a desire to bring every show into town and keep them running for as long as possible.

I started going out with Elizabeth just before we transferred. *Dial M for Murder* was the first time my name had been up in lights in the West End, and I went across the road to take a picture.

In the months following the miscarriage, with the help of a barrister who helped us without remuneration, I had been trying to change a court order that was made when I was earning good money, and I still had a large bank debt that I had only reduced by a small amount. The root cause was years of failing to set aside the money to pay the tax. So while money was coming in, my earnings over the years were reducing so paying last year's tax with this year's earnings always ended with a bigger debt. I had been doing pretty much everything that came along, but I was about to plumb new depths. I got the call from Michael Winner. I had heard the stories. Nearly every actress who auditioned for him had a story to tell. Nothing actionable, usually no more than demeaning, sexist, and occasionally sleazy. My ex-wife Sandra Dickinson had a meeting with him which he began by shouting, 'Why do they keep sending me these short actresses?'

Another friend told me of an audition where he made her stand in front of a window because he thought she was wearing a see-through dress. Then there was the naive drama student who writes to him, comes down to London to meet him, she's invited to lunch, the offer of a make-over, and then the invitation back to his place.

I may have been safe from his attentions, but I'd not managed to avoid his films. From the cheap and exploitative *Death Wish*, a rare success, to the ham-fisted disaster of *Bullseye*. In different circumstances I might have questioned whether I wanted to be in a Michael Winner film, but it was a job, and I could always justify it by imagining the stories I could tell if I ever wrote my autobiography (like that was ever going to happen).

Of course, if Michael Winner's your mate, and he makes you an offer it's a different matter I'm sure: 'Oliver, here's a few thousand quid, come along, and do a day's filming.' 'Ben, old chap, your name will be above the title, and you've only got seven lines.' But I wasn't a mate, and so I had to turn up in Holland Park to meet him. A cheerless house that copious flower arrangements failed to brighten. I climbed the stairs to his office, past the picture of him and Jenny Seagrove in her underwear, and sat down opposite him – only his huge monster of a desk between us. I noticed his chair was noticeably higher than mine.

'You do TV, do you?'

'Mostly, yes.'

'What have you done?'

I told him. He'd never seen anything I'd been in. Whether he had or not, he would have been aware of them. This was a chance to put me in my place.

'Never seen it – never seen it – never seen it.'

I wish I'd had the courage to empty a floral display over his head and walk out, but I sat there.

'Movies are different, a different world', he said.

'Yes.'

Actually movies weren't that different any more. Bigger trailers, bigger cameras, but actually, the process was the same, and . . . hang on, this is Michael Winner, so none of the aforementioned was true anyway. This was the man who made a pig's ear of *A Chorus of Disapproval*, the man who did the impossible task of getting a dodgy performance out of Jeremy Irons. He looks at me inscrutably. I begin to wonder if my shirt is see-through.

A week later my phone rang. 'Michael Winner's offered you the job.' Not even my agent sounded very enthusiastic.

'Oh, great.'

'But he does want to meet up with you again.'

'Why?'

'He wants to discuss the part.'

We met at Winner's house again, although this time in a sitting room downstairs. He explained that when he'd screen tested Chris Rea, John Alderton had played the part he was offering to me. He'd wanted Alderton to play it in the film, but he'd turned it down because the script contained violence. I nodded uncomfortably; it isn't usual for a director to tell you who he would have preferred to play the part, and so I had an idea of what was coming next.

He thrust a videotape across the coffee table at me: 'That's a copy of the screen test – I'd like you to play it exactly like John Alderton.'

It crossed my mind that he was doing this deliberately, that he'd chosen me as a target for humiliation. Quite apart from the impossibility of playing a part exactly like John Alderton, I can't imagine any director thinking it was a constructive suggestion to give to an actor. Once again I kept my mouth shut, left his house, and never looked at the tape.

Filming started a few weeks later. I'd been asked (for the sake of my own comfort of course) to provide my own clothes, and there was no sign of a make-up department, which he'd told me was a waste of money. He was of the opinion that a dab of powder was all you needed, and to administer the dabs, he brought in an ex-girlfriend. If you wanted anything more than that, you did it yourself, which is exactly what Felicity Kendall and Diana Rigg did. It was an impressive cast, I'll give him that: there was also Oliver Reed, Bob Hoskins, John Cleese, Ben Kingsley, and Joanna Lumley, all with their names above the title, though most did no more than a day on the film. The star was the rock musician Chris Rea, in his first film role. He'd been talked into accepting it by Michael Winner after a chance meeting at the exclusive Sandy Bay resort in Barbados. I was playing his best friend John, and all my scenes were with him. He was unsure what he'd got himself into, and his looks of bewilderment grew over the course of filming. He played a man who discovers he's dying, and decides to kill everyone who's done him wrong, a sort of comedy rehash of the *Death Wish* theme. Without the comedy.

Winner had developed his own style of making movies, centred on the axiom that you shouldn't have to pay anyone for anything if there was a way of avoiding it. Passers-by would be asked to be unpaid extras, we would film in locations without permission, and we even took a camera down on the Underground, hidden under a large coat. There was no security or police hired to help with pedestrian or traffic control. How could there be when no one had been told we were filming? Rather than pay an editor, he did it himself under the name of Arnold Crump, who not surprisingly was really bad at his job. Neither did he bother with ADR sessions (automatic dialogue replacement), recording any lines that were necessary on a portable recorder at home. He told me the method was his invention. He would play you the line from the original soundtrack, and then record you repeating it. Why did no one ever think of that before? It was rubbish – but so much cheaper.

There was a budget for *Parting Shots*, Winner told me that Fuji had invested heavily in the film – from which I assumed Fuji had never seen a Michael Winner film. One of the most visible expenditures was on Michael Winner's lunches. He refused to eat the catering food, and instead his driver would pick up elaborate take-away meals from local four-star restaurants. If there was a Diana Rigg, or a Bob Hoskins filming that day, they would be invited to dine in his trailer. Chris Rea and I were invited on the first day of filming, an hour and a half of Winner extolling his own virtues and telling tall tales of his 'mates', as he called them. People like Robert Mitchum, who I was told by someone on the crew had got so angry with Winner that he'd pissed down his leg in a bar in Soho, during the filming of *The Big Sleep*. I wasn't invited again until the last week of filming, when the second assistant grabbed me as I was making my way to the catering truck, and I politely turned down the invitation.

In one scene, Chris Rea's character 'Harry' decides to hire a couple of beautiful hookers for us. The day before we filmed it, Michael had been telling everybody about his problems trying to cast the girls. 'They sent me a room full of models, and I sent them back,' he complained. 'Beautiful girls, but no breasts!'

The next day our more bountiful 'Hookers' turned up. One was Nicola Bryant, 'Peri' from *Doctor Who*. It was to be my second encounter with Ms Bryant's cleavage. We shot the scene in less than an hour, which even by his standards was rushing it. Then Winner disappeared, and shortly after, the girls were also called away, still in their underwear. We sat around for half an hour or so, while Michael had his photo taken with the girls for his 'collection'.

On set he was unpleasant to anyone not in a position to fight back. His production assistants were a persistent target. When we were filming in Sonning, a pretty village in Berkshire, close to the A4, he was on particularly good form, screaming at the supporting artistes who were actually unpaid locals, telling a couple of them to get off his set. He managed to top that by firing a young female runner for failing to stop the traffic on the A4 during a take. She hadn't even been provided with a luminous jacket to make her look halfway official. He liked to have a go at me, I think, because I was television and he was motion pictures. He once lost it in the middle of a take, and screamed that I wasn't on my mark.

'This is the movies. In the movies you've got to hit your mark!'

I looked down and my toes were right on it. It's one of the few things I know I'm good at. On my feet, or in a car, I can hit a mark. I took a deep breath, and spoke loudly across the room.

'Michael, I'm on my mark. If it's wrong you can give me another one, I'll hit that one too.'

There was no response. The mark was changed, and we went again.

My hostility probably didn't even register on Winner's radar. I came to realise there were many so-called friends or 'mates' who disliked him, but he just never noticed. I was asked to lunch once more, but again politely declined. I felt sorry for Chris Rea, who was a very intelligent, friendly man who had been persuaded into a venture he wasn't keen to do. He once said to me, 'I don't understand all this, Peter.' I promised him if he ever did another film, it wouldn't be like this.

On the last day of shooting the press was invited along – why he risked it, I don't know. I was asked if I had enjoyed working with Michael Winner. I described it only as 'interesting'.

In May the following year, the film was released. There was no premiere, no advanced publicity. One day I happened to look in the *Evening Standard*, and there was a half-page advertisement for the film, showing at the Odeon, Haymarket in London. I thought I should go and see it, so I looked elsewhere but that was the only cinema showing it, and, oddly, there were no performance times listed. I called the Odeon, and asked what time it was on, I was told it was only showing on Thursday afternoons. A week later it had disappeared completely.

A few months later I was in my local video rental store in Belsize Park, and there on the shelf of new releases was a copy of *Parting Shots*. I asked the bored-looking man behind the counter if I could buy it once it had reached the end of its rental life. He looked at the untouched tape box on the shelf, and then back at me, then shrugged casually. 'You might as well take it now, mate.'

Reviews of the film varied from bad to catastrophic. *Total Film*'s review described it as 'offensive, incompetent, and bad in every possible way'; Christopher Tookey called it 'the most tasteless, abysmal comedy of all time', and according to the *Independent*'s film critic it was 'the worst film I have ever seen'; Miles Kington went further, describing it as 'possibly the worst film ever made'.

And yes, I was in it.

I might have found the whole experience disheartening, had not the intervening few months brought significant changes in my life. Elizabeth was pregnant again and everything was going well, and then, much to my surprise, I was offered the part of Amos in the West End production of *Chicago*. I was replacing Joel Grey who had done three months in the West End production, after starting the show on Broadway. After years turning up to auditions unprepared, clutching my guitar, and giving unsuitable renditions of minor pop classics, I discovered the way to succeed in musical theatre was to bite the bullet, and pay for a singing lesson, and actually do a song from a musical. Who knew?

Joel Grey seemed charming enough, despite a bad start, asking me if I wanted the beautiful throw he had bought for the dressing room. What I didn't understand was that he was inviting me to purchase, at the same price he had paid, the attractive but overpriced throw that he didn't want to take all the way back to New York, but I guess words don't always come the way we mean them to. In much the same way as I was thinking, No, I've changed my mind, I don't want it, but actually said, 'Yes I'd love to.'

At least I inherited his dressing room, which was large with a battered sofa in the middle (hence Joel's throw), and a view into offices along the Strand. I couldn't understand why I hadn't taken musicals seriously before. Maybe I had confused watching them with being in them, which I discovered was a thrilling and intoxicating experience, both doing the show and hanging around in the green room with the attractive girls in fishnets tights, talking about the stuff you'd never expect scantily dressed girls to talk about: the new kitchen their boyfriends were building for them, the various ailments of their dogs (or cats), and how many children they would one day have.

One night these distractions led me to miss an entrance. Even as I recall it, I'm reliving the terrible sinking feeling as I realised, too late, my cue had passed and memories of the Edinburgh Festival and the entire Scottish army missing its cue, came flooding back. This time it was just me and what with stage management waving their arms about, first telling me to go on and then not to, I was in a blind panic.

Moments later Clarke Peters came offstage, grinning at me and seemingly unflustered by a two-handed scene that had just become a soliloquy only raising an eyebrow as if to say, *And where were you?* I apologised profusely but he brushed it away. 'It was kind of fun – I played both parts.' Clarke Peters is a pretty cool guy.

Maria Freidman, who played Roxy Hart, would throw regular soirees in her dressing room after the show which would go on long after she had gone home. I was usually there till the bitter end, refusing to be outdone by the younger, fitter cast, who managed to look so good on a diet of cigarettes and chocolate. One night as I left the stage door and walked down the alley beside the theatre, I interrupted a couple having sex, the girl with her back against the wall, her legs wrapped around his waist. They actually weren't interrupted at all, and carried on energetically, but it was too late to turn back so I carried on resolutely and, when she caught my eye as I passed, politely wished them a good evening.

* * *

Early in the run, I had an audition for an episode of a new series called *Hope and Glory*, a vehicle for Lenny Henry who was looking to broaden his career to encompass straight acting parts. The director was Juliet May whom I had worked with before, and who was the daughter of Val May who, when I was fresh out of drama school, had resisted the temptation to offer me a job. I was up to play the outgoing head of the school Lenny's character is brought in to rescue. The part was a bitter and disillusioned teacher who loses it at his last assembly, and screams obscenities at the children. It wasn't the kind of role that usually came my way, and I wanted to do it. On the other hand, it was only one episode, and it demonstrated to me, if I needed reminding, that I was no longer in line for leading parts in shows. In the eighties I had graduated, at least as far as TV was concerned, to getting direct offers of parts, in the nineties I had slipped back to the 'they want to meet you but you won't have to read' audition. There was usually a subtext to these kinds of meetings: *We only want to meet you but may offer you the chance to read although we're not insisting, it depends on whether you want the part or not.*

This was that kind of meeting.

'You won't have to read, they just want to meet you.' I didn't even think my agent believed this.

'But I've already met them. Well, the director. I've worked with her.'

'When was that?'

'Two years ago.'

'It's a very different part for you.'

'I know . . . so they expect me to read?'

'No, they just want to meet you.'

'But I've already met them.'

I was feeling unusually bullish, and there was a reason. I used to think I was good in auditions, some naive charm combined with an ability to do something idiotic enough to imprint myself on the producer's memory. That must have been beginner's luck, and now it had worn off. Nowadays the more I wanted a job the worse I screwed it up. Admittedly a lot of these were non-job jobs. American studio execs fancying a few days living it up in a boutique hotel in Chelsea, come over to interview a few British actors, write it off on expenses, and fly home. The worst example was *As Good as It Gets*, starring alongside Jack Nicholson. Every actor in London thought they went up for Greg Kinnear's part, waiting patiently, like I did, in the lobby of the boutique hotel while the execs finished lunch.

I doubt Greg was too worried. I'm guessing he had been cast the month before.

The problem in this case was that I was taking the meeting because it wasn't about reading even though it was, and even though I didn't mind reading as long as I did it well enough to get the job, which unfortunately I didn't think I would, and knowing that if I turned down the opportunity to read . . . it was all but certain I wouldn't get the job anyway. I hope that's clear because I was confused as fuck as I sat in the meeting. Juliet May, various producers, executive and otherwise, sat around a large table in Centre House, yet another BBC building just across the road from TV Centre. Everything was very friendly, chatting about what I'd been up to, and how much I liked the script (I did actually), and exchanging the odd memory with Juliet about working together, and then came the lull, out of which came the inevitable, 'Actually, would you mind reading the scene?'

The inference is almost that we're getting on so well that we'd like to give you this special opportunity. In my case I thought, to screw it up. This was when I usually went right ahead and read, but just when I least expected it I had a light-bulb moment. It was simple. I realised I was so close to getting the part I could only lessen my chances by reading it, especially around a large imposing BBC table in West London.

'I'd prefer not to,' I said.

There was an imperceptible intake of breath.

'I think I can I play it, and I'd like to, but I don't want to read something I haven't prepared.'

Juliet looked at the faces around her, and smiled back at me, 'Yes I understand that,' she replied. The moment probably wasn't significant in their lives but for me it was a huge step forward. It was one thing being confident enough to read for them but so much better to be confident enough not to. A day later I was offered the job, and worked feverishly on the big speech. Anyone passing my dressing room door at the Adelphi Theatre might have wondered who exactly I was yelling at, and why I was calling them cretins, and filthy little whores. We filmed the breakdown scene at a school in Hertfordshire in an assembly hall packed with children, presumably some of them pupils, who seemed unfazed by the abuse hurled at them.

★ ★ ★

Monday, 16 November 2015. Two weeks left. Imelda insists it is only one, as the last week doesn't count. I struggle to get my head around this, but

I nod intelligently as she explains it to me, and then changes her mind, and says, 'No forget it, as far as you're concerned there are two weeks to go, or you might not bother turning up next week.'

A standing ovation at the curtain call again tonight. Only one man in the front row did not rise to his feet. Eventually the pressure was too much for him, and he stood, only for him to make a desperate grab for his trousers as they slipped down almost to his knees.

Judi Dench was watching tonight, and as she came backstage afterwards I was in the corridor waiting for my guests to come through. I lingered longer than I should have done, hoping that she might say something complimentary but she only said, 'What a great show.' This, in the language of actors, can mean anything from 'What a great show' to 'You were shit, but at least I didn't fall asleep.'

* * *

It looked like everything would work out perfectly. I could finish my run in *Chicago*, and concentrate on the last few months of Elizabeth's pregnancy. The only unhappy note was the deteriorating health of my father; he needed too much care for my mother to handle, and was moved to a care home close to Weybridge. He was lucid for only short periods, and circulation problems required him to have a foot amputated. He accepted it with resignation, although he probably never quite understood what was happening. On our part, the resignation was accepting that he wouldn't be around for much longer.

Two months before I finished, another TV guest part turned up in the *Mrs Bradley Mysteries*, a new series starring Diana Rigg. I was offered the part of a vicar in the final part of the series. It would have slotted in nicely between finishing in the show and Elizabeth's due date but the part wasn't great, and I wanted a break to focus on impending fatherhood. I thought it seemed an unnecessary distraction so I turned it down.

It was a time of mixed emotions. The dark cloud was my father but even then I wished only that he lived long enough to see his new grandchild born. He had suffered a slow but relentless decline over the years, and we were all of a mind that the end would be a release. When it came it hit me harder than I would realise, but for now there were other things on my mind. I was busy patting myself on the back about putting my partner and unborn child before work, for once getting my priorities right, which of course was the moment they chose to come back and offer me an infinitely better part in the series, and one that would keep me away from home for longer, and meant starting to film the following week.

It was tough enough turning down one job – to turn down two might seem like recklessness, and so I accepted the part of Inspector Christmas, a man with an unlikely crush on Mrs Bradley, and who turns out to be the villain of the piece. This series marked my first appearance alongside David Tennant, although if I'm truthful I had to be reminded that he was in it. I was only in one scene of David's episode, and it was over very quickly before the car whisked me off for the evening performance.

Working with Diana Rigg was intimidating. I'm quite prepared to accept this was all in my mind, and beneath the frosty smile and withering looks beat a welcoming heart, but she scared the hell out of me. It took me back to my unfortunate encounter with Arthur Miller and to an excruciating first-class flight with Michael Grade, and I was probably on the back foot anyway, having unintentionally wangled myself a part that I was a few years too young to play. In one intimate dinner scene I had my least favourite speech in any production I have ever done. After a few flirtatious lines to warm up.

Inspector Christmas leans over and says, 'You can be the cream in my coffee any day, Mrs Bradley.'

The withering look she fired at me may have been in character, but was more likely a more heartfelt response.

It could have been both.

My father was dying. Parkinson's disease slowly but surely closing down his mind and body and it was difficult to watch his decline. I barely noticed that on every other front, my life was looking up. Elizabeth's pregnancy was going smoothly, and I had managed to slot two TV jobs into my time in *Chicago*.

* * *

Thursday, 29 October 2015. As we sat in the darkness before the Chinese restaurant scene, Imelda leant across to me and said, 'There's no nice way of putting this, but my husband took me up the Shard last night.' We were seconds away from the scene starting and were helpless with laughter. As the truck rumbled forward, the music played and the lights came up, I buried my head in the newspaper, and whispered that I was amazed she could still walk.

The giggles were brought on by a long, tiring day. Since ten o'clock in the morning, I'd been recording a Big Finish story with the new 'Master', played by Geoffrey Beevers, who had been married to Caroline John – famous for playing Pertwee's companion Liz Shaw.

* * *

In March of 1999, I returned to *Doctor Who*.

A company called Big Finish had obtained a licence to make audio episodes of the series. The first, featuring Colin, Sylvester and myself, was recorded at Crosstown studios in London and was called *Sirens of Time*. I had almost no idea what the story was about, which was a tiny bit more than Colin and Sylvester did, but we all enjoyed the experience enormously. Big Finish went on to play a huge part in keeping the soul of the series alive and they are still going strong today. Going back to *Doctor Who* reminded me that playing leading parts on television was something I used to do and that nowadays an offer, without going through the auditioning process, was a rarity.

A couple of weeks later a large envelope of scripts arrived by courier, closely followed by a call from my agent asking me to have a read and telling me it was an offer. I read them with little expectation, only to discover it was one of the best scripts I had ever read. I called my agent back.

'Are they serious, it's an offer?'

'That's what they said. What's it like?'

'It's brilliant. Who else is cast?'

'No one at the moment.'

'Really?'

'I'll call them tomorrow, tell them you're interested?'

'Can you call them now?'

I was confused. Even going up for a series lead was rare enough these days – to be offered one, especially before anyone else had been cast, was a bit like winning the lottery. Which, in a curious synergetic way, was exactly what *At Home with the Braithwaites* was about. Even stranger was casting me as David, the irascible and unfaithful husband whose wife wins thirty-eight million pounds – a character far removed from the safety of my usual parade of nice blokes and Time Lords. I hadn't even been seen shouting at schoolchildren in *Hope and Glory*, which wouldn't air until the following month, but once the deal was done, I put the mystery to one side and concentrated on the job itself. The unanswered question was who would play Alison, the wife. Over the next few weeks it was rumoured to be one actress then another.

Then I was reliably told it was Felicity Kendall, and then, almost as suddenly, I was told it wasn't. A week later I was officially told it was Amanda Redman.

One morning in early summer we sat around a large table in the Irish Club in Eaton Square for the read-through. The project had taken five years to get to this point, carefully nurtured by Yorkshire Television. I was happy to see Lynda Bellingham again, and to finally meet the director Robyn Sheppard, who had the first and most difficult job of introducing, without the aid of a safety net, everyone around the table.

A week later we were filming in Leeds.

* * *

Tuesday, 29 March 2016. Sitting in a hotel room in Key West. The children are out with Elizabeth, jet-skiing or scuba-diving or something that I'm too old to try, so the room is quiet. An email from my sister flashes across the screen, telling me that Aunt Olga's health has suddenly declined and she is now in palliative care and not expected to last the week. I struggle to decide if this is a tragic turn of events or perfect timing, because at that moment I am struggling to write about my father's (her brother's) death. I think about driving up to Palm Bay right away, but it's a seven-hour drive and seven hours back again to pick up the family, so I call the care home and ask if they think she'll hang on until Friday when we had planned to see her, and the nurse carefully informs me that at present she isn't 'actively' dying, which sounds faintly comical and despite everything, or maybe because of it, makes me chuckle audibly. After a moment the nurse goes on.

'I think she'll make it till Friday,' she says, adding, 'but I have been wrong before.'

* * *

My father died a week before my son Louis was born, while I was away filming in Yorkshire. I borrowed a black suit from the costume department for the funeral the following week. The crematorium was across the road from my old school, where years before I had so often looked out of the classroom window and watched the grey smoke rising from the chimneys.

In the days that followed I thought about my relationship with him. I felt I hadn't appreciated him in the way I ought to have done, or at least I never communicated it to him. Perhaps the closest I came was a couple of weeks before he died, when he was to all intents, comatose. As he lay in the hospital bed, I whispered in his ear that I loved him and asked him to squeeze my hand if he understood. After a moment his hand tightened around mine, almost imperceptibly, but enough to get me off the hook.

I am more like him than I cared to admit while he was alive. I stand like he did, sit like he did, I look at my hands and see his, I look in the mirror and see his features, even though our colouring was so completely different. While I longed to look more like him, I realise I turned out as perfectly as he could have wished. Here was a man from the Caribbean who wanted nothing more than to be accepted as British, who had a son who had made a name for himself playing the typical Englishman.

I didn't do so badly either. I inherited his fatalism, his relatively easy-going nature, maybe too much of an inclination to be flirtatious, but best of all the ability to repair almost anything with a bread knife and an old coat-hanger. He was, I decided, a good, simple, and useful man.

Amanda Redman had two mobile telephones, which I thought very impressive. Sometimes she would talk on both at the same time.

Sometimes she would talk on both at the same time while smoking a cigarette – this was Amanda in power-woman mode. I remember watching her perform this feat one afternoon in the back garden of the *Braithwaites* location house, until she noticed me watching and grinned sheepishly as if she'd been caught out. From powerful woman to little girl in an instant. Not so far beneath Amanda's tough exterior, beat the soft heart of the hopeless romantic. I always enjoyed playing scenes with her, and felt we developed an understanding of the comedy and tragedy in our characters that lasted all four series.

In the evenings I would often meet up with my daughters, that is to say, my pretend daughters who were both named Sarah. Smarty and Churmy, as we called them, were inseparable, probably getting along better than real sisters. I loved them because, despite being excellent actresses, they were genuine and unspoiled. Sarah Smart, who admittedly had the juicier storyline, played Virginia with such uncluttered truthfulness that it often took my breath away. She managed what is so hard for actors to do – she discarded vanity the moment she left the make-up room. She would go on to be a favourite of Sally Wainwright's, who wrote other series with Sarah in mind.

A month after filming began we gathered in a bar in Leeds city centre to celebrate finishing the first block and to watch a rough assembly of scenes. Until then no one had been sure how it would turn out, and Amanda, in particular, wasn't convinced by the title, while there was a concern, from ITV network centre, about a series filled with such dysfunctional characters. After we saw the rough-cut, we knew it was something special. Suddenly there was a real sense of excitement and as the evening wore on I found myself talking to Hugh Warren, the producer. I asked him bluntly how I got the job. His explanation went like this:

A list of names had been put forward as possibilities to play Alison and David. The ITV controllers had rejected them all with the exception of me. Normally this wouldn't automatically lead to an offer, but ITV had come back with their own suggestion of an actress to play Alison that was so far from their own vision, the production team felt the only way to avoid a drawn-out battle of wills was to immediately cast me and tell ITV that as I was contracted, they needed an actress that, would match up with me. Perhaps it wasn't the most encouraging explanation to hear, not like they woke up one morning, blinded by a vision of me playing the part, but these twists and turns are otherwise known as 'luck', and it was me standing there chatting with the producer. Later still, I sat with Robyn Sheppard, by this time we were both fairly mellow, and after an exchange of compliments, I decided to thank her for giving me the rare chance to play an unsympathetic character.

'Well, thank you for playing him so sympathetically,' she replied.

The penny dropped in an obvious and rather painful way. Rather than being an unlikely choice, I was perfect casting to calm the nerves of a network nervous about unsympathetic leading characters, the tragedy being I had no idea that's what I was there to do. I had been giving the part every ounce of unpleasantness I could muster.

The first episode of *At Home with the Braithwaites* was broadcast in January 2000 and was an immediate hit. Elizabeth and I were on holiday in California with baby Louis and my daughter Georgia, when ITV picked up the option for a second series and by the following summer we were back filming in Leeds.

At some point during the second series I remember pointing out that the winning lottery ticket had been bought by Charlotte, the youngest daughter (played by Keeley Fawcett), and that as she was underage, the ticket was illegal. I may not have been the only one to notice this but it became the story arc of the series. Until someone challenges me, I am taking a little credit for giving Sally the idea.

LOVE AND DEATH

The series went from strength to strength, and by 2001 we were one of ITV's biggest shows. I was well and truly out of the wilderness and back on the box. In June of that year we started work on series three. The main thread centred on the teenage pregnancy of the Braithwaites' daughter Sarah (Sarah Churm) and my character's inability to deal with it.

Joel was born on the 7 August 2001. He timed his arrival perfectly in the middle of a two-week break from filming the third series of *At Home with the Braithwaites*. Joel might have been named Felix but for a strange sequence of events that began the preceding day when Elizabeth, already two weeks overdue, was finally induced. I'd taken her up to the Royal Free Hospital in Hampstead, leaving Georgia, who had spent the last few days persuading us that Felix should be at the top of our favoured names list, alone in the flat. That's how it stood as the two of us waited in the hospital room ready for action. Several hours passed and inevitably there was no action at all and eventually I was sent home with the determination that I would get a phone call when I was needed. Elizabeth went into labour around midnight. I was important enough in the scheme of things that everyone sort of forgot to call me, and when they eventually got in touch, I was more rested than I had any right to be, having missed several hours of agonising contractions and thoroughly deserved verbal abuse.

Putting up with the latter is the most useful job of the expectant father. I remember when Georgia was born, listening to the raised voices in the next delivery room that went along the lines...

'God, I fucking hate you! This is all *your* fucking fault!'

Sandra, although slightly wittier, had a similar sentiment.

Elizabeth's approach was slightly different, she stabbed her finger-nails into my arm, and looked imploringly at me and said, 'Please make it stop.'

Eventually there was Felix, or at least 8lb 13oz of 'boy', pending name confirmation. I triumphantly brought out my video camera only to discover I had triumphantly forgotten to charge the battery.

Later my mother and mother-in-law appeared. Blurry photos of newborn were taken with cheap cameras. There was much happiness and celebration. More friends dropped by. In the late afternoon, feeling exhausted, I drove my mother back to our flat. We'd been inside for only a minute, the car keys still in my hand, when I heard a loud thump from outside. I went to take a look, and discovered my car window smashed. I didn't immediately understand what had happened until a neighbour ran out calling, 'He went that way.' Quite what came over me in that moment, I don't know. My normally placid and fatalistic view of the world disappeared out of my smashed window, replaced momentarily by a kind of Super Pete. I jumped in the car, figuring that the 'he went that way' would be towards Belsize Village, and that if I went the back route I might cut him off, or at least give him a fright.

As I turned left into Belsize Avenue I saw someone run across the road. I swung the car into the parking area by the village, and jumped out, leaving the car door swinging dramatically. I looked around wildly. I only wanted the bugger to know I'd tried. Someone looked at me quizzically, and then in the direction away to my right. I set off, even though it was beginning to dawn on me that I was much closer to catching up with him than I had ever intended to be. He looked younger than me though, and as I was already running out of steam, he would almost certainly get away. That's when he made his big mistake, making his escape down Belsize Mews, a dead end.

I knew exactly where he'd gone because a helpful passer-by called out, 'He's gone down there, mate.' It struck me, what the hell do I do now? I could hardly change my mind, so down the mews I went. There was a sturdy young man in a large combat jacket walking towards me. I said, 'Did you smash my car window?' His response,

'Get away from me,' wasn't the response of the innocent. There was a momentary impasse as I blocked his way. In truth I had no idea what to do next. I had never got myself in this situation before. Then he said threateningly, 'I've got a knife,' and promptly made his second mistake. His combat jacket was long in the sleeve, and covered most of his hands so the threat could well have been real, but as he slashed out at me he imitated the noise of a knife cutting through the air, the way a child might do in a pretend fight. It was an oddly surreal moment, but I remember clearly thinking, if he's making the noise, he probably doesn't have the real thing. So I grabbed him, somehow wrestled him to the ground, and used my one great advantage to subdue him. My superior weight rendered him helpless. So we lay there. Occasionally someone popped out of the pub to take a look. My restrained new friend ran me through several scenarios, from threats of extreme violence if he got loose, to pleas that I let him go because his mum would be pissed off with him. Every couple of minutes he would struggle violently before surrendering to the effects of gravity.

Eventually a man from the pub strolled over, pint in hand, and enquired whether I might like him to call the police. I told him that was probably a fine idea, and off he went. This seemed to spur other inquisitive folk to come over, and before long there were two or three of us taking turns to sit on him. After about twenty minutes a couple of impossibly young policemen turned up. One said, 'Come on, let's be having you,' and the violent, imaginary-knife-wielding brute turned instantly into the meekest of men. They patted him down, pulling something from inside his jacket. It was my video camera, which I had left on the seat of the car, now crumpled, and broken by some idiot who had jumped on some other idiot.

Later that evening, after I had given my statement, and had gone off to collect mother and new baby from the hospital, the press rang my home. Georgia, who was babysitting Louis, answered the phone. The story was out, somehow leaked from the police station. Georgia chatted away, and finally as an afterthought they asked does the baby have a name? Georgia inexplicably replying, 'Joel.'

It must have been a slow week, because the following day the story made *News at Ten*. I was interviewed outside my flat, and the reporter walked the route of the thrilling chase. 'It was down this very cul-de-sac that the actor pursued the thief ...' etc., etc. The newspapers and TV loved the idea that I had chased the thief to recover precious shots of my newborn child. I never had the heart to tell them there was nothing on the camera.

★ ★ ★

Saturday, 3 October 2015. My daughter has given birth for the fourth time. Joel had a sleepover at their house last night, and when I spoke to him he casually mentioned Georgia had gone into labour. I called David who replied that they were at the hospital, and looked like they were staying there so he presumed she had. This morning he sent a text to say mother and daughter were well.

★ ★ ★

In the summer of 2001, Georgia left her expensive boarding school in favour of applying to Richmond Sixth Form College. She'd managed to pass a good deal more exams than I had, but it wasn't enough to propel her towards university. She resolutely dismissed any idea of becoming an actress.

'There are too many of them,' she said.

She was sitting on the sofa in our splendid, newly-moved-into home in East Twickenham. We had loved living in Belsize Park and had been sad to leave, and Elizabeth especially had been resistant to 'moving out to the sticks', as she put it, but with Joel's arrival and with Georgia undecided where she would base herself, we had definitely outgrown a one-bedroom flat.

'It's fifteen minutes from Waterloo and a safe place to live.'

It didn't impress Elizabeth, who until I introduced her to the gentrified streets of North London, was happy living with the wailing sirens and small bunches of flowers tied to lamp-posts in Shepherd's Bush. She didn't trust underground trains that didn't go underground, or didn't go around in circles. In the end she gave in because I pointed out the house was actually north of the river and a good five minutes from the unacceptable stickiness of Surrey and so a couple of weeks after Joel was born, we headed south(ish). It was a bit like coming home. We were a short walk from Richmond town centre, where I'd lived nearly thirty years before and where so many things ended and began.

Georgia, after smoking another roll-up and slipping back in from our small courtyard garden, announced she wanted to go to Richmond College and do art A level. I was happy to be supportive and so it barely crossed my mind how little of her 'art' I'd seen. We made several trips to art stores to buy paints, pencils, sketch pads, and gigantic folders with carrying handles for all the 'artwork' she would be doing and she completed the make-over by moving into our small box room and painting every inch of it a bright gloss orangey red.

The following September, back on location in Yorkshire, I had a message to call Elizabeth urgently. I sat on the steps of my trailer as the phone was picked up. I remember this moment in the same way as I remembered where I'd been only a few weeks before on 11 September 2001. This was very different, of course, but invoked the similar sense of numbness in me. Georgia was pregnant. She'd been too scared to tell me herself and asked Elizabeth to call. I was slightly wounded by this, as I couldn't recall ever being angry with her, but maybe she had paid too much attention to the television series, because this was life imitating art. One of our ongoing storylines was my teenage daughter getting pregnant and her father's inability to cope. At least the show had given me a blueprint of how not to behave, I thought, and maybe because of that, or a natural fatalistic approach to life, I took it rather well – all things considered.

Georgia wanted to have the baby. There was never any doubt in her mind.

I worried about her missing out on being young and carefree, but she insisted she wouldn't miss it at all, and after all, being young and carefree had been a hefty contributing factor to her current circumstances.

We were left with the bright red bedroom for a few years before finding a decorator brave enough to tackle the job. Georgia went to the Sixth Form college for a couple of weeks before coming up with a pretty good reason to leave. All the artwork stuff is still in our loft, unused and looking rather sad.

Instead Ty was born in late March 2002, only seven months after his uncle Joel, and remains a tribute to Georgia's extraordinary and instinctive parenting skills, almost none of it learned from her parents.

* * *

Elizabeth and I had two children and were living happily in our end-of-terrace house and planning for the future, but we had avoided the subject of marriage. Perhaps we had tiptoed around it a little, I can't be sure, but I'd convinced myself that she was OK with the status quo. Friends would ask if we were getting married and I would say that, no – she's fine the way we are. I so convinced myself of this that I can pinpoint the moment I realised she wasn't.

LOVE AND DEATH

I was walking around Leeds city centre, looking for a birthday present for her when I passed an antique jewellery shop in one of the grand arcades off Briggate. There was a ring in the window, and being a bit stupid about the significance of these things, I asked to see it. It was an engagement ring, the man said, and an unaccountable feeling welled up inside me. I realised I was perfectly happy to get married after all and that Elizabeth would never have said she'd like to if she thought there was the remotest possibility that it would make me less happy. This wasn't about staying together, that much was certain, and besides Georgia had threatened me with patricide if we ever split up. This was about me being used to more direct expressions of neediness, not seeing the bleeding obvious.

I bought the ring and gave it to her on her birthday. She was mightily impressed when she opened the small box and then a cloud of doubt crossed her face.

'It looks like a bit like an engagement ring?'

'Oh', I said in surprise. 'We'd better get married then.'

So gloriously understated was my proposal that two days later it emerged that Elizabeth hadn't realised it had happened. She'd gone out with friends for a late birthday celebration and they all examined the ring and agreed it looked like an engagement ring.

'That's what I said to him.'

'What did he say?'

'He said we'd better get married then.'

'I think that was a proposal.'

'No, I think he was joking.'

When she got home she confronted me. I was outraged and said of course it was a proposal, although I was prepared to admit it was a truly pathetic one. To this day I'm not sure she got around to saying yes.

The wedding took place in Orleans House by the River Thames in August the following year, with family and friends, a man playing the accordion and two small children baffled by all the fuss. Owing to the problems of film scheduling I only had one day off and we'd had the short honeymoon a week earlier, completing the upside down nature of the wedding: children, honeymoon, wedding. Later in the day there was a reception at Pembroke Lodge in Richmond Park, with more friends than we ever knew we had, all with their fingers crossed, thinking – third time lucky.

★ ★ ★

Thursday, 2 July 2015. Tonight, moments before the start of the second act I asked Lara if Raza, her husband of five months, was still in London. 'Only for ten more days,' she said, 'then I shall be crying into my pillow.' I said we'd cheer her up, and she looked at me as if that wouldn't help at all, and asked if I had ever been away from my wife for a long time. I replied I had, which was true, at the start of the year I was in Australia for over a month.

'Didn't you miss her?' she asked.

'Well, yes, of course, and she was away again last night,' I said still smarting that my wife had buggered off to visit her aunt in Liverpool.

'Isn't life so much better when they're there? I miss him so much when he's away,' she sighed. Lara is very much in love.

'Well, yes, but you've only just got married so of course you feel like this.'

'You mean in a couple of years I won't miss him at all?' This was a genuine question, not a hint of rebuke.

'No, I mean you'll miss him in different ways. I missed Elizabeth last night principally because she'd taken my toothbrush.'

She looked at me strangely, but I ploughed on, 'And because she'd left me with the two boys who ransacked the house and left dirty clothes and dishes everywhere.'

I could see that this wasn't the direction she'd imagined the conversation going but I was on a roll now. 'And the older one left the milk out all day, which went off, because he claimed there wasn't any room in the fridge, even though there were any number of Diet Cokes, and bottles of white wine he could have taken out.'

She was saved by the orchestra striking up with the overture.

★　★　★

I was back on the TV map as suddenly as I'd dropped off it and by the summer of that year I was a fully-fledged member of the ITV family, with two more series offers on the table. *The Last Detective*, based on the books by Leslie Thomas, and *Distant Shores*, a series that was the pet project of Carolyn Reynolds, the executive producer of *Braithwaites*.

It also meant yearly invitations to the ITV summer party, a lavish and champagne-fuelled evening, usually held at the Orangery at Kensington Palace, Kensington Gardens. I earned a bad reputation at the first one I ever attended, after gently lambasting David Liddiment, the ITV director of programmes, for making the reality show *Soapstars*. We were two hours into the party and Amanda Redman and I were whinging to each other about the idea of a show in which people competed for a chance to play regular parts in *Emmerdale*. It was a terrible idea and a terrible show, but we had also been drinking champagne for a terribly long time and when David made the mistake of stopping to chat to a group of people close to us, the die was cast. Amanda thought it would be a good idea to tell him exactly what we thought and I was inebriated enough to agree with her. What started as a good-humoured challenge was inflamed by Liddiment, who wasn't entirely sober himself, jokingly accusing us of being like all actors, precious and insecure. That's when I suggested they should have a reality show to choose the next Director of Programmes, something I thought was a good idea for about five minutes after which I sank into despair about the scuppering of my recently revived career.

I woke up the next morning with my heart and my head thumping, but David Liddiment, it turns out, is a man with a wonderful sense of humour and there were no repercussions. Either that or he had another glass of champagne and forgot all about it.

Michelle Buck, who was producing *The Last Detective* and hoping to get the green light, had observed the debacle from a short distance away. She called me the next day and said not to worry, everything was fine, but maybe hold back a little next year.

I was keen to make *The Last Detective*; it reminded me of a show I'd watched as a teenager called *Public Eye* that starred Alfred Burke. With its easy pace and gentle humour and world-weary central character, it had been a success for many years. *The Last Detective* had Sean Hughes as my eccentric sidekick, who turned out to be fairly eccentric in real life. An Irish comedian brought up in Kilburn and a passionate supporter of Crystal Palace football club. They were my team too, mostly because of my South London background and the few games my uncle John had taken me to, but the result was an immediate affinity, although I was always about ten seconds late getting his jokes and he'd raise his eyes to the ceiling as if say, Why do I bother?

* * *

Monday, 14 September 2015. Steven Moffat and Sue Vertue were in tonight. Lara (who knows them from *Sherlock*) suggested we have drinks in my dressing room on condition I tidied it first. Every moment I wasn't on stage, I was cleaning all the surfaces, chucking out rubbish and putting clutter into boxes and hiding the boxes in the cupboard. I put a bottle of champagne in the fridge, and washed the glasses, tidied my make-up space, until the room was unrecognisable as mine. This disturbed many people including my dresser, Michelle, who suspected I had been replaced by a clone with OCD. After the show I sat and waited for them to come round to the stage door. Ten minutes later I got a text saying, 'We've gone to the pub next door, see you there.'

* * *

In 2004, we were invited to dinner by a friend who wanted us to meet Steven Moffat. He was there with his wife Sue Vertue, whose mother, Beryl Vertue, had been a powerful figure in TV for more than forty years. Steven was a fan of *Doctor Who*, although that doesn't quite describe the intensity of his obsession. Over dessert our host would show Steven black-and-white photos from old *Doctor Who* episodes. He could name not only the story, the episode, but also how far into that episode the scene occurred. Now he was having dinner with one of the Doctors. This, of course, went right over my head, I was more impressed that *I* was having dinner with Sue Vertue and Steven Moffat and his amazing party tricks. We shared similar surnames, our children shared similar Christian names, and now with less than a year before *Doctor Who* returned to the TV and with Steven writing one of the stories, we shared a connection with the show itself.

* * *

The first series of *The Last Detective* acquired a loyal following and also had a strong ally in the Controller of Drama's cleaning lady. The rumour goes that Nick Elliot, eager to have the people's touch, used her as a barometer of popular ITV drama. Presumably, as she vacuumed the stairs and Nick straightened his always immaculate tie in the hallway mirror, he would casually ask what shows she liked at that moment. *The Last Detective* was right up there and as result we got the nod for more.

We made four series of *The Last Detective* and I was sad to see it finish, a casualty of an eventual change of Controller in ITV drama. It was 'TV as it used to be made', as one reviewer put it, which I'm pretty sure was complimentary, referring to the show's content rather than any technical deficiencies.

Distant Shores didn't fare so well. It took a long time to get off the ground and by the time it did, there was another series, grabbed by ITV from Sky TV that was very similar. *Doc Martin* was about a grumpy doctor who went to the wilds of Cornwall whereas *Distant Shores* was about a grumpy surgeon who went to a remote island in the North Sea. They weren't exact copies, in fact ours had an almost mystical and quirky feel to it, a bit like *The Wicker Man* without the sex or Edward Woodward going up in flames.

On the first day of filming I shared a car from the hotel with Gareth Thomas who was playing the small but regular part of the vicar. Back in the late seventies, he had starred in the sci-fi series *Blake's 7*. Despite its success, Gareth had chosen to leave after the first season, to pursue more serious work – and it hadn't worked out as he might have wished. Because I'd been in *Doctor Who* shortly afterwards, I think Gareth was feeling uncomfortable with the disparity in our career trajectories. After remarking on the early start and the beautiful Northumberland scenery he changed the subject abruptly and asked what I'd been up to recently.

I gave him a brief rundown, trying to sound offhand, which probably made things worse.

There was a lull while he considered this.

'You were much cleverer than me,' he then said with a slight edge. 'You took every job that came along. I tried to be selective.'

The rest of the journey was discomfiting and I was left wondering if this was an insult framed as a compliment, or if he really felt that way.

The first series had good ratings without setting the world on fire and after a few tense weeks they picked up our option. Series two saw a change of executive producer. Someone who should have known better thought it would be a good idea to show the first series to a focus group to see what they thought we could improve.

I don't like focus groups. Usually people with nothing better to do, some of whom will like your show while the rest will base their opinions on wanting it to be like something else. That's probably unfair but I was mad as hell about this one. They thought the first series was far too mystical and quirky and effectively questioned why it couldn't be more like *Doc Martin*, which was as quirky as they wanted anything to be. We sat down with the new exec shortly after we got the green light for the more focused second series. He'd come up with a big idea, he told us, one that would take the audience by surprise. Samantha Bond and I looked at him with great excitement, but only because actors can do this kind of thing convincingly, without meaning it at all.

'Your daughter gets pregnant,' he said and sat back proudly.

As big ideas go, this was a bit disappointing. Apart from the fact my own teenage daughter had got herself pregnant, while I was filming a TV series about my teenage daughter getting pregnant, it was apparent this whole 'pregnant teenage daughter' thing had featured in pretty much every soap opera over the last ten years and should now be put in a box marked 'overused' and buried deeper than they deposit radioactive waste.

I didn't quite put it like that, but for me I was surprisingly unequivocal.

He was unmoved. I was dismayed.

It wasn't a happy second series. The scripts were uneven to say the least, and niggling things started to annoy me. The actor that played my daughter's love interest arrives on the island, emerging from the sea in only the clothes he stands up in, and yet over the course of next few episodes – and without leaving a tiny island that has only one shop – he wears an array of fashionable clothing including a very expensive-looking leather jacket.

'He came out of the sea in his shirt,' I cried.

He could have borrowed them, said the director.

'Borrowed them? Have you seen what the other islanders are wearing?

When my daughter finds an army pistol in his house on the beach:

'Where was he hiding the gun when he came out of the sea?'

And before anyone can reply:

'. . . Don't answer that.'

* * *

The saving grace of the summer of 2005 was England winning the Ashes cricket series against Australia. A member of the sound department managed to conjure up a grainy picture on a battery-powered TV and groups of us would crowd around it between takes. After years of resolutely losing, and with every game of that summer on a knife edge, we were finally victorious by drawing the last match at the Oval cricket ground in London. Unfortunately, at that very moment, filming on a rocky outcrop on the Northumberland coast, a cliff rescue stunt went horribly wrong and the actress playing my daughter shattered her wrist when she became entangled in a rope pulling us up. For me, it summed up the series, and though we resumed production shortly after and stumbled through to the end of the series, I had huge reservations about the finished product.

LOVE AND DEATH

The second series of *Distant Shores* was never broadcast. At least not in this country. Some 'fortunate' people in Canada had the chance to see it and I once met a man in New Zealand that claimed it was broadcast there, but in Britain it sat on a shelf until 2015, when a careless employee came across it, dusted it off and suggested it should be released on DVD.

By the time *Distant Shores* wasn't broadcast there were another two projects on the go. I could hear the words of Gareth Thomas echoing in my ears. But these were good scripts and very different characters and if I did both, they would film back to back, with production schedules that overlapped. *A Complete Guide to Parenting* and *Fear Stress and Anger*. It was like going back twenty-five years when I had two other comedy series on the go. A year later I was doing *Doctor Who* as well.

I rang my agent and said yes to both.

The following year, Steven Moffat and Sue Vertue came over to lunch. Afterwards, as we sat in the garden, Steven asked if I'd consider filming a short film for Children in Need and passed me the script of *Time Crash*.

A couple of months later I was back playing the Fifth Doctor on the set of the TARDIS, alongside the upstart David Tennant.

I'd come a long way and yet, no distance at all.

13

CONVENTIONS AND HOW TO SURVIVE THEM

Saturday, 12 March 2016. Attending a convention in Lexington, Kentucky, I met a man who told me we'd last met in Tulsa in 1981. When I say a man it's misleading, because he went on to say he was five years old at the time and hadn't been able to speak on account of the 'charismatic aura'. I suggested this may have been because of the long journey and my not having time to change my shirt before coming down to meet him, but he said no, it had been the greatest moment of his five-year-old life.

★ ★ ★

On 14 August 1981, nearly five months before I appeared on television as the Doctor, I made my first appearance at a *Doctor Who* convention. It was in Tulsa, Oklahoma at the Camelot Hotel, a large, pink, concrete building, complete with a concrete moat and iron portcullis (non-functioning) that had seen much better days. My room, situated on the top floor, was enormous and smelled of damp. It had two levels, with a substantial staircase leading to the bedroom area. It was nine o'clock in the evening Tulsa time, three o'clock in the morning for me and I collapsed on the vast king-size bed and briefly closed my eyes, but there was no time to rest because JNT had agreed I would appear at the welcome ceremony. He was very keen on these *Doctor Who* conventions as a way of breaking the show in new territories, possibly leading to more co-production money and the tantalising prospect of foreign filming – that's why he was banging on my door at that very moment.

The idea of jet-setting around the world had seemed an attractive prospect, but an economy seat and the faded glory of the Camelot Hotel was hardly it. But at the time I wasn't so picky; I smiled for three days, signed autographs till my hand curled with cramp, had questions fired at me about the series that I couldn't possibly answer – and still I couldn't have been happier.

I remember my very first question was about a Patrick Troughton story, which was as baffling to most of the audience as it was to me, as very few viewers in North America had seen a Doctor prior to Jon Pertwee. It was likely that only I and the fan who'd asked the question had ever seen the episode, and I could remember nothing about it. This didn't stop the audience looking at me with high expectations, and I looked back at them, wondering how seriously they took the series.

Did they think I'd really regenerated? Or I was a time-travelling actor?

Someone asked how I prepared for the role of the Doctor and I foolishly said, they sent me the script and I learned the words. This was a bad start and there was a murmur of disapproval rippling around the grand ballroom. I was in front of an audience who would rather be listening to Tom Baker than me, and being flippant was doing me no favours, after all I was a now a role model. This had been made clear to me a few months earlier when I was told I'd have to give up a lucrative beer commercial for Yorkshire Bitter in order to play the Doctor.

In those early days I wore my costume, a vision in beige, to these events and could be reasonably sure I'd be the only Fifth Doctor around, but I was not unknown in the USA. *All Creatures Great and Small* had been a mainstay of PBS TV stations for a few years, and would be for a long time to come. If I was recognised in the street while I was there it was always for Tristan rather than the Doctor and by the end of that first evening, I had answered more questions about *All Creatures* than about *Doctor Who*.

At a crowded press conference the following day, held in the famous Red Lion nightclub in the basement of the Camelot Hotel, I was asked if I ever worried about being assassinated at these kind of events (it was less than a year since John Lennon had been killed in New York). I was speechless for a moment.

'Not until now,' I said.

★ ★ ★

Thursday, 23 July 2015. A 6.15 a.m. call for *Toast of London* to do the final scene of the episode – me and Morgana Robinson dead on a bed with drink-induced bubonic plague. Ironically a little later my son Louis sends me a link to a newspaper article saying I have been the victim of a celebrity death hoax a couple of days before. Someone in the States announced I had passed away, and opened a Facebook page inviting people to post condolences. Nearly a million posted tributes before someone thought to question why my death had not been reported on the BBC or any UK news outlets. They could also have rung the theatre, and asked if I was off that night, although Imelda said that my death would not have been a good enough excuse not to go on. The number of people mourning me has impressed my son Joel more than anything I have done in my life. I can see his point and so I recommend the death hoax experience highly. It's like having the wake before you die. I mean what's the point of people saying all those nice things about you if you're not around to hear them.

★ ★ ★

JNT pressed ahead arranging more conventions. It was slightly mad but still I didn't complain. In those heady pre-security days, a recognisable face would sometimes get an upgrade on a flight and occasionally invited into the cockpit for take-off. If the conventions happened during a production period as this one did, we would finish rehearsals on a Friday, fly out to Florida or Chicago, or some *Who*-friendly city, and leave again on the Sunday night to be back rehearsing on Monday afternoon. My first Fort Lauderdale convention took place the following year. *Doctor Who* flourished in Florida, especially in that part of the state, but that event stays in my mind because I sat in the sun too long on the first day, and had to spend the rest of the weekend sporting a bright red nose.

★ ★ ★

Friday, 17 July 2015. First day on *Toast of London*, playing myself. In this parallel world I have run off with a foul-mouthed dancer. Matt Berry reminds me we have met once before long before this series. I try to give a look that indicates that of course I remember but could you remind me anyway. He grins, and says I wouldn't remember because he was seven years old, and standing in a queue outside the *Doctor Who* Celebration at Longleat in 1983.

CONVENTIONS AND HOW TO SURVIVE THEM

★ ★ ★

The year 1983 was always going to be a bumper year, being the twentieth anniversary of the first episode. An event celebrating 'Twenty Years of a Time Lord' was planned to take place on Easter Sunday, 14 April, at Longleat, home of Lord Bath, where there was already a permanent exhibition in place, and was organised by BBC Enterprises. This meant liaising closely with producer John Nathan-Turner, which for a while they appeared to be doing. He suggested a make-up and costume tent, where the BBC make-up department would turn you into an alien or you could try on a Cyberman head, and he suggested how to sell the idea to the fans. This was meat and drink to JNT, who whilst I don't think he was necessarily the best producer for *Doctor Who* could get publicity for a passing cloud.

Enterprises reckoned on a few thousand attendees over the two days, but from the start ticket sales were excellent. He warned them they were still underestimating the numbers, but they continued to base their figure on tickets sold. He mentioned this to me on a number of occasions, and was frustrated about it. I think it's fair to say that what went well with Longleat was mostly down to him, and every cock-up lay at the door of BBC Enterprises.

As we drove into the grounds of Longleat that morning the extent of their folly was obvious. Over the two days more than 40,000 people turned up – some say the figure was nearer a 100,000. The queue from the entrance booth stretched into the distance, and it was clear even at that time in the morning only a small percentage of fans would get in. BBC Enterprises found themselves playing down the numbers attending in order to cover the extent of their miscalculation. Remembering that weekend it's hard to believe only two years later the show would be taken off the air.

IS THERE LIFE OUTSIDE THE BOX?

I had a busy schedule of autograph sessions, and panels, then at eleven o'clock I was taken to the famous Green Library, a highlight of Longleat House, which housed rare and priceless books – some dating back to before 1500. I was there, along with Lord Bath, to present prizes to the winners of a *Doctor Who* drawing competition. The two young winners were there, along with two sets of smartly dressed parents. All that was missing was the Lord Bath himself. Apparently no one had seen him that morning. His personal assistant, a stern-faced but surprisingly friendly woman was in a bit of a state, sending out search parties of footmen or whatever you call them, and apologising to us. I got the impression that Lord Bath going missing was a fairly regular occurrence. 'He knows he should be here,' she explained, and we all smiled politely. Time passed. We all had a nice cup of tea. At one point Viscount Weymouth, the elder son, wandered in, took a look at us, and wandered out.

The Viscount was quite big news at the time, as he had married what the tabloids called a porn star, although she was simply an actress who had taken her clothes off once or twice in low-budget films. He'd grown his hair long, and wore kaftans that my friend Dave would have been proud of, and had taken to painting over the famous murals of Longleat House with his own depiction of scenes from the Kama Sutra. He was also building an impressive collection of wifelets, women he'd had relationships with, who were now housed on the estate. I thought perhaps he was going to stand in for the missing Lord, but he'd also disappeared – presumably by now in the middle of another erotic masterpiece.

Twenty minutes later Lord Bath turned up, slightly dishevelled and with his trousers tucked into a pair of Wellington boots. He apologised extravagantly, announcing that he'd been cleaning out the ditches around the bottom of the estate, and had 'clean forgot' about 'this business'. He waved away the entreaties of his assistant to get on with the presentation, and instead focused on the children. He said he wanted to show them the treasures of the Green Library, and, throwing open one of the glass cabinets, pulled out a book, and handed it to one of them, 'Over five hundred years old,' he said, 'probably worth a couple of million quid. Open it, and have a look.' His assistant, stressed before he turned up, was now in hyperdrive, dancing forward, arms outstretched, and hands cupped, as if she might dramatically save the book should it slip from the boy's grubby hands.

Outside, things were not going well; the people queuing had realised their chances of getting in were diminishing, and some were becoming impatient. Jon Pertwee and Patrick Troughton were doing their stints of autographs and panels, and so I had an hour or so off before lunch. I suggested it might be a good idea for me to walk down the line of fans, saying hello, and apologising for the 'problems'. At least that they would get to meet a Doctor. There was a concern about my security but I pointed out that if anyone was going to be attacked it would be someone wearing a BBC Enterprises badge, not me. It turned out the long walk along the queue was one of the high spots of the weekend. I said 'Hi' quite a lot, and signed autographs, posed for pictures, and tousled a lot of hair. I have read accounts of these tousling incidents posted by adults who were children in 1983, and to be honest they are very complimentary – 'He was great, he signed my picture, and tousled my hair' etc. I believe I've even seen the odd photograph of tousling taking place. I never made it to lunch that day – it was a very long queue.

Easter Monday was a re-run of the previous day, without the distractions of Lord Bath. I walked the queue, signed autographs, and answered questions. I also met Christopher Thynne, the second son, who at that time ran the estate, and seemed, by far, the least eccentric of the family. Ten years later on the death of Lord Bath, Christopher found his services were no longer required by his brother, now the 7th Marquess, and he left the estate he had run for so many years.

In November of 1983, we celebrated the 20th anniversary of the show in Chicago at the Spirit of Light convention. Once again all four surviving Doctors were invited, as well an array of companions, and of course the Master. The thousands of fans that turned up had a great time, but Tom Baker's position was uncompromising: he didn't want to appear with any other Doctors on panels or photographs. Maybe he felt on safe ground because to most American fans he was the first, and probably their favourite. This annoyed the hell out of Pertwee, who was already resentful of him over *The Five Doctors* in which Baker had refused to appear. We were all of the same opinion about Tom's behaviour, but Pertwee was vociferous. Both Pertwee and Baker saw themselves as the definitive Doctor, and were determined to prove it this weekend in Chicago. I thought Patrick was definitive but then again, I was the incumbent and had nothing to prove.

This was a battle for *Who* domination.

I was more sanguine about this contest of egos, happy to defer to Pertwee as the egocentric elder statesman and never feeling Tom Baker's battle was with me. In 1983, I was at the beginning of my career, optimistic about my prospects and never imagining my success or failure would be defined by playing this part.

Patrick Troughton rose above it, more concerned with enjoying himself. This was his first convention and after years of refusing to attend them, he took to it instantly. Over the next four years he turned up at almost every event to which he was invited, culminating in his death in 1987 at a convention in Columbus, Ohio.

Despite these niggles, Chicago was a great success with a report appearing on the BBC news on Sunday night, leading many to believe the programme was hugely popular in the USA. In truth there were still many cities that didn't show it, and where it was aired it was shown on PBS (Public Service Broadcasting stations), where the ratings, compared to the networks, were very small. In those days Whovians were considered out on the eccentric edge of the geeky universe, mocked and shunned by their slightly more acceptable *Star Trek / Star Wars / Alien*-loving fellow geeks. It didn't help that the show was broadcast at odd times – late at night or early in the morning, or out of order – switching from one Doctor to another without warning. Still they watched, travelled across states and queued for hours, just to see us.

At the closing ceremony of the convention the rivalry reappeared. We were being introduced one at a time to say goodbye to the attendees. After the companions, Patrick Troughton went on, gave a little speech, and went to stand by the others, then Jon Pertwee came on to say a few words as, backstage, someone came over, and told me I was next. I had a feeling this might happen. I pointed out that usually the number four follows number three, and that therefore Tom Baker, the Fourth Doctor, should go next. There was an impasse. Beads of sweat appeared on the foreheads of the organisers, and Tom's agent lurked in the shadows like Maleficent weaving her magic. Actually I didn't feel calm at all and was sick to death of the whole thing. There was no star billing here and the idea that I was a pushover who would let them impose one, made me determined to stand my ground. Pertwee was finishing his speech and any moment we would all fall into a black hole of embarrassment so I walked away and sat down. Finally, Tom went on stage, but the fun was only just beginning. Instead of standing with Patrick and Jon, he positioned himself on the opposite side of the stage making it impossible for anyone to take pictures of the assembled Doctors and companions. When I came on,

I looked one way and then the other, and eventually joined the main group. Amid the confusion John Nathan-Turner walked over, took Tom by the arm and led him across the stage to join us.

There was a repeat of this in 2013 at the 50th anniversary event with Sylvester, Colin, Tom and me. Rather than sit with us, Tom perched himself on the arm of the sofa furthest away from us, his body turned away. This time we found it funny, and ridiculous, Sylvester taking up an identical position at the end of the other sofa until Nick Briggs, the host, persuaded him to join us.

By 1984 we'd added Colin Baker to the list of regular convention guests, and, as the incumbent, he was first choice where the first point of contact was John Nathan-Turner. I was happy to scale back. I was busy working on a couple of post-*Who* projects, and also had a child on the way, but despite this I still found time to be tempted back to Chicago in November for Tardis 21 or as I remember it being known the Spirit of Light convention. All the living Doctors turned up except for Tom.

The convention was meticulously organised, and involved every guest signing five thousand posters as part of the exhausting weekend of panels, autograph sessions, and photos. To me, the show felt as though it was set up as a money-making machine rather than a celebration for the fans, and many of us felt uncomfortable with this new regime of convention organisers. I remember the hospitality room heaving with guests ploughing through their posters, and being fed pizza and drinks of varying degrees of ethanol content. The weekend wasn't without its lighter moments: appearing on a panel of Doctors and companions, we were asked which we thought the greatest *Doctor Who* monster. Starting from left to right we listed the usual Daleks, Cybermen, Sea Devils, until Lalla Ward, with perfect timing, said simply, 'Tom Baker.' They were briefly married a few years before.

By 1984, what had started as a bit of fun on a Saturday night of most conventions, had turned into the highlight for many fans. The cabaret was a pain in the neck for the guests. It was fun to begin with, when it had been a case of getting up, and making a bit of a fool of yourself, but once expectations rose, once it became a requirement, the fun evaporated, and the task of getting a 'bit' together became an onerous one. I was fortunate in a way, I could always borrow a guitar, and sing a song: one of mine, sadly, because they were the only songs I knew. I had one that fitted the bill but how many times could I sing that? Even to an audience of *Who* fans, whose passion for repetition, both of stories, and episodes (not to mention, of meeting me), I was learning to love. In March of '85 I was in Florida singing my 'Officer McKirk' song, and in Missouri I did the same thing. On this trip, Sandra, and our tiny baby Georgia came along, making her first-ever appearance on stage at the Henry VIII Hotel in St Louis (a star quite recently born). It was a *Hitchhiker's Guide to the Galaxy* convention so I was able to take a back seat to Mark Wing-Davey and Sandra who were the stars of the show.

Reasons I Hate Conventions

- If you're busy it's exhausting.
- If you're not, you think no one loves you and you're probably right.
- Smiling for three days is hard. Your natural bonhomie will keep you going for a day and a half, but by lunchtime on day three you're struggling.
- Fans who say, 'Hi, Peter. Remember me? We met in 1982. I was six years old.'
- People who say, 'I don't want an autograph, but you look lonely so I thought I'd come and chat.'
- Anyone in a Tom Baker scarf.
- Seeing only the inside of airport hotels and convention centres, in so many famous cities.

- If it's abroad you arrive jet-lagged, and at the end of the weekend your body-clock has adjusted enough to get jet-lagged all over again.
- The last question in a Q and A, the one you want to be the killer question, the one that will bring the audience to its feet, will always be the crappiest question of the session.
- The Guest Cabaret (although these have mercifully died out).
- Moving from table to table at the VIP guest breakfast, and never managing to eat breakfast.
- Being escorted by a military-style posse when no one has any intention of harassing or harming you.
- Fans who wait until you've signed a photo to tell you their name is spelt in an unusual way (Courtney with a K).
- Fans who tell me I'm their fourth (or below) favourite Doctor.
- Fans who turn up dressed as me, only they look better than I ever did.

Reasons I Love Conventions

- How can you not love conventions?
- Visiting places you never knew you wanted to go to, where people in strange costumes and gallons of green body-paint spend the weekend telling you how amazing you are.
- Many fans know more about your life and the shows you've been in than you do. (Slightly creepy but useful if you're writing a book.)
- Wandering the dealer room like a fanboy and thinking, Hey, *I'm* the Doctor.
- Catching up with friends, and colleagues you'd never otherwise catch up with.
- Fans bringing you gifts they've made, and pictures they've drawn and sometimes . . . chocolate.
- People who say, 'You were my first Doctor.'
- People who say, 'You are my Doctor.'

- People who say, 'Hi Peter. Remember me? We met in 1982. Your Doctor saw me through a difficult time in my life. Thank you.'
- Children dressed like the Fifth Doctor, who look at you like you're a superhero.
- (They may have the identical look, while thinking, *Seriously*, this is the Fifth Doctor? What happened to the hair, and the blond highlights? And why does he look like grandpa?)

Dixie Trek, in Atlanta in '86, was, as the name might suggest, a combined *Doctor Who/Star Trek* event. Most of the Saturday evening was broadcast by Georgia Public Television, and a fair amount has found its way onto YouTube. I look like a slam dunk for a *Miami Vice* spin-off, only not set in Miami, and with very little vice. Once again I sang my 'Officer McKirk' song (somebody, somewhere, stop me!), with artist Gail Bennett, a stalwart of so many conventions over the years, draped around me holding the microphone, and a small crib sheet of the lyrics.

George Takei, who played Sulu, was the headline *Star Trek* guest at Dixie Trek. George had a permanent smile on his face, and a throaty dirty laugh, that may have been his regular disposition or perhaps he was having a particularly good time that weekend. He was a keen runner, and tried to persuade me to join him for a long Sunday-morning jog around Atlanta. I'd had an exhausting night roaming the hotel in my silk jacket with sleeves rolled up to the elbow, and so had a lie-in instead, but a good few Trekkies were persuaded to join him, and, given the fitness level of your average sci-fi fan, were lucky to survive. I came down to reception late that morning to find George, slightly more flushed than usual, a broad grin on his face, and surrounded by a jumble of exhausted, and sweaty fans stretched out across the floor, and draped untidily across the furniture.

Four days later, having returned to London, I was back at Heathrow in the British Airways business lounge sitting with Michael Grade. How the hell could this happen?

Ten months earlier, four years after the advent of *Doctor Who* conventions in the USA, it occurred to the BBC Enterprises they might be missing out. This epiphany must have coincided with Michael Grade's rather more dark-hearted decision to delay the next series until late the following year, but even so, these odd bedfellows found common ground enough to give the *Doctor Who* USA Touring Exhibition Bus Thingy a green light. It wasn't a bus of course, it was a 48-foot-long trailer filled with bits, and pieces from the series with the intention of touring around the states, and having the odd Doctor or companion turn up in particular cities, and wave to the cheering crowds.

By May of 1986 the bus/trailer thingy was freshly painted, and ready to go. A couple of weeks before the start of the tour in Washington DC, I had a call asking if I would appear alongside Michael Grade at the inauguration ceremony. I was in Atlanta the weekend before, and already had my return ticket booked. The idea of flying back to Washington a couple of days later didn't sound like fun. Unlike my usual bargain-basement travel, I figured Mr Grade was probably flying in style, and so I suggested if they flew me the same class as the BBC Controller, I would do it. The consequences of them accepting my terms only occurred to me as I sat in the Business lounge waiting to board. We were, of course, also sitting together on the flight. Me and the man who effectively ran the BBC.

For seven long hours.

With nothing to say.

It wasn't his fault that I had instantly become the dullest man on earth (or thirty-five thousand feet above it), with no conversation I came up with lasting longer than two sentences.

'Exciting'

'Mmm?'

'Have they told you what we're doing?'

'Well, I'm the one who usually decides what I'm going to do.'

'Right. Yes.'

(Forty-five-minute silence.)

'Have you been to Washington before?'

'Quite a few times, yes.'

'Hot this time of year.'

'I believe so.'

(Three-minute silence, although it feels like forty-five.)

'Very cold in the winter though. Washington.'

'It can be.'

He seemed so damned comfortable with silence. He sat there with his head in one of those inflatable neck cushions. The first time I'd seen one. When we got off the plane in Washington, Michael lit up his cigar, and, literally in a puff of smoke, morphed into a cut-and-thrust TV exec, reminding me of his uncle Lew. We were met by an ingratiating young man from Enterprises, who, in the limo from the airport, had questions fired at him until I almost felt sorry for him.

Apart from the few words at the ceremony the following day, I never heard Grade mention *Doctor Who* the entire time we were there. I never got to appear on the tour, I was busy working, but I heard it was a long arduous job for those responsible for keeping it going.

Somewhere along the convention super-highway I fell into the embrace of Ron Katz. Ron had founded the DWFCA (*Doctor Who* Fan Club of America) in 1982 by accident. He started off as a fan of T-shirts rather than sci-fi but after a chance encounter with the series on a Sunday morning high in the Rocky Mountains, and after tracking down a rather scrappy item of official BBC merchandise, Ron decided he could do better. He had been a success in the clothing business, successful enough to sell up, and retire ridiculously early, and though he thought this would make him happy, it clearly didn't. Together with Chad, the son of a close friend, he designed a *Doctor Who* T-shirt, which came to the attention of the local PBS station. Ron excused his personalised shirt by explaining that he ran a *Doctor Who* fan club, The *Doctor Who* Fan Club of America. An impressive title for a fan club which, at that moment in time, didn't exist. Ron and Chad's plan was to help promote *Doctor Who* in America by raising money for PBS stations to buy the show, and if, along the way, they made chunks of money on merchandise, and appearances, well why not?

At first, the merchandising part was theoretically unauthorised, but by 1984 he'd struck a deal with JNT to become official sellers, and the fun began. After we launched the BBC Tour Trailer Exhibition Bus Extravaganza, and watched it disappear down Pennsylvania Avenue, Michael Grade lit another cigar, shook my hand, and flew back to Britain, while I went off with Ron and Chad, and their team on a series of one-day appearances that criss-crossed the country over the course of a single week. From Denver to Minnesota via Tampa, Phoenix and Boston we slipped sky-caps extra money to ignore overweight luggage, arrived at hotels without bookings and did deals on any rooms they had left. The appearances were short and sweet, and the fans turned up in large numbers, and enjoyed the slightly hysterical nature of the events. A couple of years later Ron Katz had disappeared from the scene (I imagine he'd made enough money to retire for the second time), and no one I know has been able to track him down. I liked him. He had an engaging if slightly questionable attitude, and was up-front about his reasons for getting into *Doctor Who*. It was business.

In 1987 the series was finally taken off the air, and I assumed that fandom would slowly fade to black. I was wrong of course. The absence of the series cemented the show in the hearts of the fans. The invitations to conventions still rolled in, and now the question first out of the mouths of fans was 'Do you think the series will come back?'

No need to ask the question now . . .

14

THE
MUSICALS

Friday, 17 April 2015. The reviews for *Gypsy* have been extraordinary; one critic saying it's the best show he's ever seen. There were five stars flying everywhere, and Imelda deserves every one she gets, as does Lara. I simply stand behind them with the others trying to bask in a little of the glory. Apparently I am 'The human heart of the show', which I think is a good thing because they have stuck it on my picture outside the theatre.

* * *

In 1998, nearly thirty years after I went to drama school, I chalked up my first successful audition for a musical. Not surprisingly it coincided with the first time I'd got around to paying for a singing lesson to run through the song. *Chicago* came along at the end of my decade in the wilderness and looked like both being a saviour and heralding a new direction for me. Instead, no sooner had I opened, than television parts started popping up all over the place and blocked my path to musical stardom for another seven years. I did audition for the 1999 West End production of *The Lion King*, which would have prevented me doing *At Home with the Braithwaites*, but fortunately a combination of thinking I could get away without a singing lesson (it was that talking/singing thing that Jeremy Irons did in the movie), and the unexpected arrival on the scene of a much better candidate, meant I had to make do with television for a few more years.

Then in the spring of 2007, I got a call to audition for King Arthur in *Spamalot*. I went to see the show in London (it was Simon Russell Beale at the time), and was determined to do it. There was the slight problem of the audition, which turned into a rather enjoyable problem when Mike Nichols announced he didn't want to travel to London, so they must fly us to New York instead. The 'us' was one other actor, whose name they wouldn't reveal to me, and who was not told mine. They were determined to keep us apart. They flew us on separate flights and put us in separate hotels, even our auditions the following day were two hours apart. The secrecy was total, admirable, and was fine with me. Except that at five o'clock, someone from the Broadway production rang me in my hotel and asked if I wanted to see the show that night. I said of course. At twenty past seven I was sitting in the packed stalls with a vacant seat beside me, and still I didn't realise the potential screw-up that was about to unfold. I looked up and saw Jon Culshaw making his way along the row of seats. I looked away in panic and by then it was too late to look back at him, or to say anything casual along the lines of *Hi Jon, what a pleasant surprise it is to see you here.*

He must have seen me, but we have never spoken of it. Instead, we sat side by side and watched the first act, neither of us making a sound, in case we gave the game away. He left at the interval and I didn't see him again until he turned up to do Tom Baker's voice on *The Five(ish) Doctors* shoot, six years later.

At the audition the following day, nervous of meeting Mike Nichols and in spite of a couple of singing lessons, I made a mess of the song. I stopped after a couple of bars and said loudly, 'Oh bugger!' It was something I often said when I got things wrong, but it was lifted from the end of the 'Python's Spanish Inquisition' sketch, and Mike Nichols found it more amusing than it was. It's probably what got me the part.

★   ★   ★

Thursday, 16 April 2015. Last night was the opening night of *Gypsy* and it's fair to say it went well. After the curtain call, complete with standing ovations, we stayed on stage while a succession of famous faces arrived to heap praise on us. I didn't recognise Elaine Paige, which didn't go down too well, but honestly without my glasses it's not easy. After a while I resorted to saying 'Hi' to everyone in the joyful way you might greet a dear friend you had lost touch with for many years. This must have confused a fair number of people that I'd never met before, and reminded me of the day I was late for rehearsals at the BBC, and jumped in the lift occupied only by Les Dawson. When I saw his face I gave him the 'Hi' and he gave me one back. I asked him how he was, he asked what I was up to, and we chatted amiably. In fact, I'd realised the moment I'd opened my mouth that we had never met. He'd almost certainly had the same thought, but it was too late, we were now old mates reunited, and whenever I saw him after that we'd say, 'Hi', and exchange pleasantries.

Finally, Angela Lansbury, who last played the part in London in 1973, makes it onto the stage, and we have our photos taken with her. At one point she inclines her head in my direction and despite wearing her glasses, says in a worried tone, 'Who's that standing next to me?' 'It's Herbie,' I say, and she seems comforted. 'Oh, that's OK, then.'

IS THERE LIFE OUTSIDE THE BOX?

* ★ *

Another two years passed before I did *Legally Blonde*. The original Broadway show had fallen victim to the banking collapse and the subsequent sharp decrease in audiences. When Sonia Freidman turned up and said she wanted to put it on in the West End, the original artistic team jumped on board. Jerry Mitchell bounded around the rehearsal room like Bambi on legal highs, especially when he felt we weren't giving it our all, and he had the chance to play the entire ensemble with the sweep of his arms. Laurence O'Keefe would take me patiently through my six-minute solo song, apologising for the multiple key changes which he said he found irresistible.

Before we started previews, the main cast performed a song on Children in Need. We were a bit under-rehearsed and the resulting spiteful online comments badly affected Sheridan Smith. She had worked incredibly hard and was spectacularly good in the show, but for someone that talented, she took too much notice of idiots. It wouldn't be the last time I was sent down to her room to talk her out of a blue funk. I was given the job out of seniority (I was a good thirty years older than anyone else), rather than any skill in the pep talk area. I would tell her she was brilliant (which she was) and eventually she would recover her mojo. I wouldn't claim to be a friend of hers – I couldn't keep up – but I got to see her at close hand. She liked to have fun, that's all. If she hadn't been lumbered with all that talent she might have led a perfectly happy life, going out in Scunthorpe on a weekend, with the odd trip into Doncaster on a Saturday night. Instead she does brilliant work but still wants to enjoy herself, and who can say she doesn't deserve to. It's true that sometimes those things don't sit so well together, but I don't believe that, with Sheridan, you can have one without the other. And still her work ethic is stronger than most.

THE MUSICALS

We opened in January and got five-star reviews. Every night there was a swarm of noisy young girls at the stage door, almost none of them there to see me. But still there were many moments of delight. At the beginning of the second act, we'd assemble in the wings. If I was down early enough I'd sit in the judge's chair on stage right, and the girls would gather around me: at my feet, on the arms on either side, or sitting on my knee. It took me some time to work out that their ease was because I was now considered 'safe'. A kindly avuncular figure they could safely hug without thinking I might get the wrong idea. I hated it and loved it at the same time.

In 2011, *Legally Blonde* won Best New Musical at the Olivier Awards, and ran for two and a half years; I stayed for the entire run. Another two and a half years later and I was back at the Savoy theatre, and in the same dressing room, this time in the musical *Gypsy*. I spent most of the time hiding behind the prodigious talent of Imelda Staunton, which given her size, is no mean achievement. In recognition of that, and other extraordinary feats of song and dance, I was nominated for an Olivier award for best supporting actor in a musical at almost exactly the same time as I was invited to go on a Caribbean Sci-Fi cruise. It would possibly be the last chance to see my aunt Olga and straighten out the last kinks in the family tree, and with our children getting older and more reluctant, perhaps a last for them to willingly go on holiday with us.

It turned out the awards ceremony and the trip also clashed. Take the money or open the box. With my remarkable history in the field of winning awards, I decided to go on holiday.

My first award was given to me in my second year of senior school: an illustrated book of British racing cars which was five years out of date when I was presented with it. Mike Hawthorn's 1958 world championship-winning Ferrari was proudly displayed on the dust jacket. Unfortunately this was 1963. It was my reward for coming second in physics, an achievement that only just preceded a staggeringly quick decline in my scientific success. I never made it into the top twenty again, and my guess is that it was a horrible mistake in the first place. Our physics teacher, Mr Young, would regularly mistake the anonymous me for much brighter students, usually Roger Lawson, one of those annoying friendly boys who was good at anything he put his mind to. From physics to fighting, from football to girls, Roger was the master. The only thing he never mastered was tucking his shirt in, although that clearly didn't count against him with the blossoming opposite sex. We didn't look alike of course but Mr Young was too absorbed teaching us the wonders of natural science by reading aloud from a succession of atrophied notebooks, to notice where one child ended, and another began.

Mr Young was old and Scottish. At some point we discovered he was known as 'Jazz' to his colleagues, I assume the sobriquet was used with heavy irony, as a less jazzy bloke it would be hard to imagine. It's possible he was only in his forties (still old to a twelve year old boy), but his bald head didn't exactly shout youth and vigour, and he was as old as Scottish granite in his soul.

The distraction of Mr Young left us free to do pretty much as we pleased during lessons. Setting fire to stuff with a Bunsen burner was a favourite, and as if to encourage this, every desk in the science room was generously supplied with its own. If you had an artistic bent, and were afraid actual flames might attract his attention you could lightly singe the edges of your exercise books giving them a pleasing aged and antiquated look. I became quite good at this, occasionally taking commissions, while Mr Young talked and circled his desk, notebook in hand, and never seemed to notice. My friend Raymond's first memory of me, arriving in 3b after demotion from 3a, was attaching a Bunsen burner to the water tap, and sending a thin plume of water high into the classroom. Mr Young carried on as usual. This one event cemented my acceptance in my new class, even by those who were caught in the downpour.

It was fifteen years before I was lauded again. In 1978 the entire regular cast of *All Creatures Great and Small* was awarded a joint Variety Club Personality of the Year award, by which I mean it was one award but, each of us received a Variety Club Silver Heart on a plinth, informing us we were joint winners, and so presumably one-fifth of a personality. As the third or fourth lead in the show I was just happy to be included. Even being twenty per cent of a personality was more than I might have dreamt of a few years before, and as physical awards go it was impressive, although as often happens with me, it fell apart before the lunch was over.

That July I was invited back to the Winston Churchill School as the guest on Prize Day. (I know, strictly speaking this doesn't come under the heading 'My Awards' but there are so precious few of them I thought I could include a case of handing them out as well.) Usually this honour was reserved for retired army officers or distinguished local councillors (retired), none of whom had been to a secondary modern/comprehensive school, and who clobbered us with salutary tales demonstrating the importance of studying if we wanted to claw our way out of the evolutionary bog of the lower orders. As if to clarify his point, one year, one of these elevated gentleman (I forget if he was Army or Councillor), suffered a severe attack of incontinence after delivering his speech. He sat down, looking pleased with himself, and got down to it. The teaching staff beside him stared blankly out front, not wanting to believe what they knew was happening and listening to the steady trickle of urine falling from the seat of his chair to the stage.

Whether the quality of the prize-day guest changed in the ten years between me leaving school a loser, and triumphantly returning for prize day – and bearing the standard of a successful academic failure proudly in front of me – I don't know. But it was, in the words of one of the trendier teachers, 'a bit of a turn-up for the books'. Mr Lee and Mr Giovanni refused to attend because they didn't feel I was a suitable example of the importance of hard work.

Mrs Norris was responsible for inviting me. She had risen from being head of maths when I was at school, to becoming deputy headmistress when she sent me the letter kindly inviting me to prize day. I liked Mrs Norris, and I suspect she had a soft spot for me, even though I was possibly the worst maths student she had the misfortune to be lumbered with. When I decided to stay on in the sixth year, ostensibly because I needed to retake the many exams I had failed, and decided to give maths A level a go, I hadn't actually taken O level maths. I never gave that a second thought, and anyway I was rather taken with the idea that the A level course concentrated on the 'new' maths of binary.

Binary was the real deal, and might have been invented for me.

As I understood it, and I clearly didn't, binary maths never went beyond zeros, and ones. What, I concluded, could be difficult about a subject where you only had to deal with two numbers? It is to Mrs Norris's great credit that she didn't hit me with a large stick or at least send me to one of the aforementioned teachers who might have enjoyed doing it on her behalf. For her part, Mrs Norris was an optimist, and seriously considered that the low marks I had received in maths was because of my failure to show the 'working out' when the answers were correct, which I insisted was down to working it out in my head rather than bothering to write it all down, and therefore, she thought, I might be a bit of a mathematical genius who would grasp the binary system in a blink of an eye. It was true I had a knack for mental arithmetic, even for more complex maths, as long as you didn't need to see the working out.

But the binary system? What the fuck is that about?

By Christmas I still had no inkling of what she was talking about, and missed the numbers two to nine so much I gave up on the 'new' maths, with its bits, and bytes, and withdrew from the course.

So it was a surprise to get the letter from her. But the fact that I'd predicted the invitation all those years ago on the day I left school, meant I had to accept. I wore a suit and an old school tie and, after being introduced, noted how the place hadn't changed much except for a few more broken windows in the technical block and the grammar of the graffiti in the boys' loo could be better. I implored them to work hard otherwise they might end up like me, standing around for hours on cold Yorkshire hillsides with my arm up a cow. I concluded by reading extracts from my school report: a litany of damning remarks ending with one by Mrs Norris herself complaining she had seen no homework, no effort and no improvement, and finding it hard to imagine what purpose would be served by me remaining at school. I turned to her, looking wounded, and said, 'A little harsh?'

It probably would have gone down well simply by virtue of my not being ex-army or retired councillor, but the children, I noticed now that I was almost home and dry, were having a good time. Rather too much of a good time it turned out, as the school orchestra's rendition of something unrecognisable was mercifully rendered inaudible by the over-excited audience.

* * *

Wednesday, 20 May 2015. Imelda pops into my dressing room to tell me Meryl Streep was in last night, and was very complimentary about me as Herbie. Will have to pin her down over the exact quote as I plan to have it engraved on my headstone.

* * *

IS THERE LIFE OUTSIDE THE BOX?

In 1982 I received the *Multi-Coloured Swap Shop* Top Man award. It was a weighty piece with a large Perspex base that made it perfect for hiding things under until the multi-coloured plastic logo came off in my hand as I lifted it off a collection of bills pending, and the rest of it landed heavily on the floor, snapping off the words 'Swap Shop', and the tiny plaque with my name on it. After that the assorted pieces went into a cardboard box which is now residing in an unspecified location.

The *Multi-Coloured Swap Shop* show itself was hosted by Noel Edmonds assisted by Keith Chegwin, and Maggie Philbin, and had been running for six years on Saturday mornings. The amount of swapping on the programme, only moderate to begin with, had reduced over time, gradually being replaced by celebrity interviews, and general silliness. In fact the show was a more child-friendly version of the anarchic, theoretically for kids, *Tiswas* on ITV, which at the age of thirty-one, I was still shamefully addicted to. Shortly after I appeared to accept the award, the *Multi-Coloured Swap Shop* was dropped from the schedules. I have no idea if the two events are connected but as the Top Man award was a new category, I have the honour of being the only man to receive it, and therefore can still claim forever be the '*Multi-Coloured Swap Shop* Top Man'.

So far, my acting awards were conspicuous by not actually mentioning acting: Top Man, and Joint Personality not supplying the kind of re-assuring ego boost us sensitive needy souls need.

In 2007 all was put right when I won the Nymphe d'Or at the 47th Festival of Television in Monte-Carlo. The actual inscription on the award itself (which fell apart as I walked down the red-carpeted stairway into the banqueting hall after the presentation) read, 'Out-standing Actor, Comedy TV Series'. The series in question was *Fear, Stress & Anger*, written by Michael Aitken, and I'm confident in saying it was a good one, even if it didn't set the sitcom world on fire. However my cynical side has never been quite convinced of the veracity of the award. The fact that I was the only nominee in my category to be in Monaco publicising his show, and that I saw off all American contenders, including Larry David, has always troubled me. But only a teeny tiny bit.

A coachload of us had travelled out to Monaco (not on a coach) primarily to plug the show, with the glittering awards ceremony a frilly extra. As well as the actors, and Michael, the writer, the producer Sue Vertue came along with her husband, Steven Moffat. On the first afternoon most of us sat on the terrace relaxing with a glass of wine, while Steven sat with Mark Gatiss discussing an idea they'd just had, to do a modern-day version of *Sherlock Holmes*. It sounded a bit of a dud to me.

Also in our cast and on the trip was Pippa Heywood playing my wife, and Daisy Aitken and Georgia Moffett playing our daughters. By an amazing coincidence Daisy was Michael Aitken's daughter and Georgia was mine. If that smacks of nepotism to you, then you're a very cynical person (albeit a perceptive one).

Georgia and Daisy persuaded Armani to loan them fabulous outfits for the occasion, which was a terrific idea until my suitcase, in which the dresses, and shoes were safely packed for the return journey, was lost by British Airways in the Great British Airways Baggage Cock-up of 2007, in which the loss of over a million suitcases in one year was compounded by the disappearance, at the same moment, of the entire British Airways customer service department. There were rumours of large pits being dug in Eastern Europe (for the unclaimed baggage, not the British Airways customer service department), although nothing was ever proven. My suitcase was only one of 'the disappeared', but its loss was felt keenly because at the time it was worth just over six thousand pounds (if you count the Prada handbag belonging to my wife, and the trouser part of my nicest brown suit).

Georgia and Daisy's attempts to explain to Armani about the loss of their two expensive borrowed outfits and shoes, is a story I would love to tell, but the film rights have been snapped up, and there's nothing more I can reveal.

Finally, in a *Doctor Who Magazine* poll in 2009, *The Caves of Androzani* (my swan song) was voted best story. It isn't exactly *my* award, or even an award at all, but it's close enough for me to bask in the glory. Added to which, it annoyed the heck out of Steven Moffat, who had several stories in the running. By then my daughter Georgia had recovered from the loss of her dresses and shoes and met David Tennant, which is the sort of happy accident that will make up for many other disappointments in life.

* * *

Tuesday, 22 March 2016. I'm off to Salt Lake City Comic Con tomorrow, before meeting up with the family in Florida at the weekend. The original delivery date for this book would have meant leaving the outcome of my Olivier award nomination a mystery, which would have made a tidy cliffhanger-type ending for the book, and one in which I could have sailed off into the sunset with expectations high. Now that isn't the case. I foolishly asked for, and was given, a bit of extra time, and will have to face the consequences. Adding to my gloom, I've had to turn down a proper job (actually it wasn't that good) in order to keep the holiday intact.

This afternoon Louis came home from school and asked Elizabeth if it was true I'd been in lots of other stuff apart from *Doctor Who*. Apparently, as part of his theology revision, he'd been looking at IMDb.

* * *

THE MUSICALS

Prior to my last-ditch and fortuitous stab at acting, my family had no history of entertaining at a professional level. Now things are very different. My daughter became an actress, married an actor, and has four children who will probably all do the same. My two sons tell me they are going to sign up as well, and it doesn't stop there. My nephew is now an actor, and my niece is about to leave drama school (incidentally, her brother, who is on the production side is about to work with my son-in-law).

How did this happen?

Of course I would like to think that I've been an inspiration to them: a shining light that they have proudly followed, but I'm not so sure. Without a grand plan and with very little ambition, I've ambled through my career, pausing occasionally to look at the view, only to discover that where I was standing was exactly in the right place at the right time. And so it went on.

I have been luckier than most, but not as lucky as some, and that's fine with me. As for those in my family about to roll the dice and wondering what the future will bring, there is always me: the bloke from the vet series, the Fifth Doctor and all that other stuff that my children barely noticed. They can look at me, pictured in sci-fi magazines, immortalised in six-inch-high figures with articulated limbs, and in various re-runs on any number of cable channels, and think with some confidence – if he can do it, anyone can.

* * *

Sunday, 3 April 2016. Finally, we are on board the *Carnival Breeze*, about to leave Miami on the six-day Caribbean 'Sci-Fi' cruise. Three thousand, four hundred miles away, in London, the great and the good of British theatre, including my fellow nominees, are gathering for this year's Olivier Awards. I have made the decision to be here, rather than there, and it's a choice I'm beginning to question. It's the end of what has been a bad week. It started with two emails, one informing me that my schoolfriend Matthew was in hospital with severe chest pains, the other that my aunt Olga was now in palliative care. Despite the hospice nurse's assessment that she wasn't 'actively dying' (whatever that means), she passed away the following day, only a few hours before we were due to visit. Now I'm going to miss the funeral because it's too late to pull out of the cruise without letting everybody down.

Then the weekend gets worse. I pay $99 for shipboard Internet access only to discover England have lost the 20/20 cricket World Cup Final in the last over and Lewis Hamilton has crashed out of the Bahrain Grand Prix after being in pole position, and I realise there is only one thing left that can save the week from being a total disaster.

A couple of hours later we are sitting on the lido deck at the raucous 'leaving Miami party'; Louis has already nicked my phone (and Internet access) and I'm eating ice cream to compensate. Elizabeth turns to me.

'When will you hear about the Oliviers?'

I shrug in reply and Louis looks up and casually says,

'Oh, yeah, I forgot to tell you Georgia sent a text. She said the other bloke won.'

ACKNOWLEDGEMENTS

Grateful appreciation to my three sisters.

My father, for leaving a short memoir in an old school exercise book of mine.

My Uncle John (Hallett) and my Auntie Olga, for filling in the gaps.

Many thanks to the following for their contributions: David Tucker, Dave Clark, Janet Fielding, Joanna Kanska, Sarah Churm, and Clara Francis.

My teachers Mr Verney and Jane Walters, and also The Byfleet Players.

My friend Dave, for all the photos.

A special mention to Elizabeth, Louis and Joel, for putting up with it all.

IS THERE LIFE OUTSIDE THE BOX?

Georgia and David, for giving us a shot at a Tennant–Davison dynasty.

Andy Merriman for his encouragement, expertise and the most gentle nagging imaginable.

Finally, to all the staff at John Blake Publishing – especially my editors James Hodgkinson, Dominique Buchan and Sarah Fortune.

INDEX

INDEX

INDEX

INDEX